Cycling Great Britain

D1100466

Cycling Great Britain

Cycling Adventures in England, Scotland and Wales

Tim Hughes and Johanna Cleary

Bicycle Books – San Francisco

Printed in the United States of America

Published by:
Bicycle Books, Inc.
1282 - 7th Avenue
San Francisco, CA, 94122
U.S.A.

Distributed to the book trade by:

U.S.A.	National Book Network, Lanham, MD
U.K.	Chris Lloyd Sales and Marketing Services, Poole, Dorset
Canada:	Raincoast Book Distributing, Vancouver, BC
South Africa:	Book Distributors International, Sandton
Australia:	Tower Books, Frenchs Forest, NSW

Photographs by Tim Hughes
Maps by Eureka Cartography, Berkeley, CA

Publisher's Cataloging in Publication Data

496.6	Hughes, William Thomas, 1934–
HUG	Cycling Great Britain : cycling adventures in England, Scotland and Wales / Tim Hughes and Johanna Cleary. San Francisco, Ca : Bicycle Books, Inc., ©1996.

224 p. : col. ill., maps; 21.6 cm.
Includes index.

Summary: Gives background information and route
descriptions, with route maps, for 30 multi-day bicycle tours
throughout England, Scotland and Wales.

ISBN 0-933201-71-0
LCCN 95-76302

1. Bicycle touring - Great Britain - Directories 2. Bicycle trails -
Great Britain - Directories 3. Great Britain - Bicycle touring -
Directories I. Cleary, Johanna II. Title

796.6'4
_dc20

Provided in cooperation with Unique Books, Inc.

Introduction

This book on cycling in Great Britain, though primarily published for an American audience, is equally suitable for cyclists from other countries, including those from Britain itself.

The book uses American spellings, but much of what we have written is British in other ways. The same thing just doesn't always go by the same name on both sides of the big puddle. Even so, an American asking for a "restroom" in Britain, where that institution is known as a "toilet,"will probably figure it out pretty quickly. Just the same, we have made every effort to explain typically British terms for our American readers.

Most of the other information intended for non-British readers is contained in a separate section at the end of the book. If you're a British reader there will be some things in this book that you know already and don't have to be told. However, the general cycling guidance and the touring routes will still be useful, and you may find the rest entertaining. Wherever you come from, the essential message is the same: get out and enjoy exploring one of the world's most interesting countries in the best way there is—by bicycle.

Publisher's Disclaimer

We acknowledge that wearing a helmet while cycling can significantly reduce the risk of sustaining serious and fatal brain injury if you fall off your bike. The fact that cyclists photographed in this book are not shown wearing a helmet in no way implies that we suggest it is safe to do so.

The fact is that English touring cyclists by and large do not wear helmets. The cyclists shown are not models and the scenes depicted are not staged: the authors photographed actual cyclists, wearing the gear they were actually wearing.

About the Authors

Tim Hughes is a scientist and a lifelong cyclist turned freelance writer and photographer. He is currently the editor of the Cyclists' Touring Club's publication *Cycletouring and Campaigning*. His earlier books include *Wheels of Choice*, a photographic essay on the charms of bicycle touring in Britain.

Johanna Cleary, Ph.D., is a town planner who specializes in cycle route planning. She too is an avid touring cyclist.

Between them, Hughes and Cleary have ridden about 400,000 miles. Together, they operate a cycle consultancy, concentrating on British cycling routes.

Table of Contents

Part I
Bicycle Touring in Britain

CHAPTER 1

A Cyclist's Anatomy of Britain

Although this book outlines a number of specific routes, it helps if you know something about the cycling-specific aspects of Britain's geography. Whether you are a visitor from abroad or have lived in the country all your life, this information will help you plan your cycling tours and appreciate the terrain you are traveling through.

Looking at it geographically, Great Britain is a group of islands to the northwest of the European continent—England and France are only about 35 km (22 mi.) apart across the narrowest strait of the English Channel. The two largest islands are the British mainland—made up of England, Wales and Scotland—and Ireland. Politically, there are two countries: the "United Kingdom of Great Britain and Northern Ireland," comprising England, Wales, Scotland, and the six of the nine counties of the ancient province of Ulster that make up Northern Ireland; and the Republic of Ireland, comprising the

Near Oban in Scotland (See Tour D, Route 22, starting on page 173).

remaining 26 counties of the island of Ireland. Both are members of the European Union.

This book gives routes in mainland Britain. The mainland is about 1,000 km (600 mi.) from south to north and about 500 km (300 mi.) from east to west at its widest point. For comparison, England is about the size of Alabama, and Scotland of South Carolina, with Wales similar to New Jersey. Appropriately, the New England states together are about the size of *old* England plus Wales.

Britain divides fairly neatly into two parts: the lower, flatter, drier, more intensively cropped and more populated south and east, and the higher, hillier, wetter and wilder north and west. In geological terms, the older and harder mountain limestones and sandstones, and volcanic rocks, come to the surface in the north and west; the newer, softer deposits of clay, sand and chalk are in the south and east. Softer deposits are less resistant to the weathering that shapes a landscape, so the southeast has lower, rounded hills.

Even in the wilder parts, virtually all of Britain's landscape has been molded, sometimes literally sculpted, by its centuries of human settlers. As civilizations moved westward across Europe, they drove earlier settlers before them, and the last 2,000 years have seen Celts banished northward and westward by Romans, followed by Angles and Saxons, then much of the east settled by Danes, with other Norse incursions to north, west and east. Finally, on the climactic date in English history that everyone knows, A.D. 1066, the last successful invaders, the Normans from northern France, stumbled up an English beach. All these influences have affected Britain's culture, its language, its towns and villages with their buildings—and their names. These names, originally just descriptions of the place, encapsulate Britain's varied history.

It is easy to think of Britain's history as being enshrined in its castles, medieval cathedrals and old city centers, but in truth, history is everywhere. You don't need to turn your trip into a desperate scramble to see as many castles or cathedrals as can be crammed into three weeks. On your tours through pleasant country, on quiet roads, through small towns, villages and hamlets rather than cities, you'll see as much historic architecture in modest village churches, farms and houses as in the famous set-pieces. That's not to say these aren't worth a visit; we mention it when routes go near them, and several routes start and finish in historic cities.

Because Britain is densely settled—there are over 55 million of us, and most of those in the flatter, lower parts—distances between places are short by American or Australasian standards. Villages may be no more than 4 or 5 km (about 3 mi.) apart, and there's a lot to see, so don't be too ambitious in your daily distances. Navigating can be quite complex with so many roads, so good maps are virtually essential. See Chapter 2 for information about suitable maps.

Local administration was undergoing a radical revision at the time of writing, but currently England and Wales are divided into counties and Scotland into regions, and these are subdivided into districts. Nearly all commercial listings of accommodations, restaurants, campgrounds and so on are given by county or region, while many tourist information centers are run by district councils. In addition, information may be given to cover the whole of a national park, for example, and this may straddle several counties or districts.

Effectively all the laws that affect cyclists, particularly the traffic laws, are uniform throughout the United Kingdom. There are no changes at state or other boundaries; apart from slight differences in the opening hours of pubs and bars, it's unlikely that you'll be affected by the differences between the Scottish and English legal systems. Nevertheless, keep in mind that the Welsh and Scottish are fiercely proud of their different cultures. Don't say how glad you are to be in England if you are actually in Wales or Scotland.

The Regions of Britain

A convenient dividing line is the 250 m (800 ft.) contour, and the map shows shaded all the land over that height. The map shows the main physical regions of Britain, and below you'll find a short description of the types of countryside, villages and towns you may expect. The narrative on each of the routes in the next chapters fills out this information and suggests places of interest.

Berkshire and Wiltshire Downs
- [ ] rolling chalk landscape, culminating in high chalk downland
- [ ] often open with wide views, including highest point in southeast England, Walbury Hill (297 m/974 ft.)
- [ ] many prehistoric sites
- [ ] racehorse-training country

Central Highlands
- [ ] often neglected area of wild high mountain and lakes
- [ ] wildlife

Chilterns
- [ ] chalk ridge with 250 m (800 ft.) escarpment looking northwest over rolling clay plains
- [ ] highest parts are heavily wooded (mainly beech)
- [ ] brick-and-flint-built villages

Cotswolds
- [ ] limestone ridge (highest point 330 m/1083 ft.) overlooking Severn Valley to the west
- [ ] rolling limestone country sloping down to River Thames
- [ ] stone walls to fields
- [ ] chocolate-box golden stone villages
- [ ] clear streams
- [ ] university city of Oxford at southeast edge

Dartmoor
- [ ] often dour granite moorland rising to over 600 m (2,000 ft.)
- [ ] some heather cover with distinctive rocky outcrops ("tors")
- [ ] pretty villages on southern fringe

East Anglia
- [ ] gentle rolling country, largely cultivated, often open
- [ ] lazy river valleys, some wetlands (e.g., Norfolk Broads) and nature reserves, especially near coasts
- [ ] often decorative villages

Exmoor

- [ ] upland England comes to the south: heather-covered sandstone moorland, rising to over 470 m (1,550 ft.)
- [ ] pretty villages in wooded valleys
- [ ] coastal cliffs

Fens

- [ ] dead flat and geometrical landscape, rarely rising above 5 m (15 ft.)
- [ ] marvelous under tall cumulus clouds, bleak when grey
- [ ] reclaimed marshland, with slow rivers
- [ ] wetlands including sample of undrained fen, Wicken Sedge near Soham
- [ ] magnificent and magnificently sited cathedral at Ely
- [ ] colleges at Cambridge

Galloway

- [ ] broad range of hills, many above 600 m (2,000 ft.)
- [ ] highest point, Merrick, at 824 m (2,703 ft.)
- [ ] castles
- [ ] open moorlands, many forests, lakes
- [ ] mostly gentle coastal scenery

Grampians

- [ ] highest continuous stretch of land over 900 m (3,000 ft.) in Britain
- [ ] often bleak, but exhilarating under the right conditions
- [ ] few roads

Isle of Man

- [ ] surprising variety for 50 x 15 km (30 x 10 mi.) island: dunes in north, mountainous center (Snaefell, 620 m/2,034 ft.), rolling hills in south
- [ ] cliffs
- [ ] Scandinavian and Celtic cultural mix

Isle of Wight

- [ ] the nearest mainland counties in miniature but with steeper cliffs
- [ ] southern coast is sunniest place in England
- [ ] some showpiece villages
- [ ] genteel coastal resorts
- [ ] distinct "island" atmosphere

Lake District

- [ ] England's most mountainous area
- [ ] spectacular lake and mountain scenery, including England's highest mountain, Scafell Pike, 977 m (3,205 ft.)

Lincolnshire Wolds

- [ ] rolling chalk upland, mostly cultivated
- [ ] workmanlike but nevertheless attractive villages
- [ ] sparsely populated (miles without a pub)

Mendips

- [ ] high, rounded limestone ridge
- [ ] open country with some forest
- [ ] caves
- [ ] fine cathedral at Wells

Mid Wales

- [ ] rolling upland plateau, mostly around 500 m (1,600 ft.), dissected by river valleys
- [ ] much remote and wild country
- [ ] open space
- [ ] man-made lakes and forests

New Forest

- [ ] the hunting forest of King William I (William the Conqueror of 1066 fame), so it's not that new

- ☐ now a mix of open heath-
land and mixed forest
- ☐ quiet villages
- ☐ semi-wild ponies

North and South Downs and the Weald
- ☐ mixed landscape of chalk
hills (North and South
Downs) and sandy heath-
land (Weald)
- ☐ much wooded, with wide
variety of trees, although
South Downs have fine
open stretches
- ☐ some picturesque villages
- ☐ spectacular white cliffs
where Downs reach the sea

Northumberland
- ☐ includes much wild upland
moor with picturesque river
valleys
- ☐ highest point, Cheviot, is
815 m (2,674 ft.)
- ☐ coastal area includes sea
"ford" to Holy Island
- ☐ fishing villages
- ☐ border castles

North Wales
- ☐ high mountain and plateau
country
- ☐ highest point, Yr Wyddfa
(Snowdon), 1085 m (3,560 ft.)
- ☐ waterfalls, lakes
- ☐ Llyn peninsula to west is
gentler with coves, beaches
- ☐ Clwydian and Berwyn hills
to east more rounded
- ☐ many Welsh-speaking areas

North Yorkshire Moors
- ☐ heather-covered upland
with some new afforestation
- ☐ highest point 454 m
(1,490 ft.)
- ☐ coastal fishing villages and
towns
- ☐ "bracing" (i.e., windy) coastal resorts

Pennines
- ☐ the "backbone of England"
and first taste for
southerners of northern
landscapes
- ☐ limestone plateau, rocky
upland heath or grazing, dissected by deep river valleys
- ☐ grey stone walls divide
fields
- ☐ solid-looking stone villages
- ☐ caves, miniature gorges
- ☐ harder gritstones take over
as you move north, and tops
of hills become more bleak
and barren

Quantocks
- ☐ high and largely forested
sandstone ridge

Roman Wall
- ☐ built across country from
sea to sea to protect Roman-
held territory from
marauding Scots
- ☐ spectacular views in places
along top of craggy cliffs
- ☐ atmospheric

Somerset Moors and Levels
- ☐ largely flat wetland area dissected by water channels
("rhynes")
- ☐ extensive bird life
- ☐ pretty villages in surrounding countryside

South Wales
- ☐ mix of mountain and
upland moorland, with
lower agricultural country
in south
- ☐ Black Mountains, Brecon
Beacons and Carmarthen
Vans all over 800 m (2,600 ft.)
- ☐ fine cliffs on west and southwest coasts
- ☐ wooded valleys

Trossachs
- ☐ compact area of forests,
lakes, castles

Welsh borders

- [ ] sometimes also known as the "Welsh Marches"
- [ ] hilly wooded country
- [ ] heather-covered moorlands of Long Mynd and Stiperstones
- [ ] lush river valleys
- [ ] "black-and-white" timber-and-plaster cottages
- [ ] broad views
- [ ] the counties of Shropshire and Herefordshire are poet A. E. Housman's "colored counties."
- [ ] our favorite part of Britain for cycling—but you'll need low gears

Western Highlands

- [ ] high mountains, including Britain's highest point, Ben Nevis, 1,344 m (4,409 ft.)
- [ ] sea lochs (many almost fjords), cliffs, beaches, islands—you can hardly go wrong

Yorkshire and Durham Dales

- [ ] upland mountain limestone plateau, sometimes cultivated to surprising heights
- [ ] dissected by deep, sometimes wooded, attractive river valleys known as dales
- [ ] limestone features—limestone pavements, grit-topped peaks
- [ ] grey stone solid villages and towns
- [ ] farther north in Durham Dales (Weardale, Teesdale), upland is heather-covered moorland with deep cultivated valleys

Yorkshire Wolds

- [ ] quite abrupt chalk hills with attractive small villages tucked into the folds
- [ ] sea cliff at Flamborough Head

National, Regional and Forest Parks

England and Wales have a number of national parks; some of the routes described in this book pass through them, and you might care to make side trips to visit others. Unlike some American, Canadian, Australian or New Zealand national parks, these are not wilderness zones but rather areas in which the management of the human-influenced landscape is controlled. They are also much smaller than those of other countries. Most are in upland or mountainous areas, but two—the New Forest and the Norfolk Broads ("broad" is the local term for the marshy, reedy lakes that are the main feature of the area)—are in lower country. In addition, a number of other forests have been designated as forest parks. Scotland has no national parks as such, but a number of areas are designated as regional parks and forest parks.

Some of these parks are immensely popular with visitors. For example, at most seasons of the year the relatively few roads in the Lake District are very busy with tourist traffic. If you are traveling to Britain other than during the main summer holiday months, the best times to visit such places is spring, after the Easter crowds have dispersed, or autumn, which is quite late in Britain, extending into early November. Traditionally, British schools have a week's vacation at the end of May and the end of October, and there are more surges of visitors then. Even late winter—with snow on the mountain-tops and signs of spring in the valleys—can be a good time to visit.

English and Welsh National Parks

1   Dartmoor
2   Exmoor
3   New Forest
4   Pembrokeshire Coast
5   Brecon Beacons
6   Norfolk Broads
7   Snowdonia
8   Peak District
9   Lake District
10 Yorkshire Dales
11 North Yorkshire Moors
12 Northumberland

Scottish Regional Parks

13 Pentland Hills Regional Park
14 Loch Lomond Regional Park

Forest Parks

A   Dean Forest and Wye Valley
B   Thetford Forest Park
C   Grizedale Forest Park
D   North Riding Forest Park
E   Galloway Forest Park
F   Border Forest Park
G   Argyll Forest Park
H   Queen Elizabeth Forest Park
J   Tummel Forest Park
K   Glenmore Forest Park

Several other smaller areas with distinctive landscapes are designated as Areas of Outstanding Natural Beauty (ANOB) and are subject to some control on developments likely to affect their character.

CHAPTER 2

Orientation: Roads, Maps and Finding the Way

Although some of the information included in this chapter is most relevant to foreign visitors, and could therefore have been included in the separate section in the back of the book, much of it is so essential to traveling by bike that it should be considered essential reading for all who plan to tour Britain by bike.

Types of Roads

British roads are classified into four groups: M-roads (motorways), A-roads, B-roads and unclassified roads.

Cycling is not permitted on motorways. They are prominently marked with blue signs and the European car-only road symbol: two ribbons of uninterrupted roadway with a stylized overbridge, together with the road number, e.g., "M23." If you do inadvertently find yourself about to join a motorway, walk carefully back up the shoulder of the slip road until you are back on the general road system.

The A-road classification is a wide one, from roads that are motorways in all but name to lightly trafficked but nevertheless principal roads in remote rural areas. There's a world of difference between, for example, the six lanes and shoulders of the A40 as it leaves London and the same A40 400 km (250 mi.) later as it approaches Fishguard in west Wales, by now a two-lane winding country road. Nevertheless, there is a system in the numbering.

Learning to read the signs of the map is part of the fun of cycletouring in Britain.

The original classification of the principal A-roads in the 1930s was based on a clockwise radial pattern from London. The A1 headed north for York and Edinburgh, the A2 headed southeast to Dover, the A3 southwest to Portsmouth and so on round to the A6, which headed northwest to Carlisle on the Scottish border. The system was completed by the A7 from Carlisle to Edinburgh, A8 from Edinburgh to Glasgow, and A9 from Edinburgh to the northeast tip of Scotland, John O'Groats.

The next tier of roads in the hierarchy was numbered as they diverged from these single-number roads: for example, the A10, A11, A12, and so on lie in the sector between the A1 and the A2, and the A20, A21, A22, A23, etc. between the A2 and the A3. Further subdivisions down to three- and four-figure A-numbers filled in the network. Our general advice is that, although cyclists have every right to use A-roads, it's best to avoid at least one- and two-figure A-roads wherever possible. (Indeed the original concept of this book arose from a wish to show cycling visitors to Britain that the best route on a bike from London to Oxford was not the A40, nor the A34 the best route from there to Stratford-upon-Avon.) Some important A-roads are designated "trunk" roads and have special green signing; these are likely to be busy and carry a higher proportion of heavy trucks. A-roads are busier—and usually wider—within about 60 km (40 mi.) of London or near to other large cities.

With B-roads we begin to come to more comfortable cycling, although B-roads also within about 60 km (40 mi.) of London and close to some other big cities can be busy. B-roads usually have a four-figure number and fit generally though less precisely into the same numbering system. Several of our routes use sections of quiet B-road.

Finally we come to the thousands of miles of unnumbered minor roads—approximately 250,000 km (150,000 mi.) of them. These are Britain's real bikeways, covering almost the whole country in a fine mesh and carrying relatively little traffic. These minor roads are the backbone of the routes in this book.

The road system is continually evolving. A new bypass round a village or town will probably take on the number of the road that formerly went through the settlement, while the original road may be given a new number rather lower in the hierarchy (downgraded from A to B and renumbered, for example) or even no longer be numbered at all. If your map and the new road number disagree, this is the reason. Follow the map. In the route directions, we've used the latest maps available at the time of writing—but some of the changes are rapid.

In England and Wales you can also legally ride on "public bridleways"—paths originally designated for horseriders. These really belong in the off-road section later, but it's worth noting that quite a number of these follow minor paved roads and drives and are hardly off-road at all. Many of these roads and drives are privately owned and are misleadingly but legally correctly marked "Private Road" but nevertheless have a public path following their line—it's only the road that's private. If your map shows the appropriate right of way (below), then you can use the road or track whatever the (often deliberately) discouraging sign says.

Maps for Cycling in Britain

Because Britain is heavily populated and the network of minor roads so dense, an accurate map is nearly essential, especially if you wish to make side trips off any of the routes. The sketch maps showing the routes are really intended to help you place yourself on a real map. A good map can give you all the information you need, plus a mind's-eye picture of the landscape it depicts. You merely have to learn the conventions.

The first characteristic of a map is its scale. A small-scale map shows a large area but lacks detail; large-scale maps show more detail but cover a much smaller area. The map scale you choose has to be a compromise between showing detail and what is practical.

For cycling, scales from 1:250 000 (about ¼ in. on the map representing 1 mile on the ground, or 1 cm representing 250 000 cm, i.e., 2.5 km) to 1:25 000 (where about 2½ in. represent 1 mile, or 1 cm represents 250 m) are the most useful. The 1:250 000 scale is adequate for following most on-road routes but is short on detail in cities, towns and even large villages. The 1:100 000 scale would be ideal for most cycling purposes, but there is no British map at this scale covering the whole country. The 1:50 000 scale (where about 1¼ in. represents 1 mile, or 1 cm to 500 m) is detailed enough to show virtually every road and track, together with details of villages, towns, churches, individual farms, woodland, streams, lakes and rivers, and other landmarks. Unfortunately, to cover the whole of Britain at this scale would require 188 maps, even if you didn't visit the remote Scottish islands, with a total weight of about 19 kg (41 lb.), and costing over £840 ($1,350). The larger-scale 1:25 000 maps show even more detail and can be very useful off-road—but of course need even more sheets and cost more than the 1:50 000.

Britain's national maps are made by the Ordnance Survey, colloquially known as the "O.S.," who give each scale fancy names: 1:250 000 are "Travelmasters" in blue covers, 1:50 000 are "Landrangers" in bright magenta covers, and 1:25 000 are "Pathfinders" in green covers. For a visitor to Britain using this book we'd recommend the Travelmaster map for general navigation and following our routes. Eight sheets cover Great Britain (the ninth sheet in the series is a double-sided sheet covering the whole of Britain at the smaller scale of 1:625 000—you might find this a useful map to buy at home to plan your trip in outline before coming to Britain). Then, if you want to explore an area in more detail for a few days, you can buy the 1:50 000 Landranger sheets locally.

A slightly enlarged version of the Travelmaster—at a scale of 3 miles to the inch or 1:190 080 (except for the Scottish Islands, which are at the smaller scale of 1:316 800)—is published in revised form each year as the O.S. Motoring Atlas, at a cost of less than two Travelmaster individual sheets. This is hardly the appropriate form for carrying on a bicycle—it's an A3 (16 x 11 in.) paperback book,

10 mm (⅜ in.) thick—but it could be economical to buy one and detach the pages you need.

The 2-miles-to-the-inch (1:126 720) maps recently introduced by Goldeneye are designed for cyclists. They give much the same road information as the Travelmaster, but the larger scale permits what is in our view a more attractive presentation and appreciably more topographical detail and tourist information. One feature of these maps is that they are designed with tall, thin panels that concertina out to display an almost square shape (covering about 20 x 22 miles) without having to make the awkward double fold needed with O.S. maps, and which results in the latter's premature wear at the corners of panels. Further, these maps are printed with a waterproof lamination (you can make temporary notes on it with a Wet-Wipe pen) on tear-resistant paper.

Goldeneye Cyclists' Road Maps so far cover thirteen tourist areas of England; for more details, contact Goldeneye Map-Guides (address given in Appendix 1). We mention in our route description if there's a relevant Goldeneye map.

The maps sold by Tourist Boards, at varying scales around 1:100 000 depending on the size of the area they have to cover, can also be useful.

Map symbols and conventions

Travelmasters and Landrangers use similar color codes for roads, showing their status.

Motorways, banned to cyclists: blue

Designated "trunk" roads:

> Travelmaster—green
> Landranger—red

A-roads: red

Divided highways ("dual carriageways") are also distinguished from two-way roads on both maps.

B-roads: orange-brown

Unclassified minor roads:

> Travelmaster—uncolored, and some very minor roads may be omitted, but you may take it that any road shown with a solid line edging is paved.

> Landranger—yellow for paved hard-surfaced roads, shown in two different widths on the map, according to whether they are wider or narrower than 4 meters (about 13 ft.) on the ground. This is a bit academic to an unhurried cycle tourist except that the narrower ones are usually likely to carry less traffic.

Very minor roads of perhaps indifferent surface, minor streets in towns and unpaved tracks:

> Travelmaster—usually not shown

Landranger—uncolored

The Landranger also shows roads that are unfenced (or unhedged or unwalled) with a dotted edge: on both sides if completely unfenced, on the appropriate side if the road is open only to that side. Unfenced roads may offer more open views but less shelter.

Both maps also show what every cyclist needs to know: how hilly the route is going to be. Grades in Britain are often given on road warning signs as a ratio—a 1:6 hill (not uncommon) is 16–17%, a 1:4 25%, and so on. These are spoken of as a "1-in-6" or a "1-in-4." The steepest either of us has ever seen and ridden up is a short 1:2, 40%, between the upper and lower parts of the small town of Harlech in Wales. Don't panic—as far as we know it's unique.

Travelmaster maps show hills by:

☐ marking highest points of hills or mountains (but not road passes) with altitude in feet, with a single arrow or chevron pointing down hills steeper than 14% (1-in-7) on A- or B-roads only. Cyclists generally want to be warned if the road goes up: it takes a while to accept that these warning arrows or chevrons point downhill.

☐ layer shading—land in different height bands is tinted with a different color. Low-lying land is tinted green; higher ground is marked by a series of yellowish-browns of increasing depth of color. The exact heights at which the bands change are shown on the key panel down the side of the map.

History at the roadside. Sometimes you may find an old milestone beside a now almost forgotten road, dating from the days when this was the main coach route between two important places.

☐ shadowing hills as though the sun were low in the northwest, giving an immediate impression of relief in hilly country.

Landranger maps show topography in three ways:

☐ Heights above sea level in meters ("spot heights") are shown at varying intervals, including at the top of road and off-road passes.

☐ Contour lines—imaginary lines, marked in brown on the map, which link points of the same height—are plotted at 10-meter (about 33 ft.) intervals. The more closely grouped the contour lines, the steeper the slope.

☐ Steep road grades are shown (on colored roads only) by a more elaborate system of arrow or chevron marks, once more pointing downhill: one chevron indicates grades between 14% and 20% (1-in-7 and 1-in-5); two mark a grade steeper than 20% (1-in-5). Such quite steep grades are not uncommon.

On Goldeneye maps, hills are shown by layer shading, and B-roads are shown in yellow; road coloring is otherwise similar to the Travelmaster maps. Heights are in meters.

Using the map: finding your way

With Britain's—or at least lowland Britain's—intricate network of roads, finding your way can call for quite a lot of attention. Fortunately, because the network is so dense, if you make a mistake it is usually possible to get back onto the right road without too many extra miles. Don't forget what we wrote earlier about changes in road numbers following new roadbuilding.

British road signing is usually good, but don't forget that signs are nowadays addressed mainly to car drivers, and policy is usually to direct cars to the nearest A-road route.

Roads are not usually named other than in towns and villages—though it's a fair bet that if a road in a village is named, say, "Muddyford Road" then it is indeed likely to lead to Muddyford. On the other hand, "Muddyford Street" in a town is much more likely to be named after His Grace the Duke of Muddyford, commemorating his part in some minor military skirmish in the 1870s, or after the pub "The Muddyford Arms," which is at one end of it.

The easiest way to navigate is to avoid trying to memorize more than two or three intersections ahead, and to make a mental note from the map how far it is to the next one: "Make a left in the direction of Lower Muddyford after about 2 miles, then right after another ½ mile." Your cycle computer is then helpful for checking how far you have traveled since the last landmark and to show when you should be close to the next.

Off-Road Cycling

In Britain there is a long tradition of riding on unpaved roads, and the introduction of the mountain bike has increased this form of riding in recent years. Most of the unsurfaced roads and paths actually lead somewhere, and it is entirely possible to cover large sections of a longer tour this way.

Where you can ride: rights of way

Cyclists are specifically permitted to ride on bridleways—paths for horses—giving way to walkers and horseriders where necessary.

"Byways open to all traffic," known colloquially as "BOATs," are also obviously available to cyclists. These have road status, but the local authority is not required to maintain them as paved highways.

A third category, "road used as public path," is gradually disappearing as these "RUPPs" are regraded as byways, bridleways or footpaths.

Certain long-distance trails incorporate long stretches of cyclable bridleway. Bridleways are marked on the ground in a variety of ways where they leave a road and at intervals along them. The commonest sign is a small green fingerpost, either reading "Public Bridleway," or showing a rider on a horse or sometimes just a horseshoe. In some areas, wooden signs are used as being less obtrusive. At gates and so on, many bridleways are marked by a discreet (sometimes very discreet) pale blue arrow sign (similar pale yellow signs indicate footpaths).

Byways may be marked "Byway" or in some places "Field Road," sometimes giving the destination—or they may not be signed at all. Any gates you find on any of these paths or byways should be left as you find them—closed if they were closed, open if they were not.

The surface condition and "cyclability" of these paths and tracks varies enormously. Farmers are permitted to plow over bridleways that cross fields, provided they reinstate them afterwards. The reinstatement may be no more than a rolled strip of earth across the furrows. Because Britain's lowlands often have clay soils, lowland bridleways can be very muddy, particularly if they are much used by horseriders. Upland bridleways tend to be harder surfaced and much better for cycling. There are of course many exceptions to both of these generalizations.

The O.S. Landranger 1:50 000 maps and the Pathfinder 1:25 000 maps mark and distinguish all these public rights of way. Note that these indications on the map and all the information given so far apply only to England and Wales; under Scottish law, right of way can depend on evidence of long and continuous use.

☐ Bridleways are marked as lines of dashes, red on Landranger maps and green on Pathfinders.

☐ BOATs are indicated as a line of alternating short dashes and crosses in red on Landranger maps, and by a line of small crosses in green on Pathfinders.

☐ RUPPs are shown as a line of alternating short and long dashes in red on Landranger maps; this class is not marked separately on Pathfinder maps.

The rise of the mountain bike has caused some conflict between off-road cyclists and walkers, in particular on some popular routes in areas already close to saturation by walking visitors. There is now an advisory Mountain Bike Code intended to inform new mountain-bike purchasers of the rights of way open to them and to give some practical advice on travel in wild places. The mountain-bike bodies have proposed voluntary restraints on mountain-bike usage on certain popular routes at peak times. The position is finely balanced, and it is up to off-road cyclists to act reasonably if restricting legislation is to be averted.

Cycling on footpaths is a sensitive issue. Apart from sidewalks, and paths with the standard red-bordered circular no-cycling sign showing a black bicycle symbol on a white ground, it is not (at the time of writing) a criminal offense to ride a bicycle on a footpath, but riders might leave themselves open to legal action for damages by the owner of the land over which the path passes. Note that on footpaths you will almost certainly encounter obstacles, especially stiles, over which a bike and its load have to be lifted.

Access concerns are not based solely on possible pedestrian-cycle conflict. It is now widely recognized that many of Britain's (indeed, the world's) wild and upland areas are fragile, and their flora, fauna and very character vulnerable. Too great an influx of visitors, no matter by which means they arrive, could easily destroy the wildness they come to seek. Many of these environmentally sensitive areas and nature reserves are now effectively closed to casual visitors, and off-road cyclists should respect this. Many upland paths are showing signs of overuse. Take them gently and avoid skidding or wheel-spinning on soft ground—best of all, seek out other areas and routes. Our remote and solitary places should be treated with care.

Permissive paths and bike trails

In addition to rights of way there are "permissive" routes over which cycling is allowed by the landowners, without any implication of right. These include most canal towpaths owned by the British Waterways Board. These flat routes are a fine introduction to out-of-the-ordinary off-road riding and, by their nature, often reach into urban areas. The late 18th and early 19th century narrow canal system was just beginning to establish a network when canals were overtaken by railways as the means of freight transport in the 1840s and 50s. Many have disappeared, but enough remain to offer some interesting possibilities. As with bridleways, surfaces vary widely in quality. To use most towpaths you need a (free) permit from British Waterways.

Britain's national forests are owned by the Forestry Commission, which has recently adopted a policy of opening up many of its

forest roads (of which there are over 19,000 km/12,000 mi.) for cycling. The surface quality of these varies. Many are hard-based and
scarcely qualify as off-road at all but are nonetheless superb for
away-from-it-all cycling. Some of them are waymarked as cycle
routes. The only shadow on the horizon is that some forests are
being sold off to private owners who may not maintain access.

A number of routes have been designated from the start as cycle
routes, many following the beds of former railway branch lines,
often winding a gently graded way into the hills. Railway routes
offer a mix of embankments, cuttings and even the odd tunnel or
two, so views are varied. The charity Sustrans has developed a number of such routes, and many local authorities are now following
Sustrans' lead (or combining with them) to create routes.

There are many other cycle routes, frequently associated with
country park and reservoir developments, and often combined with
a cycle hire center.

The CTC/Countryside Commission booklet *Cycle A-Way* lists
these off-road cycle routes as well as on-road waymarked ones. It is
obtainable from the CTC (see Appendix 1). Some on-road bike
routes are marked on the Landranger map. Local Tourist Information Centers will also be able to supply details.

Maps for off-road

For following well-defined or waymarked tracks, the O.S.
Landranger 1:50 000 series is adequate, but sometimes you need
more detail. Paths in lowland areas can be just as tricky to trace, or
even more so, than ones on the uplands. The best map for the job is
the O.S. Pathfinder 1:25 000 series, in green covers. At this scale,
each kilometer on the ground is represented by 4 cm on the map, or
each mile by about 2 in. Standard sheets cover an area 10 km by
20 km (about 6 x 12 mi.), but the map is also used as the basis for a
number of larger Outdoor Leisure Maps (in yellow covers) covering
popular tourist areas. These latter have extra "tourist" information
added.

The map shows enhanced detail such as field and woodland
boundaries—fences, hedges or walls—marked as fine black lines. As
already noted, rights of way are marked in green: footpaths as
dotted lines, bridleways as lines of longer dashes, and BOATs as a
line of crosses. The Pathfinder map also shows, and often names, isolated buildings and features such as cairns, chimneys and standing
stones, all invaluable for determining your position. Other map indications are the positions and boundaries of areas of loose rock,
boulders and scree; the map also distinguishes between scrub
vegetation, heath, and bracken and rough grassland, warns of
marshy areas and differentiates between coniferous woodland,
broad-leaved trees, coppice and orchard. How all this essential information is depicted is explained by the key panel at the side of the
map: study it.

Safety in remote places

Never overestimate your ability or speed off-road. Daily mileages are in any case low in tough country, and even on a day spent wholly on a canal towpath, the total feasible distance may be between half and two-thirds of what you would expect to do on-road over the same terrain. In hilly country you may not average much more than brisk walking pace.

Follow the same guidelines as everyone else who ventures into wild and, particularly, high country. Although Britain's hills and mountains are not high, a combination of high winds and damp can make the risk of exposure and wind chill very real if the weather turns nasty. Have enough clothing, including waterproofs, and sturdy shoes. Take enough food and drink for your normal needs on a trip of the duration you plan (time is more important than distance) plus some high-energy reserve food for an emergency.

Check the bike carefully before leaving to make sure that everything is in order, and carry at least tools and spares to deal with tire troubles and broken gear and brake cables.

Make sure somebody knows where you are going, by what route, and when you expect to return or reach your destination. Certainly think at least twice before making a wild crossing alone. Weather can change fast in the hills—if it gets worse suddenly, take the fastest practicable route to low ground.

If you change your plans for this or any other reason, make sure that those who might otherwise raise the alarm know that you are safe. Plan to be back to paved roads before dark, but carry a flashlight (UK = torch) and emergency whistle, just in case. The standard code for distress signals in the hills is one long blast of the whistle and showing of the lamp repeated at one-minute intervals.

CHAPTER 3

Introduction to the Routes

The routes (in England pronounced "root," never "rowt") described in this book are divided into two groups.

The first and most important group is a series of linear point-to-point itineraries. These link easily accessible centers, including airports and sea-ports, to the historic cities and other regions that are on most visitors' lists. These places are already linked by signed highway routes designed for cars, but these usually carry heavy traffic and are most unpleasant for cycling. Our routes are designed to offer bike-friendly alternatives that are on mainly quiet minor roads. Our bike routes also pass through or near a good sample of the interesting villages, towns and landscapes of England, Wales and southern Scotland. Together, these 18 point-to-point routes form a loose mesh over the country, and you can use them in whole or in part, alone or in combination with others to make up almost any number of circular trips and diversions.

The second group is made up of circular routes. There are five long and entirely rural tours in less populated parts of highland England, Wales and, particularly, Scotland. These link up to the point-to-point routes or to each other and are designed to introduce you to what we feel are some of the best of our British landscapes. Finally, there is a chapter with suggested combinations of point-to-point routes that can be used to create circular tours.

Each route includes the following:

☐ A summary of most important facts about the route.

☐ A descriptive narration about the terrain and the sights.

☐ A locator map and one or more route maps. Each route map has a North arrow, since it may not be aligned the conventional way. Use this route map only in conjunction with a detailed road map as listed for each route. In general, we recommend at least the Ordnance Survey Travelmaster map at scale 1:250 000.

☐ Detailed route directions. To keep these as short as possible, we use the standard abbreviations shown in the table on page 28.

☐ Additional details, such as access by rail or by bike.

Two of the conventions used in these descriptions call for explanation: where a description indicates that the route goes "through" a town or village, the route passes through or close to the center; where it is stated to go "by" a village, it passes close to or through the outlying parts of the settlement.

Note that for the urban sections of Routes 3, 6 and 8—from the three main London airports into central London—directions are given by road and street names rather than by road numbers.

☐ Please beware that things do change. The information given was correct as far as we could determine at the time of going to press. Neither we nor the publishers can be held responsible for subsequent changes, but we will be grateful for any updated information the reader can provide.

R.	make right turn
L.	make left turn
S.O.	continue straight ahead
L. and R.	turn left and very soon after, right; jog left jog right
R. and L.	vice versa
T-junct.	T-junction (three-way intersection with right or left choice)
rbt.	roundabout (traffic circle)
mini-rbt.	mini-roundabout
x-rds.	crossroads (four-way intersection)
O.S.	Ordnance Survey map
N., S., E., W.	north, south, east, west
uc.	unclassified (road—i.e., not numbered as a class A-, B- or M-road)
P.H.	public house
rly.	railway (railroad)
stn.	railway station
l.c.	level crossing (railroad grade crossing)
In place names the following abbreviations may be used	
Br.	Bridge
Gt.	Great
Lt.	Little
St.	Saint

CHAPTER 4

Route 1

London-Heathrow Airport to Church Stretton

Via Oxford and Stratford-upon-Avon (with link to Birmingham International Airport)

Distance: 291 km (181 mi.)

Intermediate distances:
Heathrow Airport–Oxford:
    87 km (54 mi.)
Oxford–Stratford-upon-Avon:
    82 km (51 mi.)
Stratford-upon-Avon–Tenbury
    Wells: 79 km (49 mi.)
Tenbury Wells–Church Stretton:
    43 km (27 mi.)

Terrain:
Begins gently but becomes hillier beyond Oxford

Maps:
O.S. Travelmaster (1:250 000) sheets: 6, 7
O.S. Landranger (1:50 000) sheets: 138, 139 (for Birmingham
    Airport link), 150, 151, 164, 175, 176
Goldeneye (1:126 720) sheet: Cotswolds (covers part of route)

Access:
By train: Reading (8 km/5 mi. W. of route), Oxford, and Worcester
(10 km/6 mi. S. of route).

By bike, Routes 2 and 3 connect with this route at Heathrow Airport,
and Route 9 in Oxford.

Summary:
If you're coming from overseas, this is an ideal route to start exploring the English countryside. It links London's main international
airport to the nearby royal town of Windsor, the university city of
Oxford, and Shakespeare's Stratford-upon-Avon, and then goes on
to the very attractive cycling area of the Welsh border country.

Description

The small town of Eton is famed for its public school (a term that in Britain means, quite illogically, an exclusive and expensive private school) whose pupils can expect to go on to high positions in business and politics. The picturesque narrow High Street leads to the River Thames and Windsor, dominated by the 11th-century round tower of Windsor Castle. Ironically—since it is now one of the Queen's official residences—it only avoided the destruction that overtook many castles in the English Civil War of the 1640s by being occupied by anti-Royalist forces throughout.

From Windsor, the road passes through quiet villages of the county of Berkshire (say it "Barksheer") to cross the River Thames again at the pretty village of Sonning. From the Thames, the road climbs steadily to the village of Nettlebed through beechwoods for which these chalk hills, the Chilterns, are famed. There's a fine swoop down to the hamlet of Britwell Salome, followed by several more villages, including Chalgrove, site of a Civil War battle in 1643. Following the Civil War, England was for a short time effectively a republic, known as the Commonwealth.

The pattern of small hedged fields is typical of much of southern and central England. These are in Shropshire.

The next leg of the route leads into Oxford, home of the oldest British university, with its many attractive college buildings. (For a general description of Oxford, see Route 9, Chapter 12.)

The building materials of the villages and towns have changed: the golden stone of the Oxford colleges is a foretaste of the next 50 km (30 mi.) or so, across the Cotswold Hills. From the end of the 13th to the 16th centuries, this was one main center of Europe's wool industry, and many of the now-small stone villages have almost cathedral-like churches dating from the prosperity of that time. Take the time to have a look round the village of Great Tew, one with the least evidence of modern development.

Another village, Hook Norton, has quite another claim to fame: a village brewery. Many of the pubs and inns that you pass in this part of the world will proudly proclaim that they serve Hook Norton ales. The route follows very rolling countryside from here to Stratford-upon-Avon, with many of the fields separated by the traditional Cotswold "dry-stone" walls—built entirely without cement. Stratford is nowadays very much a tourist center, and often busy with visitors. The Shakespeare legend brings tourists from all over the world; Shakespeare's birthplace (he lived from 1564 to 1616) is now a museum, while one of the other showplaces is the thatched cottage where his wife, Anne Hathaway, was born in nearby Shottery.

From Stratford, the route heads west through quiet farming country, passing between the city of Worcester and the former spa town of Droitwich. Droitwich was from Roman times the source of much of England's supply of salt and the maps show many old "salt roads" radiating far and wide from the town. Here, too, you will cross two canals. These narrow canals with their "narrow boats" were the arteries of supply during the early days of the Industrial Revolution at the end of the 18th century.

The route crosses the River Severn, Britain's longest river, at Holt Fleet and then climbs steadily to Great Witley. This is now sandstone country, with the earth a deep red, while the villages and towns feature many black-and-white timbered cottages. From Great Witley the road follows the valley of the little River Teme—though that doesn't mean it's flat. One of the features of the Teme valley are the hopfields, with their geometrical rows of hop plants. Hop flowers are dried and used to impart the flavor to bitter beer—quite possibly some from the Teme valley find their way into those Hook Norton ales.

Tenbury Wells and Ludlow, the next two towns, are gems of black-and-white architecture. Both are on the River Teme, but the route climbs over a low spur between the two. Ludlow was a 12th-century planned town, with many early black-and-white timbered buildings, perhaps the most notable being the Feathers Inn, dating from 1603. The Norman castle, built in 1085, was one of a chain built to defend the border between England and Wales.

From Ludlow, the route climbs over another wooded limestone ridge, Wenlock Edge, before dropping to Church Stretton. About 5 km (3 miles) west of the route, near Craven Arms, there is another

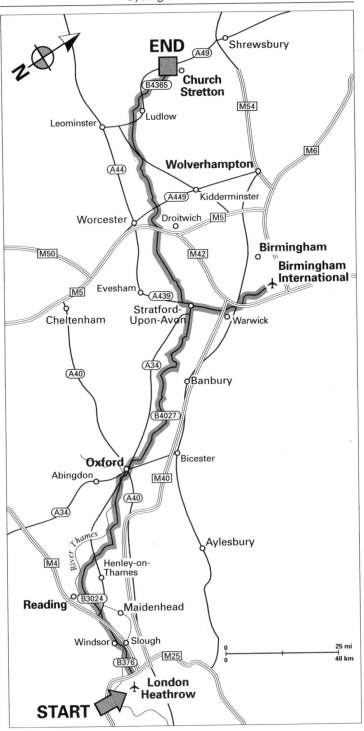

interesting castle, Stokesay. Dating from the 12th and 13th centuries, this is a fortified timbered manor house rather than an out-and-out military installation. The route ends at Church Stretton, a small town nestling at the foot of the high whaleback ridge of the Long Mynd.

Directions

1. From Terminals 1, 2 and 3, take tunnel or bus to N. of airport, then join A4. From Terminal 4, do not join A30 but follow Airport Perimeter Road E. to Hatton Cross Underground stn., then follow Airport Perimeter Road E. then N. round airport to rbt. exit to A4.

2. W. on A4 (Bath Road), then after 1.5 km (1 mi.), at "Peggy Bedford" pub, fork L. on uc. road (Bath Road) to rbt. junct. with A3044.

3. S.O. (2nd exit) on uc. road (Bath Road) into Colnbrook, then L. on Horton Road to Horton.

4. R. to B376, S.O. on B376 into Datchet.

5. S.O. through village, then fork L. on B3026 to B3022.

6. L. on B3022 through Eton to cross River Thames at cycle-pedestrian bridge to Windsor.

7. S.O. into Thames Street, R. under castle walls, R. again, then L. into Barry Avenue beside river.

8. Follow cycle route under rly. into Stovell Road and A332 into Clewer Court Road.

9. L. into Mill Lane and S.O. across Maidenhead Road, A308, on uc. road (Parsonage Lane) to B3024, Dedworth Road.

10. R. on B3024 through Oakley Green; keep L. on B3024 by Fifield to A330.

11. L. on A330 to Touchen-End, then fork R. on B3024 through Paley Street to pass over M4 by White Waltham to Ruscombe.

12. S.O. on B3024 to A3032, then L. through Twyford to rbt. junct. with A4 at Charvil.

13. S.O. (2nd. exit) on B478 opposite; follow B478 through Sonning and over River Thames to A4155 at Play Hatch.

14. L. on A4155, then after 500 m (0.3 mi.), R. on uc. road to B481 at Emmer Green.

15. R. on B481 through Sonning Common, Rotherfield Peppard and Highmoor to rbt. junct. with A423.

17. L. on A423 into Nettlebed, then R. on B481 to Cookley Green.

18. 1 km (0.6 mi.) after Cookley Green, L. on uc. road to B4009 at Britwell Salome.

19. L. on B4009, then 1st R. through Brightwell Baldwin to B480 at Cuxham. L. on B480 to A329 at Stadhampton.

20. L. on A329, then at T-junct., R. on B480 to cross River Thames and through Chiselhampton to outskirts of Oxford.

21. 800 m (0.5 mi.) after start of built-up area on L., L. into Blackbird Leys (Cuddesdon Way), then R. (Blackbird Leys Way) to pass over A4142 to rbt. junct. with B4495.

22. R. on B4495 (Between Towns Road) to B480 at church.

23. (For Oxford city center, L. on B480 or follow signed cycle route.)

24. R. on B480 (Oxford Road, Cowley), then L. on B4495 (Hollow Way) to T-junct.

25. L., still on B4495 (The Slade, becoming Windmill Road), to A420.

26. S.O. on uc. road (Old High Street, Headington).

27. L. on St. Andrews Road, becoming Dunstan Road, then L. into Saxon Way, which becomes Copse Lane.

28. Just after school on R., R. into Brookfield Crescent to T-junct. with Marsh Lane, B4150.

29. R. on Marsh Lane, B4150, keeping R. to avoid joining A40; pass over A40, then L. on uc. road through Woodeaton to B4027.

30. L. on B4027 through Islip, passing over A34 to Bletchingdon, where R. on uc. road to A4095 at Kirtlington.

31. R. on A4095 through village, then L. on uc. road (effectively S.O. where A4095 goes R.) to B4030.

32. L. on B4030 through Lower Heyford to A4260 at Hopcroft's Holt. (Route 10, Cambridge to Bath joins for a short stretch here).

33. R. and L. across A4260 on B4030 through Middle Barton to Westcott Barton.

34. R. on uc. road at church (effectively S.O. where B4030 goes L.) through Sandford St. Martin.

35. 2 km (1.2 mi.) after Sandford, L., and after 2 km (1.2 mi.), R. through Great Tew to B4022.

36. R. on B4022 to A361.

37. L. on A361, then R. on uc. road through Swerford, Hook Norton (a very complex village—look for signs) and Sibford Ferris.

37. L., L. and R. through Sibford Gower to B4035.

38. L. on B4035 through Lower Brailes, then R. on uc. road to Whatcote.

39. L. and R. in village through Fulready, then R. and L. on uc. road to B4455.

40. R. on B4455 to A422.

41. L. on A422 through Ettington, S.O. at rbt. junct. with A429, still on A422 to A34 on outskirts of Stratford.

42. R. on A34 to cross River Avon into Stratford-upon-Avon.

43. (Link to/from Birmingham International Airport joins/leaves at Stratford-upon-Avon—see below.)

44. Immediately after bridge over Stratford Canal, L. into Waterside, which becomes Southern Lane.

45. At T-junct., R. into Old Town, then L. into College Street, R. into College Lane, which becomes Sanctus Street.

46. S.O. over A4390 into Sanctus Road to B439, Evesham Road.

47. After 1 km (0.6 mi.), L. on uc. road through Luddington to B439.

48. L. on B439, then R. on uc. road through Binton, then L. at x-rds. through Temple Grafton to Ardens Grafton.

49. R. at next x-rds. to B4085 at Wixford.

50. S.O. on B4085, then L. on uc. road (effectively S.O. where B4085 goes R.) to A435.

51. L. on A435 to Dunnington, then R. on A441. After 1.5 km (1 mi.), L. on uc. road by Abbots Morton and through Radford to A422 at Flyford Flavell.

52. L. on A422 and 1st R. past Grafton Flyford church, then L. on uc. road through Huddington to cross rly. at l.c. and then over Worcester and Bromsgrove Canal.

53. After 300 m (0.2 mi.), L. then R. to pass under M5.

54. Immediately after M5 bridge, L on uc. road, S.O. at x-rds. to A38 at Copcut.

55. S.O. across A38 on uc. road over rly. bridge, then immediately L. After 800 m (0.5 mi.), R. to pass over Droitwich Canal and after 1.5 km (1 mi.), R. to A4133 at Hadley.

56. L. on A4133, passing under A449 to Ombersley.

57. S.O. at rbt. in village center, still on A4133, to cross River Severn at Holt Fleet, then to A443/B4196 at Holt Heath.

58. R. on B4196 to Shrawley, L. at church on uc. road to A443 at Structon's Heath.

59. R. on A443 to Great Witley, then L. opposite Hundred House Hotel on B4203, crossing River Teme at Stanford Bridge, to Stanford on Teme.

60. R. on uc. road by Orleton and through Rochford to B4204.

61. S.O. on B4204, then R. on A4112 into Tenbury Wells.

62. S.O. on A4112 to recross River Teme to T-junct. with A456.

63. L. on A456, then R. on B4214; after 300 m (0.2 mi.), L. on uc. road through Greete to Caynham.

64. S.O. in Caynham, then after 1.5 km (1 mi.), R. to pass over A49 and under rly. into Ludlow.

65. Leave Ludlow N. on B4361, but immediately before bridge over River Corve, R. on uc. road (effectively S.O. where B4361 goes L.).

66. R. under rly. and immediately L., still on uc. road, to pass over A49, then L. through Stanton Lacy to B4365.

67. R. on B4365 through Culmington to B4368.

68. L. on B4368, then R. on uc. road through Westhope over Wenlock Edge through Harton, then R. to Ticklerton.

69. L. in Ticklerton through Soudley to B4371 at Hope Bowdler.

70. L. on B4371 to cross A49 into Church Stretton.

Link to/from Birmingham International Airport to Stratford-upon-Avon:

1. Leave airport terminal S. on Airport Way to rbt. junct. with A45.

2. S.O. (2nd exit) on B4438 (Catherine-de-Barnes Lane) to rbt. junct. with B4102 in Catherine-de-Barnes.

3. S.O. on uc. road (Friday Lane, becoming Barston Lane) to Barston. R. in Barston to B4101.

4. L. on B4101, then after 1 km (0.6 mi.), 2nd. R. on uc. road to A4141 at Chadwick End.

5. L. on A4141 to Baddesley Clinton, R on uc. road and 1st L. through Shrewley to B4439.

6. S.O. across B4439, passing over rly. at Hatton stn. and M40, then immediately L. to B4095. S.O. across B4095 on uc. road through Norton Lindsey to Snitterfield.

7. In village, L., R. and L. to pass over A46 to A439.

8. R. on A439 into Stratford-upon-Avon to join main route.

CHAPTER 5

Route 2

London-Heathrow Airport to Cambridge

Total distance: *150 km (93 mi.)*

Intermediate distances:
Heathrow Airport–Leighton
    Buzzard: 68 km (42 mi.)
Leighton Buzzard–Cambridge:
    82 km (51 mi.)

Terrain:
Moderate, gentle toward
    Cambridge

Access:

By air: Heathrow Airport

By train: Cambridge

By bike: Routes1 and 3 link at
    Heathrow; Routes 7, 10, 13,
    14 link at Cambridge

Maps:
O.S. Travelmaster (1:250 000)
    sheet: 6
O.S. Landranger (1:50 000)
    sheets: 153, 154, 165, 166, 176

Summary:
Skirting Greater London itself,
this route leads from London's
main international airport through quiet rural country to the university city of Cambridge, hub of several of our other routes.

Description

The first few miles of this route pass through thinning suburbs and then by affluent residential areas: Gerrards Cross, for one, is a much sought-after address. On the way, just after Iver, you pass by Pinewood Studios, at one time the center of the British movie industry and setting for many of the James Bond films. Most of the sets and stages are now hidden away indoors, however.

Soon after Gerrards Cross, the route passes within about 2 km (1.2 mi.) of the Quaker village of Jordans, west of the route. William Penn, founder of Pennsylvania, lived here from 1670 and is buried in the burial ground of the Meeting House, which dates from 1687. The adjacent Mayflower Barn is claimed to be largely built from the timbers of the Pilgrim Fathers' ship, the *Mayflower*.

The next village, Chalfont St. Giles, also has historic connections. It was here that the poet John Milton came from London to escape the Plague in 1665, writing his epic *Paradise Lost* while living here. Milton's Cottage is now a small museum. From here the route follows quite hilly and narrow lanes across the chalk Chiltern Hills, known for their beechwoods. You may get glimpses of the small muntjac deer that have colonized the forest.

Leaving the Chiltern Hills for the lower, rolling Vale of Aylesbury, the route passes over the proudly named Grand Union Canal, which was built just before the rail age to link the River Thames near London with the River Trent, which passes several midland cities, and with the largest midland city, Birmingham, in the heartland of the Industrial Revolution. One of industrial Birmingham's boasts is that it has a greater mileage of canals than Venice. Just before the village of Ivinghoe there is a well-preserved windmill. This type was known as a "post-mill" because the whole mill body rotated on a central wooden pillar to face the wind; 18th-century Pitstone Mill is one of the oldest in Britain.

The Vale of Aylesbury is pleasant undulating agricultural country, restful rather than spectacular. Looking back to the Chiltern

Windmills were used to grind wheat or to power drainage pumps in marshy areas.

Hills from Mentmore, you can see a large white figure of a lion cut into the chalk of the hillside. Unlike the ancient ones near some of the other routes, this hill figure dates from the mid-20th century and marks the site of Whipsnade Zoo, a large open-air animal park, now largely devoted to preserving rare species.

There is another notable park about 5 km (3 mi.) off the route, north of the town of Leighton Buzzard. This is Woburn Abbey, traditional and current home of the Dukes of Bedford. The palatial 18th-century house is one of the most impressive of English stately homes. The fine open grassy park is surrounded with superb trees of many species and has herds of rare deer. There is also a safari park.

As the route passes northeastward, you move away from agricultural grazing country into wide open fields, some devoted to specialized market gardening—at the right time of year you can see miles of cabbages—but becoming more and more planted with wheat, oats, barley or oil-seed rape.

Beyond the busy A1 divided highway, the modern embodiment of the romantic Great North Road that led from London to Edinburgh in Scotland, you pass through compact and increasingly attractive small settlements, culminating in the lovely village of Ashwell—well worth a detailed look round for its plaster-decorated and timbered cottages. Ashwell has a small museum and a large church with a dominant spire. This is church spire country, and from points on the next part of the route you can see sometimes five or six of them soaring above the fields.

The final run into Cambridge is mainly gentle, through more pretty villages. Just off the route, about 1.5 km (1 mi.) to the south, is the village of Granchester, associated with the young poet Rupert Brooke.

Cambridge is one of Europe's ancient university cities, the oldest college, Peterhouse, being founded in 1285 by dissidents who had found the slightly older Oxford inhibiting their freedom of expression. The compact college area in the center is fascinating and well worth a day's exploration of its architectural treasures, ranging from the 13th century to the late 20th. Despite a recent city-center ban, Cambridge is a city where everybody bikes, with the highest level of cycle commuting in Britain. Traditionally, bikes have been the students' means of transport: the morning mass ride to 9 A.M. lectures can be quite spectacular. However, the best way to explore the colleges themselves is on foot, so that you can penetrate the many fascinating alleyways and footbridges over the River Cam to enjoy the superb prospect from the west side of the river, known as "The Backs."

Directions

1. From Terminals 1, 2 and 3, take tunnel or bus to N. of airport, then join A4. From Terminal 4, do not join A30 but follow Airport Perimeter Road E. to Hatton Cross Underground stn.,

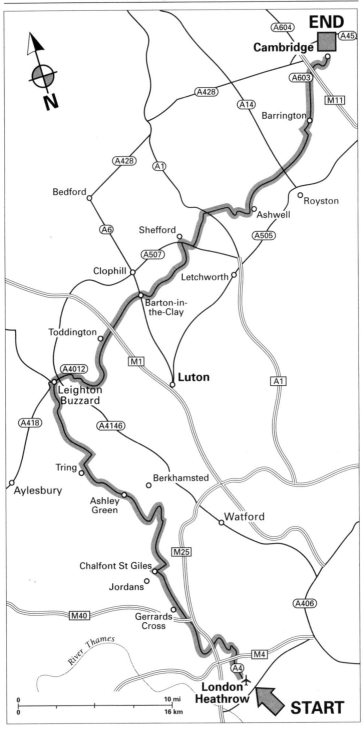

then follow Airport Perimeter Road E. then N. round airport to rbt. exit to A4.

2. W on A4 (Bath Road), then after 1 km (0.6 mi.), R. on A3044 (Hatch Lane) through Harmondsworth.

3. L. on uc. road (Harmondsworth Road) to pass over M4 to Sipson Lane, West Drayton.

4. L. on Sipson Lane, then L. opposite school to Thorney Mill Road.

5. L. into Thorney Mill Road to pass over M25 to Richings Park.

6. R. on uc. road (Thorney Lane North) to B470 (High Street) in Iver.

7. L. on B470 (High Street, becoming Langley Park Road).

8. At 3rd main turn, R., at Iver Grove, into Wood Lane.

9. Follow Wood Lane to 5-way rbt. junct. with A412/A4007.

10. S.O. (2nd exit) on uc. road (Pinewood Road) past movie studio to T-junct.

11. R. through Fulmer, passing over M40 to A40 at Gerrards Cross.

12. S.O. across A40 on uc. road, then at T-junct. R. on B416 over rly.

13. 1 km (0.6 mi.) after rly., fork L. on uc. road (effectively S.O. where B416 sweeps R.), then after 800 m (0.5 mi.), L. at Gold Hill Common (again effectively S.O.) to Three Households, Chalfont St. Giles.

14. R. at mini-rbt. through Chalfont St. Giles village center to mini-rbt. junct. with A413.

15. S.O. across A413 on B4442, then after 1.5 km (1 mi.), fork R. on uc. road, S.O. at x-rds. under rly. to A404.

16. S.O. across A404, S.O. at x-rds. at foot of hill through Latimer to Flaunden.

27. L. at x-rds. in Flaunden, then 1st L., S.O. at x-rds. to T-junct. at Bovingdon Green.

28. L. at T-junct. to B4505.

29. L. on B4505 to Orchard Leigh, where fork R. (effectively S.O. where B4505 sweeps L.) to A416 at Ashley Green. S.O. across A416, keeping left along Hog Lane to T-junct., L. then R. at foot of hill to Wigginton.

20. In Wigginton, R. down hill, under A41 to A4251.

21. S.O. across A4251 on uc. road, then immediately L.

22. At T-junct., R. over Grand Union Canal and rly., then 1st L. to B488.

23. R. on B488 to Ivinghoe, S.O. on B489 to rbt. at Pitstone Green.

24. R. on uc. road, then R. at T-junct. immediately after rly. bridge and over Grand Union Canal through Cheddington to Mentmore.

25. In Mentmore village center, R. on uc. road to T-junct. at Ledburn, R. to junct. with B488/A418.

26. Pass under A418 on path to rejoin paved road to Linslade/Leighton Buzzard.

27. R. on A4012 through Leighton Buzzard and S.O. at rbt., still on A4102, for 3 km (2 mi.).

28. R. (effectively S.O. where A4102 goes L.) through Eggington, then R. through Stanbridge and Tilsworth to A5.

29. L. on A5, then 1st R. through Tebworth to A5120 at Toddington.

30. L. on A5120 to pass over M1, then R. on uc. road through Harlington and under A6 to T-junct. in Barton-le-Clay.

31. L. and then R. at N. outskirts of village on uc. road through Higham Gobion to T-junct.

32. R. to Apsley End, L. at x-rds. through Shillington and Meppershall to T-junct. with A600 at Shefford.

33. R. on A600, then at mini-rbt., L. on A507 to Clifton.

34. At x-rds. in center of village, L. for 500 m (0.3 mi.), then R. at x-rds. to A6001.

35. L. on A6001 over River Ivel into Langford, then R. on uc. road (effectively S.O. where A6001 sweeps L.) to A1 by water tower.

36. L. on A1 then 1st R. (great care) on uc. road, then R., still on uc. road, through Edworth and Hinxworth to T-junct.

37. L. through Ashwell to T-junct., then L. and R. to Steeple Morden.

38. R. at church through Littlington and Bassingbourn to A1198 at Kneesworth.

39. S.O. across A1198 on uc. road through Meldreth to Shepreth, then L. over rly. level crossing through Barrington and Haslingfield to A603 at Barton.

40. R. on A603 to pass over M11 into Cambridge.

CHAPTER 6

Route 3

London-Heathrow Airport to Central London

Total distance: 29 km (18 mi.)

Terrain:
Mainly flat, with urban traffic

Maps:

O.S. Travelmaster (1:250 000)
sheets: 6 and 9 cover the
route but are unlikely to be
of much practical help for
navigation

O.S. Landranger (1:50 000)
sheet: 176—detailed enough
but does not give road
names or one-way streets

Access:

By air: Heathrow Airport

By train: London Mainlike stations

By bike: Links with Routes 1 and 2 at Heathrow, with Routes 6 and 8
in London.

Summary:

An entirely urban route to get you to central London from the
country's major airport.

Description

This route may not seem like your perfect bike tour at first, but after
all, if you are coming to England by air, you may want to to spend
some time in London, and this route is a good one for getting into
the city. Once you get used to riding in traffic, you will find cycling
an excellent way to get around in London. It's faster than any other
mode of transport, and you see where you are going, making it ideal
for sightseeing.

Directions

1. From Terminals 1, 2 and 3, take tunnel or bus to N. of airport;
then do not join A4 but follow Airport Perimeter Road E. round
airport to rbt. at Hatton Cross Underground stn. From Terminal
4, do not join A30 but follow Airport Perimeter Road E. to
Hatton Cross Underground stn.

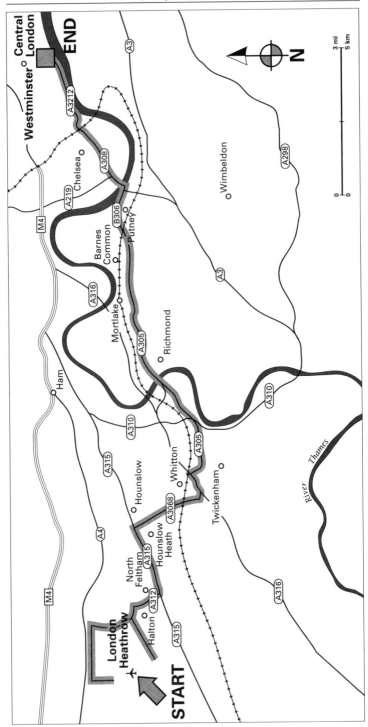

2. Cross A30, then fork L. to join Fagg's Rd.

3. L. onto Staines Rd. (A315).

4. After 1.7 km (1 mi.), R. onto Wellington Rd. South (A312).

5. S.O. across Hounslow Rd. (A314) onto Nelson Rd., bearing R. into Hospital Br. Rd.

6. 700 m (about 1/2 mi.) after second rly. br., L. at library into Percy Rd., 1st R. into Ross Rd.

7. At end of road, R. across bridge over A316 to rejoin other portion of Ross Rd., L. to intersection with Meadway.

8. R. onto Meadway, then L. onto Staines Rd. (A305), which becomes The Green, then Heath Rd., King St., York St. and Richmond Rd., still A305.

9. S.O. to Richmond Br. over River Thames, L. after br. into Hill St., R. onto Red Lion St., which becomes Paradise Rd., then Sheen Rd. and Upper Richmond Rd. West (still A305).

10. At junction with Rocks Lane and Roehampton Lane (A306), bear L. into Queens Ride (B306), which joins Lower Richmond Rd.

About as typical a cycletouring photograph as you'll find anywhere.

11. S.O. to Putney Br. over River Thames, L. over Putney Br., bear R. on New Kings Rd. (A308).

12. After 2.4 km (1.5 mi.), cross Finborough Rd. (A3220, northbound), then R. on Edith Grove (A3220, southbound), then L. onto Cheyne Walk (A3212). This becomes the Chelsea Embankment, then Grosvenor Rd., then Millbank, following the L. bank of the Thames to Westminster Abbey, Houses of Parliament and "Big Ben," about 6 km (4 mi.) after joining road beside Thames at Chelsea.

CHAPTER 7

Route 4

Harwich and Felixstowe to Cambridge

Total distance: 110 km (68 mi.)

Intermediate distances:
Harwich–Lavenham:
  47 km (29 mi.)
Lavenham–Cambridge:
  63 km (39 mi.)

Terrain:
very gentle

Maps:
O.S. Travelmaster (1:250 000)
  sheets: 6 or 9
O.S. Landranger (1:50 000)
  sheets: 154, 155, 167 (for
Stansted Airport link), 169
Goldeneye (1:126 720)
  sheet: Suffolk
  (covers part of route)

Access:

By train: Harwich Parkeston Quay and Cambridge.

By bike: Routes 2, 7, 10, 13, 14 link at Cambridge; link to Stansted
  Airport at Balsham.

Summary:
This route links the seaports of Harwich and Felixstowe on the east
coast of England to the university city of Cambridge, hub of several
of our other routes, and offers a gentle ride through the part of
England known as East Anglia, named for its early settlers, the
Angles.

Description

The first few miles lead inland beside the tidal estuary of the River
Stour to Manningtree, a small town that owes its existence to its
strategic position at the first practicable crossing of the Stour. Immediately after leaving the main A137 you enter "Constable Country,"
named for the landscape painter John Constable (1776–1837), who
lived in East Bergholt. The subjects of several of his paintings, notably
Flatford Mill and Willy Lott's cottage, have been preserved much as
he saw them and are now used as field study centers.

  The great joys of this route, however—apart from the warm and
gentle agricultural landscape—are the picturesque villages and
small towns. Hadleigh, the next small town, is a jewel. Here the

houses, the earliest dating from the 14th and 15th centuries, are timber-framed with ornate plaster decorations, brightly colored with warm reds, golds and pale yellows; many carry molded emblems testifying to their earlier uses.

Although the route as described goes straight from Hadleigh to the next small town, Lavenham, it is worth making a short side trip of no more than 3 km (2 mi.) to the west of the route to visit the villages of Kersey and Lindsey. Kersey has a particularly fine main street of white plastered houses leading down to a little watersplash.

Lavenham is another gem, with virtually the whole town center consisting of 16th-century timber buildings, several of which are open for visiting. Like the Cotswold Hills (Chapter 4), the county of Suffolk was one of the great European wool centers in medieval times, and the Guildhall at Lavenham has a museum covering 700 years of the wool trade. As in the Costswolds, too, this prosperity manifested itself in enormous cathedral-like churches, of which those at Lavenham and Brent Eleigh are notable.

The remaining villages on the route may be less spectacular than Hadleigh and Lavenham, but they, too, contain many fine buildings and are superbly set and settled in their gentle landscape. Just before the final run down to Cambridge from Balsham, there is a broad view out over the dead flat landscape of the Fens to the north. The link route from London's Stansted Airport also passes through several fine towns and villages, notably Saffron Walden with its timber-framed buildings, one of them now a youth hostel.

For a general description of Cambridge, see Route 2, Chapter 5.

Directions

1. Leave Harwich Parkeston Quay S. by Parkeston Road to rbt. junct. with A120.

2. R. (2nd exit) on A120 to Ramsey, then R. at rbt. on B1352 through Bradfield and Mistley, keeping R. after rly. bridge along coast to rbt. junct. with A137 at Manningtree.

3. R. on A137 to cross River Stour, then in Cattawade, L. on B1070 through East Bergholt to pass under A12 through Holton St. Mary and Raydon to Hadleigh.

4. S.O. in town center still on B1070 to A1071.

5. L. and R. on A1141 through Monks Eleigh and Brent Eleigh to Lavenham.

6. L. on B1071, then R. on uc. road (effectively S.O. where B1071 goes L.) to A134 at Bridge Street.

7. R. and L. across A134 on uc. road, then R. to Shimpling, L. at T-junct. at N. end of village, then R. to B1066 at Hartest.

8. L. on B1066 to Boxted, then R. on uc. road through Hawkedon and Denston to A143 at Stradishall.

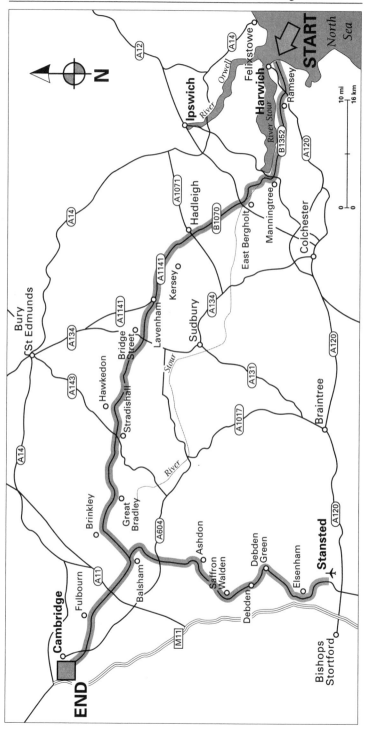

9. L. on A143, then R. on uc. roads through Farley Green, then at T-junct., L. through Cowlinge to B1061 at Great Bradley.

10. R. on B1061, then after 3 km (2 mi.), fork L. to B1052 at Brinkley.

11. L. on B1052 through Weston Colville and West Wratting to Balsham.

12. (Link to/from London-Stansted airport leaves/joins at Balsham—see below.)

13. At W. end of Balsham village, R. on uc. road to A505.

14. R. and L. across A505 through Fulbourn and Cherry Hinton.

15. Follow cycle route signs over cycle suspension bridge to Cambridge city center.

Link to/from London-Stansted Airport:

1. Leave airport terminal and L. on uc. road at rbt., then L. and L. by Molehill Green to B1051 at Elsenham. R. on B1051, then L. on uc. road to Henham.

2. R., still on uc. road, to T-junct at Debden Green, L. through Debden to B1052 in Saffron Walden.

3. R. and L. on B1052, then R. on uc. road through Church End to Ashdon.

4. L. on uc. road through Bartlow to A604.

5. R. and L. across A604 on uc. road, then after 4 km (2.5 mi.), L. at x-rds. to Balsham to join main route.

From Felixstowe (port for Belgium):

1. Take ferry across estuary of Rivers Stour and Orwell to Harwich.

2. After ferry, R. on Quay, then L. into George Street to junct. with Main Road.

3. R. on Main Road (B1352), which becomes High Street, then Main Road once more, through Dovercourt to rbt. junct. with A120.

4. S.O. on B1352 through Bradfield and Mistley, as main route.

CHAPTER 8

Route 5

Dover and Folkestone to Bath

With link to/from London-Gatwick Airport

Total distance: 396 km (246 mi.)

Intermediate distances:
Dover–Robertsbridge:
  84 km (52 mi.)
Robertsbridge–Horsham:
  74 km (46 mi.)
Horsham–Liphook:
  66 km (41 mi.)
Liphook–Overton:
  48 km (30 mi.)
Overton–Marlborough:
  48 km (30 mi.)
Marlborough–Bath:
  76 km (47 mi.)

Terrain: Quite hilly

Maps:
O.S. Travelmaster (1:250 000) sheets: 9 and 8 (just)
O.S. Landranger (1:50 000) sheets: 172, 173, 174, 179 (barely), 185, 186, 188, 189, 197, 198, 199
Goldeneye (1:126 720) sheets: Kent, Sussex (cover part of route)

Access:

By train: Dover and Haslemere (5 km / 3 mi. N.E. of route).

By bike: Link with Route 7 between Brightling and Punnett's Town; Route 9 crosses at Overton.

Summary:

This route sweeps across southern England, linking the seaports of Dover and Folkestone and the new Channel Tunnel rail terminal at the southeastern tip of England with the Georgian city of Bath. It crosses the varied landscapes of the Weald and several areas of chalk downland before reaching the golden limestone of the hills around Bath.

Description

This route traces the footsteps of some of the earliest settlers in Britain some 10,000 years ago as they migrated from a land link with continental Europe along the chalk hills toward the west.

The chalk range known as the North Downs reaches the sea at Dover and Folkestone, giving rise to the famed and sentimental White Cliffs. For the first part of the route from any of the three starting points, you cross the Downs through a very domestic landscape.

One of Britain's few dead flat areas, Romney and Walland Marshes, lie to the south between Bilsington and Ham Street. Now largely cultivated, this was once true marshland, and the area is still crisscrossed by small rivers and drainage channels, romantically known as "sewers." Between the road and the Marsh is a military curiosity: the Royal Military Canal. This was hurriedly constructed in the early 19th century as a defense against the expected invasion by the French Emperor Napoleon. The invasion never came, so the Canal was not tested; nowadays a haven for wildlife, it certainly does not look a very formidable obstacle.

The route climbs away from the marsh through Stone-in-Oxney and Wittersham, where there is a very fine windmill, and begins on its crossing of the Weald. This Saxon name is very much like the modern German *Wald* (wood), and where the sand- and clay-based Weald retains some of its natural state, it is indeed heavily wooded with oaks and chestnuts. Nowadays there are extensive clearings and meadows around most of the villages.

About 8 km (5 mi.) south of Wittersham, and worth the side trip if you have time, is the pretty village of Rye, one of the small towns known as the Cinque Ports—ancient seaports enjoying special privileges from medieval times. Rye is now no longer a port: gradual build-up of sands and marshes over a couple of centuries have left it about 4 km (2.5 mi.) from the sea.

The next landmark is a superb castle, Bodiam. Built in 1385 to stem another French invasion that never materialized, this is one of the most castle-shaped of castles, with massive walls and robust round corner towers, all properly set—as a castle should be—in a broad moat. Just 13 km (8 mi.) to the south of here lies the site of the Battle of Hastings (or Senlac) where the French King William the Conqueror did succeed in invading in 1066. The next small town, or large village, of Robertsbridge has some fine examples of typical Wealden houses, with white weatherboarding or hung with red pantiles. Near here, as well as in other places along the route, you may see a number of "oast-houses": barn-like buildings with conical roofs capped with white-painted wooden cowls. These were used for drying the hop flowers grown to flavor bitter beer. With Herefordshire (on Route 1), Kent is one of the few places where hops are grown, and up to about 50 years ago the traditional family holiday for people living in the poorer parts of east London was to go down to Kent for the hop-picking season at the end of August. Sadly, perhaps, the hops are now harvested mechanically and kiln-dried, and many of the oast-houses have been converted into unusually shaped holiday homes or country retreats.

From here to the fair-sized town of Horsham, you are in typical Wealden woodland, quite hilly with steep-sided river valleys and many trees. England is not a very wooded country (apart from Ireland, it's the least wooded in Europe) so this is a relatively unusual experience in Britain. At Freshfield the route crosses a preserved steam railroad, known as the "Bluebell Line" because of the masses of these flowers that carpet the woodlands in spring. Much of this area, and particularly the towns such as Haywards Heath, Cuckfield and Horsham itself, is very affluent and settled by people who commute daily by rail to London.

From Horsham, the route heads south toward the chalk range of the South Downs. Nestling under the north side of the Downs, beside the meandering River Arun, is the village of Amberley, with its castle overlooking the river. There is also a museum at Amberley.

A few miles farther on, at Bignor, there are the remains of a Roman villa. Dating from the 2nd to 4th centuries, it was discovered by chance by a farm worker and excavated in 1811 to reveal some of the finest mosaic tiling in Britain. There is a site museum nearby.

From here, a series of delightful little lanes, mainly through woodland, lead to Liphook. A few more wooded miles bring you to the end of the western extension of the Weald and you are back in chalk country. The next village, Selborne, dominated by its "hangers" (steep wooded hillsides), achieved fame through the publication in 1788 of *The Natural History of Selborne*, the painstaking narrative diary of its vicar, Gilbert White (1720–1793), tracing the life of the village over many years. Now the route runs through quiet, rolling, cultivated country with typical beech woods on the small hills, and a succession of pleasant small villages. The style of building has changed, and there are a number of cottages and even churches built with a combination of the local stone, flint, and brick or stone.

At Great Bedwyn, the route crosses a picturesque canal, the Kennet and Avon. Dug in 1810, this was one of the last canals to be constructed before they were superseded in the 1840s by rail (the rail route runs close by, following the same easy contour), and was intended to link London with the western seaport of Bristol, one of the major ports for trade with the Americas. The engineers were a little too ambitious in the number of locks on the canal, however, and natural water feed was not enough. So a powerful steam-beam-engine was constructed at Crofton, 4 km (2.5 mi.) southwest of Great Bedwyn, to pump water up to the canal. It is now open to visitors.

Shortly after this, the route follows a magnificent avenue of trees through the ancient Savernake Forest, before dropping to the small town of Marlborough. Marlborough boasts one of the widest high streets (main streets) in England and is also home to a famous "public school." This area is also one of the centers of English racehorse breeding, and you will pass several stables and exercise gallops. The area is rich in prehistoric antiquities, and about 10 km (6 mi.) west of Marlborough lies the Neolithic stone circle of Avebury, virtually enclosing the small village. Dating from about 1500 B.C., it is considered second only to the better-known Stonehenge, which is of similar age and lies about 30 km (19 mi.) to the south. Unlike Stonehenge, Avebury is built of local stones, the largest weighing over 60 tons. Nearby are many ceremonial burial mounds or "barrows" dating from the same era, and the still unexplained artificial Silbury Hill. A steady climb brings you to the edge of the Marlborough Downs and the steep drop to the vale below.

A series of quite complex little lanes winding round the foot of the downs brings you eventually to the village of Lacock (say it "Laycock"). This is a delightful and carefully preserved village, tended by the National Trust and well worth a look round. It was here at Lacock Abbey around 1840 that the English scientist William Henry Fox Talbot invented the negative/positive process which is the basis of all modern photography. The Abbey houses a Fox Talbot museum.

The final part of the route from Lacock to Bath involves a couple of quite steep grades over two limestone ridges, the southern end of the Cotswold hills, calling en route at the picturesque golden-stone small town of Bradford-on-Avon. Note that this River Avon is not the same as the one in the Shakespeare country: England has several Avons—the word comes from the Celtic word for "river," found also as the Welsh word *afon*.

Bradford-on-Avon has a claim to fame in the cycling world as the home of the Moulton bicycle, the ingenious small-wheeled design that pioneered the use of suspension on bicycles.

Bath is on the list of every visitor to Britain. Its modern aspect is that of a graceful neoclassical planned city, with many of the creamy-stone buildings dating from the 18th century, including the elegant and striking curved "crescents" high on the hillside. But Bath was founded as a city much earlier than this: the Romans discovered the hot springs here and built villas and a bath complex in the town they called Aquae Sulis. The Roman baths and many of the later (Georgian) buildings are open to visitors; there are many other galleries and museums.

Directions

From Dover car ferry terminal (Eastern Docks):

1. S.O. (2nd exit) at rbt. at exit on Townwall Street, signed A20. At next rbt., R. (2nd exit) into York Street (A256). From Hoverport terminal, S.O. to rbt., then R. on Snargate Street, then L. (1st exit) at next rbt. into York Street (A256).

2. Follow York Street to next rbt., then L. on Folkestone Road (B2011).

3. After 1 km (0.6 mi.), R. into Eaton Road (uc. road), and almost immediately L. on uc. road to West Hougham.

4. In West Hougham, R. to x-rds. just after passing under power lines. L. for 2km (1.2 mi.) to Hockley Sole, R. to A260 in Hawkinge.

5. S.O. across A260 on uc. road, then R. to Paddlesworth.

6. From Paddlesworth, S.O. to Etchinghill, R. on uc. road.

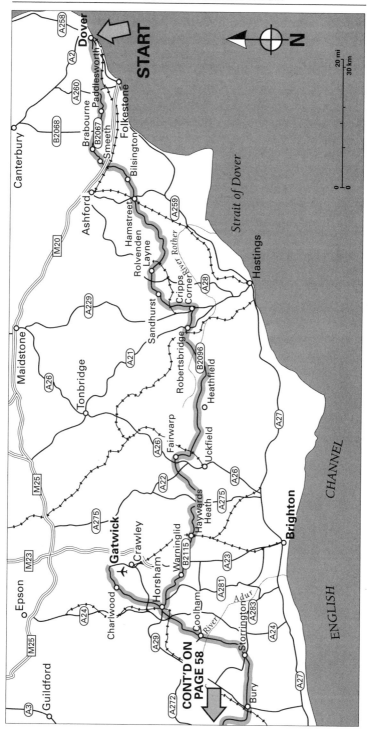

CONT'D ON PAGE 58

From Folkestone car ferry terminal:

1. Follow one-way system into Tontine Street, then R. into Dover Road, A260, then L. into Canterbury Road (uc. road, becoming A260) to cross former A20 (also now A260).

2. Immediately before A20 rbt., L. on uc. road to pass over A20, then R. through Gibraltar, R. and L. to Paddlesworth.

3. From Paddlesworth, S.O. to Etchinghill, R. on uc. road.

4. From Channel Tunnel: Follow exit to M20 Junct. 11a.

5. Pass over M20 and at rbt. junct. with A20, S.O. on uc. road through Beachborough to Etchinghill, continue S.O. on uc. road.

All routes:

1. About 1 km (0.6 mi.) after Etchinghill, S.O. on uc. road to B2068.

2. S.O. on B2068, then L. on uc. road by Stowting, L. to Brabourne, then L. through Brabourne Lees and Smeeth to A20.

3. S.O. across A20 on uc. road to pass over M20 and rly. through Aldington and Bonnington to B2067.

4. R. on B2067 through Bilsington and Ruckinge to Hamstreet.

5. S.O. to pass under A2070 on B2067 to Kenardington, then L. on uc. road through Appledore Heath to B2080.

6. S.O. on uc. road by Stone in Oxney to B2082 in Wittersham.

7. S.O. on B2082, then 1.5 km (1 mi.) after village, L. on uc. road (effectively S.O. where B2080 goes R.) to Rolvendon Layne.

8. L. to A28; cross A28 L. and R. on uc. road, then L. to A268 at Sandhurst.

9. R. on A268 through Sandhurst, then L. on uc. road to Bodiam, R. on uc. road to A229.

10. S.O. across A229 on uc. road, then L. through Salehurst and pass over A21 into Robertsbridge.

11. R. in Robertsbridge on uc. road, then L. through Oxley's Green to Brightling.

12. R. in village, then L. at x-rds. to B2096.

13. R. on B2096 through Dallington and Punnett's Town to A265.

14. L. on A265 through Heathfield to A267.

15. R. on A267, then after 1 km (0.6 mi.), L. on B2102 (effectively S.O. where A267 goes R.), then after 3 km (2 mi.), R. on uc. road through Pounsley to A272 at Buxted.

16. L. on A272 under rly. bridge, then R. on uc. road to Parkhurst, then L. on uc. road to A26.

17. R. and L. across A26 on uc. road to B2026 at Fairwarp. S.O. across B2026 on uc. road, then L. to A22 at Horney Common.

18. R. and L. across A22 on uc. road, then L. and R. through Splayne's Green to A275.

19. S.O. across A275 on uc. road to Freshfield rly. stn. on steam rly. 1 km (0.6 mi.) after rly., R. to B2028. L. on B2028 to Haywards Heath rly. stn.

20. At rbt. by stn., R. on uc. road, then L. under rly. to B2036.

21. R. on B2036 into Whitemans Green, then L. on B2114 to Slough Green, then L. (effectively S.O. where B2114 goes R.) on B2115 to pass over A23, then through Warninglid to A279.

22. L. on A279 to Lower Beeding, then R. on uc. road through Plummers Plain, then 2nd L. to Horsham.

23. (Link to from London-Gatwick airport joins/leaves at Horsham—see below.)

24. Leave Horsham town center S. on B2237, then after passing over rly., R. on uc. road to pass under A24 and continue to A272 at Coolham.

25. S.O. across A272 on B2139 by Thakeham to A283 at Storrington.

26. R. on A283, then L. on B2139 by Amberley to cross under rly. at Amberley rly. stn. and over River Arun to Houghton.

27. R. on uc. road to A29 at Bury.

28. Cross A29 R. and L. on uc. road through West Burton, Bignor and Sutton.

29. 2 km (1.2 mi.) after Sutton, L. to A285.

30. L. on A285, then R. on uc. road through Selham to A272.

31. L. on A272, then R. on uc. road through Lodsworth to Lickfold, then L. to A286 at Fernhurst.

32. S.O. across A286 on uc. road to Elmers Marsh.

33. R. to B2131 in Liphook.

34. L. on B2131 to rbt. junct. with A3; take 3rd exit, B3004, then after 3 km (2 mi.), L. on uc. road to A325 at Whitehill.

35. S.O. across A325 on uc. road to Blackmoor, R. to B3006 in Selborne. L. on B3006, then R. on uc. road to A32 at East Tistead.

36. L. on A32, then 1st R. on uc. road to 5-way x-rds. at Hawthorn; R. (3rd exit) to A31.

37. Cross A31, L. and R. on uc. road through Medstead by Lower Wield to B3046 at Preston Candover.

38. R. on B3046 to Axford, then L. on uc. road to pass under M3 to A33.

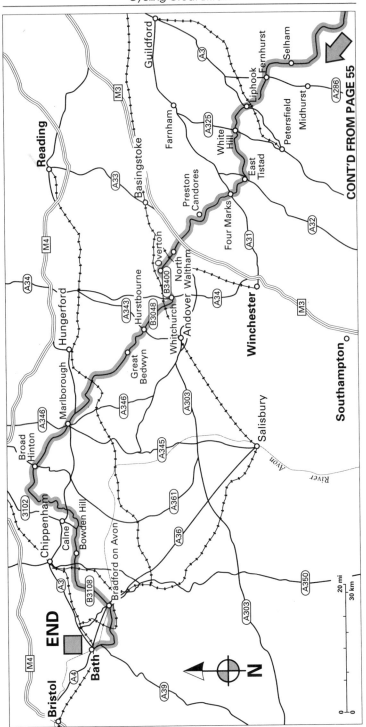

39. S.O. across A33 on uc. road through North Waltham to B3400 in Overton.

40. L. on B3400 through Whitchurch to pass under A34 to Hurstborne Priors.

41. R. on B3048 through St. Mary Bourne and Stoke to A343 at Hurstbourne Tarrant.

42. S.O. across A343 on uc. road through Ibthorpe, Upton, Vernham Dean and Oxenwood to A338.

43. S.O. across A338, still on uc. road, to cross rly. and Kennet and Avon Canal at Great Bedwyn.

44. S.O., and after 3 km (2 mi.), L. on uc. road, then 1st R. (after road to St. Katharine's on L.) along Grand Avenue through Savernake Forest to A4.

45. L. on A4 down hill to Marlborough.

46. In town center, R. on A345 by church, then L. on uc. road (effectively S.O. where A345 goes R.) over Hackpen Hill to A4361.

47. Cross A4361 R. and L. on uc. road to Broad Hinton.

48. At T-junct. in village, L., then 1st L. to Clyffe Pypard.

49. L. and R. in village to x-rds. at Bushton.

50. L. through Compton Bassett to A4.

51. R. on A4, then 1st L. on uc. road to Blackland, R., then L. to Stockley, R. to A3102.

52. L. on A3102, then after 5 km (3 mi.), R. on uc. road to A342 at Sandy Lane.

53. R. on A342, then 1st L. on uc. road through Bowden Hill to Lacock. In Lacock, L. and 1st R. to A350.

54. S.O. across A350 on uc. road to B3353 at Gastard.

55. S.O. on B3353, then after 800 m (0.5 mi.), L. on uc. road to Neston, L. on uc. road to A365 at Atworth.

56. S.O. across A365 on uc. road to B3109 at Bradford Leigh.

57. L. on B3109 to A363 by church in Bradford-on-Avon.

58. R. on A363, then L. on B3108 through Winsley to cross River Avon and Kennet and Avon Canal to A36.

59. S.O. across A36 on uc. road, then over Claverton Down into Bath.

Link from London-Gatwick airport to Horsham:

From Gatwick South Terminal:

1. Immediately after clearing customs, L. to lifts (elevators).

2.   Take lifts 15, 16 or 17 to street level (G = ground floor).

3.   L. on Perimeter Road East to rbt.

4.   Follow signed route S.O., now Perimeter Road North, signed "West Side Cargo Centre" through underpass to rbt.

5.   S.O., signed "North Terminal, Long Term Car Park," passing Ramada Hotel on R.

6.   After 800 m (0.5 mi.), R. past barriers signed "Permit holders only" over bridge over River Mole into Povey Cross Road.

7.   R. to x-rds., L. on uc. road to Charlwood.

From Gatwick North Terminal:

1.   Exit at street level, then L. to rbt.

2.   Take 4th exit signed "South Side" (Gatwick Way).

3.   At T-junct., R. on Perimeter Road North through underpass as for route from South Terminal.

4.   In Charlwood, L. past road to church through Russ Hill to T-junct.

5.   L. through Jordans to T-junct., L. through Rusper to rbt. junct. with A264. S.O. on uc. road, then L. to center of Horsham to join main route.

Return route to airport:

1.   From center of Horsham, E. on B2195 past Horsham rly. stn.; after crossing over rly., L. on uc. road to 5-way rbt.

2.   Take 2nd exit over rly. level crossing by Little Haven rly. stn. to T-junct., R. on uc. road to rbt. junct. with A264.

3.   S.O. to Rusper; at N. end of village, fork R., signed "Newdigate," then after 1.5 km (1 mi.), R for 3km (2 mi.), then R. to Charlwood.

4.   R. through village, then S.O. to Povey Cross, R. into Povey Cross Road, L. past barriers signed "Permit holders only," L. on Perimeter Road North to rbt. by Travel Inn.

5.   S.O. (2nd exit), still on Perimeter Road North, through underpass, then:

For North Terminal:

1.   L. on Gatwick Way to rbt., L. following signs to North Terminal.

For South Terminal:

1.   S.O. on Perimeter Road North to rbt.

2.   S.O. to follow signs "South Side." At beginning of terminal building underpass, dismount, cross road to ramp, take lifts (elevators) 15, 16 or 17 to departure/arrival areas.

CHAPTER 9

Route 6

Gatwick Airport to Central London

Total distance: 66 km (41 mi.)

Intermediate distances:

Gatwick Airport–Epsom:
32 km (20 mi.)
Epsom–Westminster:
34 km (21 mi.)

Terrain:

Rolling but with steep climb to cross Downs at Pebble Coombe.

Maps:

O.S. Travelmaster (1:250 000) sheets: 9 covers the route but is unlikely to be of much practical help for navigation on the urban section

O.S. Landranger (1:50 000) sheets: 187, 176 (adequate overall detail but lacks street names and one-way street detail in urban section)
Goldeneye (1:126 720) sheet Sussex (covers part of route)

Access:

By train: Gatwick and London mainline stations.

By bike: Link to Routes6 at Gatwick, Route 8 at Oxford Circus, Route 3 at Putney Bridge.

Summary:

This route is essentially utilitarian, but the first few rural miles pass through a cross-section of the largely domestic countryside of the counties of West Sussex and Surrey.

Directions

From Gatwick South Terminal:

1. Immediately after clearing customs, L. to lifts (elevators). Take lifts 15, 16 or 17 to street level ("G" = ground floor).

2. L. on Perimeter Road East to rbt.

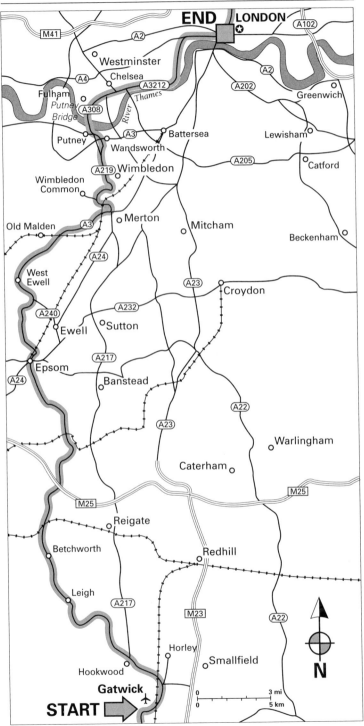

3. Follow signed route S.O., now Perimeter Road North, signed "West Side Cargo Centre" through underpass to rbt.

5. S.O., signed "North Terminal, Long Term Car Park," passing Ramada Hotel on R.

6. After 800 m (0.5 mi.), R. past barriers signed "Permit holders only" over bridge over River Mole into Povey Cross Road.

7. R. to x-rds., S.O. signed Hookwood and Reigate to join A217 to Hookwood.

From Gatwick North Terminal:

1. Exit at street level, then L. to rbt.

2. Take 4th exit signed "South Side" (Gatwick Way).

3. At T-junct., R. on Perimeter Road North through underpass as route from South Terminal.

4. At N. end of Hookwood, fork L. on uc. road, then 2nd L. after 4 km (2.5 mi.), through Nalderswood to T-junct.

Combined route:

1. R. on uc. rd. through Leigh to Betchworth.

2. L. and R, still on uc. road, to rbt. at crossing of A25.

3. S.O. on B2032 past Betchworth rly. stn. up steep climb of Pebble Coombe.

4. At top of hill, L. on B2033, then R. after 1.5 km (1 mi.) on uc. road to Headley. 400 m (0.3 mi.) after end of village, R. on uc. rd. under M25, then R. and L. on uc. rd. to join A24 in Epsom.

5. R. on A24, and at 3rd rbt., L. past Epsom rly. stn. on uc. rd. to join B284 after 1 km (0.6 mi.)

6. Continue on B284, Chessington Rd. to West Ewell.

7. From here the route is urban.
In West Ewell, R. onto Ruxley Lane (still B284), then L. on Kingston Rd. (A240).

8. After 600 m (0.4 mi.), R. into Worcester Park Rd. (B284), which becomes Church Rd.

9. At A2043, Malden Rd., L. and then 2nd R. into Motspur Park (do not cross rly. level crossing), which becomes Claremont Rd., to join Burlington Rd. West (B282).

10. This becomes Barnes Lane and passes under Bushey Rd. to intersection with Coombe Lane (A238).

11. R. and L. into Durham Rd. (B281), which becomes in succession Cottenham Park Rd., Woodhayes Rd., West Side Common and Cannizaro Rd. This joins Wimbledon Parkside (A219).

12. After 1.5 km (1 mi.), R. on Inner Park Rd., then 4th R. into Augustus Rd., then 6th L. onto Beaumont Rd. to cross A3, West Hill (pedestrian subway: walk bike) onto Putney Heath Lane.

13. At end of Putney Heath Lane, R. on Putney Hill (A219), which becomes Putney High St., leading to Putney Br. over River Thames.

14. After Putney Br., bear R. on New Kings Rd. (A308).

15. After 2.5 km (1.5 mi.), cross Finborough Rd. (A3220, northbound), then R. on Edith Grove (A3220, southbound), then L. onto Cheyne Walk (A3212).

16. This becomes the Chelsea Embankment, then Grosvenor Rd., then Millbank following the L. bank of the Thames to Westminster Abbey, Houses of Parliament and "Big Ben," about 6 km (4 mi.) after joining road beside Thames at Chelsea.

Return route to airport:

Because the main entrance to the airport is via the busy A23 or M23 motorway, it is necessary to follow a different route for the last few miles when returning to the airport.

From Hookwood:

1. R. on A217 to rbt.

2. S.O. on uc. road to Povey Cross, S.O. into Povey Cross Road. L. past barriers signed "Permit holders only," L. on Perimeter Road North to rbt. by Travel Inn.

3. S.O. (2nd exit), still on Perimeter Road North through underpass, then:

For North Terminal:

1. L. on Gatwick Way to rbt., L. following signs to North Terminal.

For South Terminal:

1. S.O. on Perimeter Road North to rbt.

2. S.O. to follow signs "South Side."

3. At beginning of terminal building underpass, dismount, cross road to ramp, take lifts (elevators) 15, 16 or 17 to departure andarrival areas.

CHAPTER 10

Route 7

Newhaven to Cambridge

With a link to London-Stansted Airport

Total distance: 251 km (156 mi.)

Intermediate distances:
Newhaven–Hailsham:
26 km (16 mi.)
Hailsham–Goudhurst:
40 km (25 mi.)
Goudhurst–Gravesend:
56 km (35 mi.)
Ferry to Tilbury, then
Tilbury–Great Dunmow:
68 km (42 mi.)
Great Dunmow–Cambridge:
61 km (38 mi.)

Terrain:
Quite hilly south of the Thames,
flat north of it

Maps:

O.S. Travelmaster (1:250 000) sheet: 9

O.S. Landranger (1:50 000) sheets: 154, 167, 177, 188. 198, 199

Goldeneye (1:126 720) sheets: Sussex; Kent (covers southern part of route)

Access:

By train: Cambridge (main line but not InterCity).

By bike: Routes 2, 4, 10, 13, 14 link at Cambridge.
Route 5 crosses at Dallington.
Link to Stansted Airport joins/leaves at Great Dunmow.

Summary:

This route links the port of Newhaven, on the southeast coast of England, with the university city of Cambridge.

Description

Newhaven is a small seaport, at one time an important crossing point for overnight travelers from London to Paris, but whose importance declined as Dover, Folkestone and now the Channel Tunnel took the everyday car-ferry traffic. Nevertheless, the Newhaven-Dieppe crossing has the advantage for cyclists of having pleasant cycling country close at hand at either end.

Newhaven nestles at the foot of the South Downs, a line of chalk hills, and the route follows the gap carved through the Downs by the Cuckmere River. As though resting from its ancient labors, the Cuckmere now reaches the sea by a series of placid and picturesque meanders. The pretty village of Alfriston with its wooden-steepled church lies in the middle of this natural gap. About 10 km (6 mi.) to the southeast (there is an off-road bike route from Alfriston) a short side trip takes you to the spectacular 200 m (about 600 ft.) vertical chalk sea-cliff of Beachy Head. Also just off the route, about 4 km (2.5 mi.) to the east, is the enigmatic figure of the "Long Man of Wilmington," a large human figure holding two vertical poles carved into the chalk of the hillside. Its origin and purpose are unknown.

After leaving the chalk Downs and passing through the small town of Hailsham, the route plunges for a few miles into the undulating wooded landscape of the Weald (see Chapter 8). Just before the village of Burwash, Bateman's, the home of the poet and writer Rudyard Kipling (1865–1936) has been kept by the National Trust largely as he left it; it is open to visitors.

After a short length of the rather busy main A21 road, then 4 km (2.5 mi.) along the B2079, a few hundred metres (or yards) to the east of the route is the Bedgebury Pinetum, a striking collection of trees

The southern edge of England: the chalk cliff of Beachy Head, east Sussex, about 10 km (6 mi.) southeast of Alfriston.

in a lakeside setting—mostly conifers but with some colorful broad-leaved species as well.

Goudhurst is a typically Weald-style village, with many of the house walls covered with hung semicircular tiles or with overlapping weather-boarding. About 5 km (3 mi.) to the west of Goudhurst lies another typically Wealden village: Lamberhurst, which boasts the largest vineyard in England. Although the Romans and later some of the religious orders had grown grapes for wine in England, English winemaking effectively ceased for 400 years following the closing down of many of the monasteries under protestant King Henry VIII in the 1500s. Now there are over a hundred mainly small English vineyards producing usually dry and semi-dry white wines. Also near Lamberhurst is 14th-century moated Scotney Castle, now a ruin but surrounded by one of England's most romantic landscaped gardens.

The next part of the route passes through a much more intensively cultivated area, where you may see some of the characteristic white-cowled "oast-houses" (see Chapter 8). This is an area of mainly fruit- and vegetable-growing, activities that earned for the county of Kent the name "The Garden of England."

Leaving the garden appropriately enough at West Malling, one of the country's largest horticultural research centers, the route climbs over the chalk North Downs. At the top of the ridge you cross the Pilgrims' Way, the old pilgrim route to the cathedral city of Canterbury—setting for Geoffrey Chaucer's earthy *Canterbury Tales*, written in the 14th century.

The final part of the route in Kent, to the River Thames at Gravesend, is rather urban for some 8 km (5 mi.). Gravesend was at one time the key English port for emigrants to America: George Fox sailed from here in 1672, and John and Charles Wesley in 1735. An 18th-century chapel in Gravesend is a memorial to Princess Pocahontas who died nearby.

With the coming of steam, Tilbury, the port on the opposite shore, became more important, and the last view of England that many later emigrants to America or Australia had was the flat misty coastline of Essex. Now Tilbury is another port that, like Newhaven, is less busy than it used to be when it was the closest to London that large passenger liners could venture.

There has long been a ferry across the estuary of the River Thames from Gravesend to Tilbury; until very recently the lowest bridge was some 33 km (20 mi.) in a straight line (and much more by road) farther upstream at Tower Bridge in London. New motorway bridges and tunnels at nearby Dartford threatened the continuation of the Tilbury-Gravesend ferry, but it now seems secure as a foot-passenger and bike crossing.

From Tilbury for some 30 km (18 mi.) or so, the countryside is flat and there is a fair amount of industry.

Beyond Ongar, you are back in gentle rural countryside once more, but this part of what is known as East Anglia is quite different from Kent, south of the Thames. The joy of this part of the route—apart from the easy cycling and the fact that a village in this county,

Essex, boasts the lowest rainfall in Britain—is the succession of attractive villages. The typical classic Essex style of cottage has white-painted weather-boarding and often decorative plaster-work, known as "pargetting." There is a pleasing mixture of styles of different ages. Of the small towns, Great Dunmow is outstanding with its many timbered houses.

Other quite frequent landmarks are the wooden windmills which remind you that the three counties of Essex, Suffolk and Norfolk have for some centuries been the centers of cereal-growing in Britain. The village of Finchingfield is an often-pictured one, with its open green descending to a small stream, with the rising village street and church framed in the background. The small town of Linton is another architectural showpiece with its timbered and plastered buildings along a winding high (main) street.

Some of the countryside is remarkably quiet on these later sections of this route, with longer gaps than you may have become used to between villages. Some of the names—Helions Bumpstead, Castle Camps and Shudy Camps—sound rather intriguing, but like all English place-names they stem from straightforward descriptions of the places in an earlier language, in this case Old English. Bumpstead is the "homestead by the reeds" owned, in 1086 when William the Conqueror's Domesday Book listed who held what, by Breton Tihel de Helion; *camps* were fields, Castle refers to the medieval castle that was here, and Shudy comes from the Middle English word for nothing more pretentious than a shed.

From here the route continues to Balsham to follow Route 2 for the final run in to Cambridge. For a general description of Cambridge, see Chapter 5.

Directions

1. Leave Newhaven Harbour N. on uc. road to A259.

2. R. on A259 through Newhaven town center, Denton and Seaford, then L. in Sutton on uc. road through Alfriston to rbt. junct. with A27.

3. Take 2nd exit (effectively S.O. on uc. road) to x-rds., R. through Arlington and Caneheath, then R. to A22.

4. L. and R. across A22 on uc. road, then L. on A295 through Hailsham town center to T-junct. with A271.

5. R. on A271, then fork L. on uc. road through Cowbeech and Foul Mile to Rushlake Green; fork R. to B2096.

6. R. on B2096, then L. at Wood's Corner on uc. road to A265 at Burwash.

7. R. and L. across A265 on uc. road, cross rly. level crossing to B2099 at Ticehurst.

8. R. on B2099, then L. on B2087 to A21 at Flimwell.

9. L. on A21, then R. on B2079 to A262 at Goudhurst.

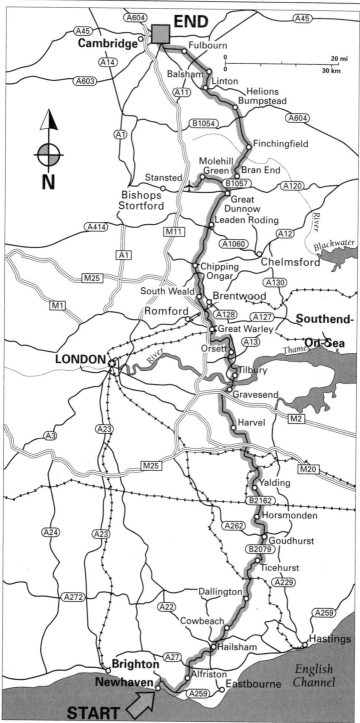

10. (Pleasant off-road alternative is to fork R. 300 m/0.2 mi. N. of junct. with A21 on bridleway through forest to B2079 at Bedgebury Cross, then R. on B2073 to Goudhurst.)

11. S.O. across A262, still on B2079, then after 2 km (1.2 mi.), L. on uc. road to B2162 at Horsmonden.

12. R. on B2162 through Collier Street and Benover to T-junct. with B2010.

13. R. over River Beult on B2010 through Yalding to West Farleigh, L. on B2163 to A26 at Teston.

14. L. on A26, then R. on uc. road.

15. After 3 km (2 mi.), L. at x-rds., still on uc. road, then L. at T-junct. to pass over A228 into West Malling.

16. S.O. to rbt. junct. with A20, L. then R. on uc. road to Birling. R. past church, then L. to climb to top of down.

17. S.O., avoiding turn to Vigo Village, through Harvel to A227 at Meopham.

18. R. on A227, then L. on B260 through Longford Hill.

19. R. at New Barn on uc. road to rbt. junct. with B262.

20. S.O. (2nd. exit) on B262 to pass over A2, then R. at next rbt. to A226 in Gravesend.

21. S.O. to ferry.

22. Cross River Thames by ferry to Tilbury (for ferry details, call (01474) 566 220).

23. From ferry terminal, R. on uc. road over rly to West Tilbury.

24. L. to Chadwell St. Mary, R. at church, then L. and R. through Orsett Heath.

25. Cross A1013, S.O. on B188, and pass under slip road and A13 to Baker Street.

26. R. on B188 through Orsett, then L. (where B188 goes R.) on uc. road to Bulphan.

27. S.O. on uc. road, then after 1.5 km (1 mi.), R. to x-rds.

28. L. at x-rds. to B186; R. on B186 to pass over A127 to Great Warley.

29. S.O. on uc. road in Great Warley (where B186 goes R.) to pass over rly. to A1023.

30. L. on A1023, then R. on uc. road passing over A12 to South Weald.

31. L. through Coxtle Green to A128 at Bentley, L. on A128.

32. R. on A113 into Chipping Ongar.

33. At rbt. junct. with A414, take 2nd exit (effectively S.O.) on B184 through Fyfield to A1060.

34. R. on A1060, to Leaden Roding.

35. L. on B184 through High Roding, L. over A120 into Great Dunmow; at N. end of town, R. on B1057.

36. (Link to London-Stansted airport leaves/joins here—see below.)

37. Follow B1057 through Bran End and Great Bardfield to Finchingfield.

38. In center of village opposite windmill, L. on uc. road to cross B1054.

39. L. and R. through Helions Bumpstead, Castle Camps, by Shudy Camps and Bartlow to A604.

40. Cross A604 R. and L. on uc. road into Linton.

41. R. on B1052, then on W. outskirts of Balsham, L. on uc. road to A505.

42. R. and L. across A505 through Fulbourn and Cherry Hinton.

43. Follow cycle route signs over cycle suspension bridge to Cambridge city center.

Link to/from London-Stansted Airport:

1. Leave airport terminal and L. on uc. road at rbt.

2. L. and L. to Molehill Green, then R.

3. 2 km (1.2 mi.) after Molehill Green, R. and R. at Brick End through Butcher's Pasture to B184.

Wine-growing in Britain has a tradition going back to medieval monasteries and beyond. This modern vineyard is at Goudhurst, Kent.

4. R. on B184 to junct. with B1057 on outskirts of Great Dunmow
    to join main route.

Note:

If you are traveling northward, a more direct link from Stansted Airport to Cambridge is given in Route 4, Chapter 7.

CHAPTER 11

Route 8

London-Stansted Airport to Central London

Total distance: 78 km (48 mi.)

Intermediate distances:

Stansted Airport–Epping:
  35 km (22 mi.)
Epping–Oxford Circu:s
  43 km (26 mi.)

Terrain: gentle

Access:

By train:
  London mainline stations.

By bike: Stansted Airport:
  Links to Routes 4 and 7.
Central London: Routes 3 and 6
  link at Westminster Abbey.

Maps:

O.S. Travelmaster (1:250 000)
  sheets: 6 and 9 cover the route but are unlikely to be of much
  practical help for navigation on the urban section.

O.S. Landranger (1:50 000) sheets: 167, 177 (adequate detail but no
  street names)

Description

This route is essentially a utilitarian one, but the first 20 km (12 mi.)
or so, as far as North Weald, pass through open countryside and
pleasant Essex villages. Epping Forest, some 10 km (6 mi.) farther
on, is the remains of one of the old royal hunting forests of Essex.

Directions

1. Leave airport terminal and L. at rbt., then R. to Takeley.

2. Cross A120 S.O. onto B183 to Hatfield Broad Oak.

3. S.O. on uc. road at entrance to village, then L. on uc. road to
   A1060.

4. L. and R. on uc. road through Manwood Green to Matching
   Green, S.O. past village green, L. at end of green on uc. road to
   High Laver.

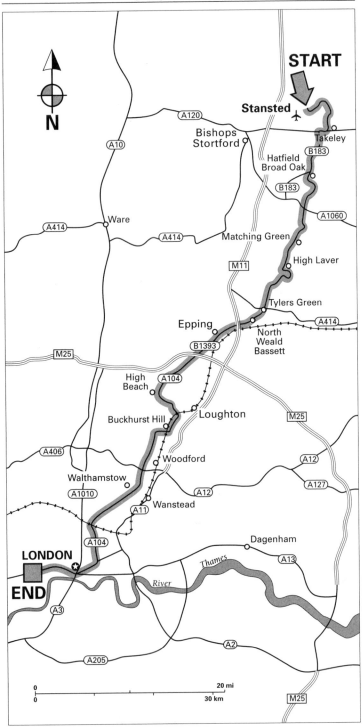

START

Stansted ✈

Takeley

Bishops
Stortford

A120

A10

Hatfield
Broad Oak

B183

B183

A1060

A414

Ware

A414

Matching Green

M11

High Laver

N

A414

Tylers Green

Epping

North
Weald
Bassett

M25

B1393

High
Beach

A104

M25

Buckhurst Hill

Loughton

A406

Woodford

A12

A12

A127

Walthamstow

A1010

A11

Wanstead

Dagenham

A13

A104

LONDON ★

Thames

END

River

A3

A2

A205

M25

0   20 mi
0   30 km

5. S.O. in High Laver, then 1st R. to Weald Lodge.

6. L. on uc. road to Tylers Green rbt. on A414.

7. S.O. on B181 through North Weald Bassett to join B1393 through Epping, over M25 to rbt. intersection with A121 and A104.

8. R. on A121 and immediately L. on uc. road through forest to Epping Forest Conservation Centre, High Beach.

9. Bear L. on uc. road, L. again to cross A104 at rbt.

10. S.O. on uc. road to Loughton, S.O. across A121 toward Loughton rly. stn.

11. L. and then R. under rly. br. past school, then R. on Loughton Way to Buckhurst Hill. (From here on, the route is urban.)

12. R. on Palmerston Rd. (B170) over rly., then L. onto Victoria Rd.

13. L. onto Forest Edge, R. onto Farm Way, which becomes Monkham's Lane to join A104, High Road, Woodford Green.

14. After 1 km (0.6 mi.), bear left, still on High Road, Woodford Green (A11), over br. over A406 (M11 approach road); rd. becomesWoodford Rd.

15. 1.5 km (1 mi.) after A406 br., R. onto Snaresbrook Rd., to intersection with Woodford New Rd. (A104).

16. L. on A104, S.O. at Whipps Cross rbt. onto Lea Bridge Rd., still A104 to cross River Lea.

17. At rbt. intersection with Lower Clapton Rd. (A107), L. on A107.

18. After 1 km (.75 mi.), R. still on Lower Clapton Rd., A107, under rly. br.

In summertime in central and southern England, you may find one of these teams of Morris Dancers performing their ritualized medieval dance in a village or a town.

19. Immediately after rly. br. at Hackney Central rly. stn., R. on Graham Rd. (A1207), to join Dalston Rd. (A104).

20. S.O. across Kingsland Rd. (A10) and after 1 km (.75 mi.), L. onto Essex Rd. (still A104) to join Upper St. (A1).

21. Cross Pentonville Rd./City Rd. (A501) at the "Angel" and continue S.O. on St. John's Rd., then bear R. on Roseberry Avenue to join Clerkenwell Rd.

22. S.O. across Grays Inn Rd. into Theobald's Rd.

23. L. into Drake St., becoming Procter St., and follow one-way system into High Holborn and St. Giles High St.

24. L. into New Oxford Street, which becomes Oxford St. leading to Oxford Circus.

CHAPTER 12

Route 9

Southampton and Portsmouth to Oxford

Total distance: 166 km (104 mi.)

Intermediate distances:

Portsmouth–Alresford:
    51 km (32 mi.)
(Distance from Southampton is
    18 km/11 mi. less)
Alresford–Overton:
    27 km (17 mi.)
Overton–Streatley:
    45 km (28 mi.)
Streatley–Oxford:
    43 km (27 mi.)

Terrain: Rolling

Maps:

O.S. Travelmaster (1:250 000) sheet: 9
O.S. Landranger (1:50 000) sheets: 196, 185, 174, 175, 164

Access:

By train: Oxford, Portsmouth, Southampton.
By bike: Routes 1 and 10 cross near Oxford; Route 5 crosses at Overton.

Summary:

This route links the ports of Portsmouth and Southampton on the south coast of England to the university city of Oxford by way of the rolling chalk-hill countryside of southern central England.

Description

Portsmouth is a naval city; one of the sights is the historic naval dockyard, which houses several vessels, including H.M.S. *Victory*, the flagship of Admiral Horatio Nelson at the Battle of Trafalgar against the French in 1805. The vessel has a special place in British heroics because Nelson won the decisive engagement but was killed just as victory was his. Also housed at Portsmouth is a less fortunate vessel, the ill-fated 16th-century *Mary Rose*, which sank soon after its launch. Portsmouth docks had their origins in the 12th century, and the world's first dry dock was built here as early as 1495.

Southampton, by contrast, gained its fame from commerce. Before the days of air travel, Southampton was the home port for luxury trans-Atlantic liners, and cruise liners still call here. Large cargo vessels also use the port and there is nearly always an impressive international array of ships lined along the wharves, the biggest towering over the nearby buildings.

From the point where the routes from Southampton and Portsmouth merge, the route climbs steadily through farming country to reach the summit at Stephen's Castle Down. Although you are only about 100 m (some 300 ft.) above sea level, there is an extensive open view over fields and hedges back toward the sea. The top of the Down has some fine beech woods, which border the road on the run down to Cheriton and New Alresford.

(If you want to make a side trip to visit the historic cathedral city of Winchester, at one time the capital city of England and some 13 km (8 mi.) to the northwest, you can turn west at the top of the Down, through Morestead. The same section also indicates a route out of Winchester to rejoin this route at Micheldever rail station.)

New and Old Alresford are centers of watercress-growing. This salad plant is very sensitive to water pollution and can be grown successfully only in broad lagoons or "beds" fed by the clear waters of chalk streams, such as the infant River Itchen here. New Alresford is also the terminus of a preserved steam railroad, linking it to the town of Alton 20 km (12 mi.) to the northeast, where it links to the main rail network. Not surprisingly, the little railroad is popularly known as the "Watercress Line."

You will have discovered that chalk country is not flat, and most of the rest of the route is a series of climbs out of the valley of one stream before dropping to the next. The grades are not steep, and there are often wide views at the tops of the ridges. At Overton, the route crosses another chalk stream, the River Test, known for the

Bridleways (horseriding paths) offer easy off-road riding. In England and Wales, cyclists are legally entitled to use the bridleways. This one is part of the Icknield Way, the pre-Roman trackway that runs from southwest to northeast across southern England.

quality of the trout fishing in its middle reaches. After Overton, the route climbs to its highest point, about 180 m (600 ft.), at the little village of Hannington, before the long and gentle descent through woods, mainly of silver birch, to the water-meadows of the River Kennet and the Kennet and Avon Canal (see Chapter 8).

There is another gentle and wooded climb after crossing the main A4 road, the Bath Road—the original coach route from London to Bath—and a series of delightful but very winding lanes before you join the broader road for the 16% grade down to the River Thames. The twin villages of Streatley and Goring stand either side of the bridge over the river. To make the Thames navigable, and to control flooding, the river now has a series of weirs at intervals, each bypassed by a lock to allow boats to pass from one level to the other. Goring Lock is just upstream of the bridge and a popular and picturesque picnic spot.

There is a complete change of countryside after you have crossed the Thames as the route follows a series of tiny lanes skirting some of the biggest open fields in southern England, with—in places—nothing to be seen in high summer but the rise and swell of the low hills covered in golden wheat.

For a short distance, the route follows the line of the ancient Icknield Way, a long pre-Roman trackway that led from the prehistoric settlements near Marlborough (see Chapter 8) northeastward to the coast. One of the next villages, Ewelme, was another watercress-growing center but, although the stream is as clear as ever, the old beds lie abandoned. Shortly after, near the village of Chalgrove, is the site of one of the battles in England's Civil War in 1643. It was here that one of the anti-royalist "Roundhead" leaders, John Hampden, whose protest at paying taxes into King Charles I's coffers sparked the war, lost his life; there is a monument about 500 m (0.3 mi.) northeast of the village.

The final leg of the route leads into Oxford by way of a short unpaved stretch of about 1.5 km (1 mi.) over Shotover Hill, then steeply down to the center of Oxford. Oxford is England's oldest university city, the first college, Merton, being founded in 1264—by students expelled from the Sorbonne in Paris. Another notable college is Balliol, also dating from the 13th century. The colleges are built around open courts known as "quadrangles"; the most spectacular and largest is in Christ Church. Magdalen College, by the River Isis, is generally held to be the most attractively sited. As with Cambridge (Chapter 5), the best way to appreciate the intricate detail of the colleges is on foot. There has always been a (fairly) friendly rivalry between the universities of Oxford and Cambridge—the Yale and Harvard of England—with annual sporting and other events. The most famous encounter is the Boat Race between the universities' eights, held every year around Easter over a traditional 6 km (4 mi.) course on a tidal stretch of the River Thames west of London (the actual date depends on the tides).

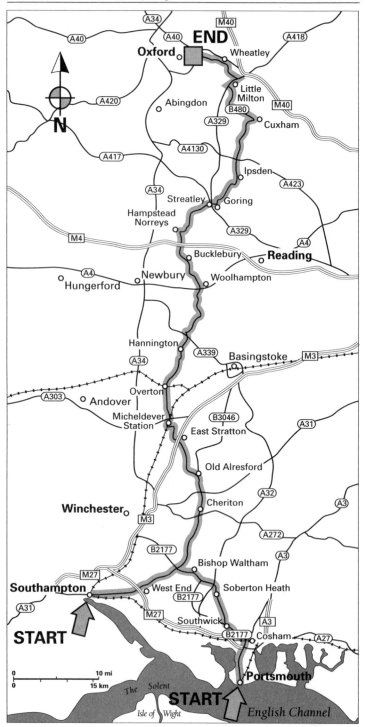

Directions

From Portsmouth:

1. From Continental Ferry Port, follow signed cycle route avoiding busy rbts. to Cosham.

2. From Cosham, go W. up Hill Road (B2177) to Southwick Road (still B2177); follow this to rbt., R. on uc. road into Southwick.

3. In Southwick, L. at church, then R. on uc. road through Newtown to T-junct. in Soberton Heath.

4. R., then 1st L. under disused rly. to A32.

5. S.O. across A32 on uc. road through Swanmore to Bishops Waltham.

6. In village center, L. to B2177.

7. R. on B2177 (Winchester Road) for 1 km (0.6 mi.) to x-rds. with uc. road.

From Southampton:

1. From Ferry Terminal at Town Quay, E. on Platform Rd., then Canute Rd. to rbt. at W. end of Itchen Bridge (A3025).

2. Take 3rd exit on A3025 to cross River Itchen, then L. into Bridge Rd. (uc. road).

3. This becomes Peartree Avenue, then West End Rd., which passes over A3024 in Bitterne.

4. At rbt., R., still on West End Rd. to A27.

5. S.O. across A27, still on West End Rd. to B3025 (High Street, West End).

6. R. on B3025, then L. on Moorgreen Rd. (uc. road) just before hospital, to pass over M27 through Moorgreen to B3342.

7. L. on B3342 (Bubb Lane) to rbt. junct. with B3354.

8. S.O. on uc. road by Durley and through Wintershill to B2177.

9. From Portsmouth R., from Southampton R. and L. across B2177, on uc. road over Stephen's Castle Down to A272.

10. S.O. across A272 on uc. road to B3046 in Cheriton.

11. L. on B3046 to pass over A31 to B3047 in New Alresford.

12. R. on B3047, then L. on B3046.

13. At N. end of town after crossing River Itchen, L. on uc. road, keeping R. at next two juncts. to East Stratton.

14. L. to pass over M3 to A33, R. on A33, then L. on uc. road through West Stratton to Micheldever rly. stn.

15. R. just before rly. to pass under on uc. road to B3400 at Overton.

16. R. on B3400, then after 2 km (1.2 mi.), L. on uc. road through Ashe, North Oakley and Hannington to A339.

17. L. on A339, then R. just before Kingsclere on uc. road through Wolverton Common and Axmansford.

18. 500 m (0.3 mi.) after Axmanford, L. on uc. road through Inhurst to B3051.

19. S.O. on uc. road, then R. and R. again to cross River Enborne, then River Kennet, Kennet and Avon Canal and rly. to A4 at Woolhampton.

20. L. on A4, then 2nd R. on uc. road to Bucklebury Common, L. to Upper Bucklebury, R. down hill to T-junct.

21. L., then 1st R. through ford, keeping L. to pass Frilsham church and pass under M4 to T-junct.

22. L. and R. to B4009 on outskirts of Hampstead Norreys.

23. R. on B4009 through Aldworth to A417 at Streatley.

24. S.O. across A417 on B4009 to cross River Thames into Goring.

25. At T-junct. just after rly. bridge, L., still on B4009, then after 500 m (0.3 mi.), R. on uc. road, then 1st L. to A4074.

26. S.O. across A4074 on uc. road, then L. through Ipsden to A423.

27. S.O. across A423, still on uc. road to Ewelme, L. at foot of hill through village to T-junct.

28. R. on uc. road, then 1st L. to B4009.

29. S.O. across B4009 on uc. road to Chalgrove.

30. L. through village to B480.

31. L. on B480, then R. on uc. road to A329 in Little Milton.

32. R. on A329, then 1st L. after village to Wheatley.

33. In Wheatley, fork L. past church and follow signs for Shotover Country Park.

34. When road becomes unpaved, track S.O. across open common until road becomes paved again.

35. S.O. down hill on uc. road to pass over A4142.

36. S.O. at rbt. junct. with B4495 in New Headington to join A420.

37. L. on A420 to Oxford city center.

CHAPTER 13

Route 10

Cambridge via Oxford to Bath

Total distance : 292 km (181 mi.)

Intermediate distances:

Cambridge–Olney:
  79 km (49 mi.)
Olney–Middleton Stoney:
  60 km (37 mi.)
Middleton Stoney–Stanford-in-
  the-Vale: 58 km (36 mi.)
Stanford-in-the-Vale–Bath:
  95 km (59 mi.)

Terrain:

Rolling, hillier toward Bath

Maps:

O.S. Travelmaster (1:250 000)
  sheets: 8 and 9
O.S. Landranger (1:50 000)
  sheets: 154, 153, 152, 164, 163, 173, 172
Goldeneye (1:126 720) sheet: Cotswolds (part of route)

Access:

By train: main line rail stations at Cambridge, Milton Keynes
(10 km/6 mi. S. of route), Oxford (8 km/5 mi. E. of route), Swindon
(4 km/2.5 mi. N. of route), Chippenham (7 km/4 mi. N. of route),
and Bath.

By bike: Cambridge: Routes 2, 4, 7, 13, 14; Bath: Routes 5 and 11; Oxford (8 km/5 mi. E. of route): Route 9. Route 1 crosses at Rousham
Gap, between Middleton Stoney and Wootton.

Summary:

This route links the university city of Cambridge—hub of several of
our routes—to the Georgian and Roman city of Bath, by way of
Cambridge's rival university city, Oxford.

Description

The first part of this route across the very gentle arable landscape of
Cambridgeshire soon offers a contrast between new and old technol-
ogy. As you turn off the main A603 road onto the B1046 through

Comberton, you can catch glimpses of the space-age radio-telescope dishes and aerial arrays of the Mullard Radio Astronomy Laboratory. It was here that the regularly changing radiation from pulsars was discovered in the 1960s, leading to advances in our knowledge of the universe.

By contrast, in two of the next villages, Bourn and Great Gransden, are two very well preserved corn-grinding windmills. Bourn Mill was mentioned as far back as 1636, which makes it the oldest surviving British windmill. It is of the type known as a "post-mill," in which the whole wooden body of the mill rotates about a central post so that the sails face the wind.

This is a countryside of broad arable fields and functional villages, sloping very gently down to and then up away from the River Ouse. Just as we have several rivers Avon, England has several Rivers Ouse—the name derives from a very old root word for water, with derivatives cropping up in many languages (including the Gaelic *uisge*). Shortly after crossing the A1 trunk road—the old Great North Road that led from London to Edinburgh—the route passes Grafham Water, a storage reservoir that now has picnic areas, bird-watching hides and an almost entirely off-road bike route round it.

The villages become more appealing on the rolling grain-growing plainlands of Bedfordshire county, Riseley in particular having some attractive cottages in a pleasing setting. The road drops gently to the River Ouse again, much smaller now, at Sharnbrook, and follows the ridge above its left (north) bank through to the pleasant small town of Olney. Olney is another of those towns with a prominent broad main street and a towering church spire, a landmark for miles around. It also has associations with the poet William Cowper (1731–1800).

From here the route passes close by the fringes of one old hunting forest, Yardley Chase, and through the remains of two more, Sal-

The 4,000-year-old burial chamber of Wayland's Smithy on the Wessex Downs, in Oxfordshire, is 2 km south of this route.

cey Forest and Whittlewood Forest. These are remnants of a vast forest that covered virtually the whole of what is now Northamptonshire county.

Just before the village of Grafton Regis, you pass over the Grand Union Canal (see Chapter 4); about 3 km. (2 mi.) north of here is the village of Stoke Bruerne with an extensive national canal museum, with the possibility of canal boat trips.

Just before Whittlewood Forest, at Paulerspury, you can head northward for an optional side trip to Sulgrave Manor, rejoining the main route near Stowe. Sulgrave Manor started life as a 13th-century farmhouse and was bought by Lawrence Washington in 1539; the Washington family lived there until 1610. The Manor was restored in 1914 as a museum to George Washington. The village of Silverstone on the return leg has achieved fame as an international grand prix car-racing circuit.

Shortly after the village of Chackmore, north of the small market town of Buckingham, the route passes the entrance to Stowe School, another well-known public (i.e., private) school. The construction of the 18th-century palladian neoclassical buildings brought together all the distinguished architects of the time: Adam, Sir John Vanbrugh and Grinling Gibbons, while the grounds—like so many—were laid out by Capability Brown. The grounds and, at times, the buildings are open to visitors.

The next section leads by a succession of small roads through a quiet landscape and sleepy villages to Middleton Stoney and Lower Heyford. It has not always been so peaceful, however: beside the adjacent village of Upper Heyford was one of the largest U.S. air bases in Britain during World War II and the subsequent uneasy peace. The route crosses in rapid succession a rail route, the Oxford Canal and the River Cherwell, before climbing left past Rousham House, a Jacobean building dating from 1635 and a Royalist stronghold in England's Civil War.

A suggested link to the center of Oxford leaves here: see Chapter 4. For a general description of Oxford, see Chapter 12.

Now you are effectively in the foothills of the Cotswold Hills, famed for their golden-stone villages and small towns. The village of Wootton, with a steep hill in and a steep hill out, is a pretty one, the first of a succession. To the south of Wootton, about 5 km. (3 mi) away, is the small, elegant, mainly 18th-century town of Woodstock, and the entrance to Blenheim Palace.

Blenheim Palace is held to be the masterpiece of the architect Sir John Vanbrugh and was built for John Churchill, Duke of Marlborough, as a reward for his defeat of the French and Bavarians at the Battle of Blenheim in 1704. The British wartime Prime Minister, Winston Churchill, was born here in 1874, and is buried in the churchyard of the nearby village of Bladon. Blenheim Palace grounds and house are open to visitors but cycling is not always allowed in the park—which was, of course, designed and laid out by the ubiquitous Capability Brown.

The route passes to the west of Oxford, passing close by the large village of Eynsham just to the west. Eynsham has an attractive village center, a small art gallery and some pleasant pubs.

If you made the detour to visit Oxford city center, it is possible to rejoin the route at one of the next villages, Cumnor.

From here, the next section of the route lies in the Vale of the White Horse, so named for the prehistoric chalk figure carved on the hillside of the Downs above the village of Uffington. The stylized horse—it could almost as well be called the "Uffington White Cat"—has recently been dated to at least 2,500 years old and is thought originally to have been a symbol of the victory of good over evil. The route passes close under the 264 m (865 ft.) Whitehorse Hill surmounted by its earthwork, Uffington Castle. It's well worth a detour up the miniature pass that leads south of the B4507 to the top, if only for the spectacular views across the Vale and the striking small valley known as the Manger.

Just before this point, where the route joins the B4507 at Kingston Lisle, there is another curiosity: the Blowing Stone, claimed—with no real substantiation—to have been used by King Alfred (the 9th-century monarch who allowed the famous cakes to burn and was born in nearby Wantage in 849) to summon his troops. You can, with the right technique, blow it to give a rather melancholy horn note. You're expected to make a small donation to charity for the privilege.

One of the best-known groups of houses in the Cotswolds—Arlington Row at Bibury in Gloucestershire, about 25 km (15 mi.) south of Stanford in the Vale.

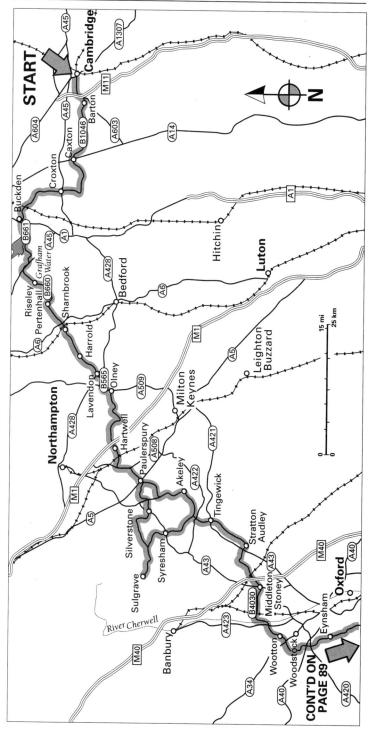

CONT'D ON PAGE 89

The route skirts the foot of the downs through a series of pleasant villages, eventually climbing up from the large village of Wroughton, then dropping through Broad Hinton and Clyffe Pypard to follow the same roads as in Route 5 to the village of Lacock (see Chapter 8 for a description of this village and the route to it).

From the village of Neston, some 7 km (4 mi.) after Lacock, we suggest an alternative final leg to that quoted in Chapter 8. It is appreciably less hilly but does not visit the delightful small town of Bradford-on-Avon and involves rather more main road in the final few miles. Either way in to Bath can of course be used with either route. For a general description of Bath, see Route 5, Chapter 8.

Directions

1. Leave Cambridge city center W. on Barton Road (A603).

2. After passing over M11, R. on B1046 through Comberton and Toft.

3. R. on uc. road (effectively S.O. where B1046 goes L.) through Bourn, then L. to A1198 at Caxton.

4. L. and R. across A1198 on uc. road to B1046 at Great Gransden.

5. R. on B1046, R. and L. across B1040, then after 1 km (0.6 mi.), 1st R. on uc. road to A45 at Croxton.

6. L. and R. across A45 on uc. road past Toseland to Graveley.

7. L. on uc. road to B1043 at Offord D'Arcy.

8. R. on B1043 to Offord Cluny, where L. on uc. road under rly. and over River Great Ouse to Buckden.

9. In village center, L. to rbt. junct. with A1.

10. Take 2nd exit on B661 past Grafham Water through West Perry, then 1st R. on uc. road to A45.

11. R. on A45 through Stoneley, then at W. end of village, L. on B660 through Pertenhall to Keysoe.

12. At Brook End, Keysoe, R. on uc. road to Riseley. L. in Riseley, then R. at S.W. end of village, still on uc. road to A6.

13. R. on A6, then L. on uc. road to Sharnbrook.

14. In center of village, L. past church through Odell to T-junct.

15. L. to Harrold, then R. through village to A428 at Lavendon.

16. R. on A428, then L. on uc. road to B565.

17. R. on B565 to A509, L. on A509 into Olney.

18. At S. end of town, R. on uc. road through Weston Underwood, R. at church to Ravenstone.

19. R. in village to B526 at Stoke Goldington.

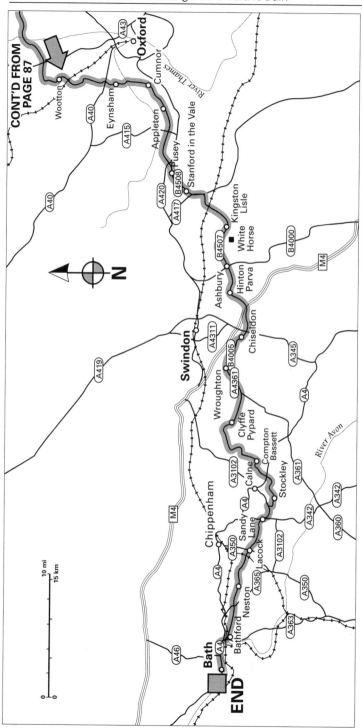

20. R. on B526, then L. on uc. road through Salcey Forest and over M1 to Hartwell.

21. R. in village, then L. under rly. by Ashton.

22. Immdediately after rly., S.O., then 1st. R. at Bozenham Mill to cross River Tove, then Grand Union Canal, to A508 at Grafton Regis.

23. R. on A508, then L. on uc. road through Alderton to A5 at Paulerspury.

24. Cross A5 S.O. to x-rds. on outskirts of village.

25. (Optional side trip to Sulgrave Manor leaves here—see below.)

26. L. through Whittlewood Forest, L. at T-junct., then after 2 km (1.2 mi.), R. to Lillingstone Lovell.

27. Just before village, L. to A413 at Akeley.

28. L. on A413, then 1st R. through Chackmore to x-rds. with Dadford–Water Stratford road by entrance to Stowe Park.

29. L. to A422, S.O. across A422 on uc. road through Water Stratford to A421 at Tingewick.

30. S.O. across A421 on uc. road by Barton Hartshorn and Chetwode to Stratton Audley.

31. R. to A421, R. and L. across A421 on uc. road, then at x-rds. after 3 km (2 mi.), L. to B4100.

32. L. and R. on uc. road through Bucknell and over M40 to B4030.

33. R. on B4030 to B430 at Middleton Stoney.

34. S.O. on B4030 by Caulcott and through Lower Heyford to cross rly., canal and River Cherwell.

35. Immediately after river bridge, L. on uc. road past Rousham House to A4260.

36. (Link to Oxford leaves/joins here: see Chapter 4.)

37. L. and R. across A4260 on uc. road, then 1st L. to B4027.

38. S.O. into Wootton, L. at church, keep R. after bridge to A44.

39. R. and L. on A44 to B4437, then 1st L. (effectively S.O. where B4437 goes R.),

40. 1st L. through Combe and past Combe rly. stn. to A4095 at Long Hanborough.

41. L. on A4095, then R. on uc. road through Church Hanborough, then R. at T-junct. to rbt. junct. with A40.

42. Take 2nd exit B449, then L. at 2nd rbt. on B4044 to Farmoor, then R. on B4017 to Cumnor.

43. At entrance to village, R. on uc. roads through Appleton and by Fyfield to A415.

44. S.O. across A415 still on uc. road by Longworth and Hinton Waldrist to A420.

45. R. on A420, then L. on B4508 through Pusey.

46. L. on uc. road (effectively S.O. where B4508 goes R.) to A417 at Stanford in the Vale.

47. L. on A417, then R. on uc. road.

48 1st L. under rly. to Kingston Lisle, L. in village to B4507.

49. R. on B4507 below Whitehorse Hill to B4000 in Ashbury.

50. S.O. on uc. road through Idstone and Bishopstone, then L. to pass over M4 to B4192.

51. R. and L. across B4192 to A345.

52. R. on A435, then L. on B4005 through Chisledon to A4361 at Wroughton.

53. L. on A4361, then after 6 km (4 mi.), R. on uc. road through Broad Hinton.

54. L. after village to Clyffe Pypard, L. and R. in village to x-rds. at Bushton.

55. L. through Compton Bassett to A4.

56. R. on A4, then 1st L. on uc. road to Blackland, R., then L. to Stockley, R. to A3102.

57. L. on A3102, then after 5 km (3 mi.), R. on uc. road to A342 at Sandy Lane.

58. R. on A342, then 1st L. on uc. road through Bowden Hill to Lacock.

59. In Lacock, L. and 1st R. to A350.

60. S.O. across A350 on uc. road to B3353 at Gastard.

61. S.O. on B3353, then after 800 m (0.5 mi.), L. on uc. road to Neston, L. on uc. road through Wadswick.

62. L. and R. across B3109 to A365.

63. S.O. across A365 on uc. road over Kingsdown to A363 at Bathford.

64. R. on A363, then L. on A4 to Bath.

Optional side trip to Sulgrave Manor:

1. S.O. through Paulerspury and Pury End, then L., still on uc. road, to A413.

2. L. on A413 to Whittlebury, R. on uc. road to A43 at Silverstone.

3. S.O. across A43 on uc. road into Silverstone village.

4. L. and R. in village for 4 km (2.5 mi.) to x-rds., L. through Abthorpe and Wappenham to Helmdon.

5. S.O. at N. end of village to Sulgrave; in village, R. to Manor.

6. To return to main route, retrace outgoing route through Helmdon, then, about 3 km (2 mi.) after Helmdon, R., still on uc. road, to A43 at Syresham.

7. R. and L. across A43 through Biddlesden, keeping L. to x-rds. with Dadford–Water Stratford road, where you rejoin main route.

CHAPTER 14

Route 11

Bath to Chester via Church Stretton

Total distance: 313 km (194 mi.)

Intermediate distances:

Bath–Chepstow:
    47 km (29 mi.)
Chepstow–Hay-on-Wye:
    84 km (52 mi.)
Hay-on-Wye–Presteigne:
    34 km (21 mi.)
Presteigne–Church Stretton:
    51 km (32 mi.)
Church Stretton–Chester:
    97 km (60 mi.)

Terrain:

Mostly hilly, less hilly run in to Chester

Maps:

O.S. Travelmaster (1:250 000) sheets: 7 and 8 (very small part)

O.S. Landranger (1:50 000) sheets: 172, 171, 161, 148, 137, 126, 117

Access:

By train: Rail stations at Bath, Chester.

By bike: Bath: Routes 5 and 14; Church Stretton: Routes 4 and 12.

Summary:

This route links the Roman and Georgian city of Bath with the city of Chester, with a short excursion into Wales and the Welsh Border country—some of the finest lowland cycling in Britain. This isn't the shortest nor the flattest route between Bath and Chester, but we think you'll enjoy it.

Description

For a general description of Bath, see Route 5, Chapter 8.

    The route starts off as it intends to continue: with a stiff uphill grade. Compensations are the fine view over the city and the closer views of some of the elegant curved "crescents" of 18th-century buildings. This is the southern end of the limestone Cotswold Hills, and although the top of this climb, at 233 m (764 ft.), is the highest point you'll cross east of the River Severn, the road is quite hard until the plunge from Rudgeway through Tockington to the Severn Bridge.

This bridge, built in 1966, was at the time one of the world's largest single-span suspension bridges. It has a separate cycle track, which you reach by following the signs past the motorway service area. There are in fact two bridges here: the Severn Bridge leads directly to a smaller bridge over the mouth of the River Wye.

The compact town of Chepstow, just east of the route after the bridges, occupies a strategic position on a spur in a bend of the River Wye, still today the boundary between England and Wales, and has remnants of the defensive town walls, as well as a superbly sited castle, built originally in 1070 and extended in 1245.

The route follows the main A466 road for about 5 km (3 mi.), then leaves it for minor roads. This main road can be very busy at times with holiday and sightseeing traffic, since the next 11 or 12 km (7 mi.) section of the Wye Valley is a popular and spectacular scenic attraction. The main A466 road runs mostly on a shelf high above the river in its gorge but drops to river level at Tintern, where there is a superbly situated ruined abbey, which is open to visitors. From Tintern there is a stiff climb up through woods for 4 km (2.5 mi.) to regain the route at Trelleck Grange. If traffic is not too heavy and you have the time, this side trip is well worth the effort.

From Trelleck Grange to Llanfihangel Crucorney, some 30 km (20 mi.) or so, the route is decidedly hilly, with some very up-and-down stretches. But the rewards are many. The landscape is a delightful mix of small fields, some grazing, some with crops, and neat hedges with small patches of woodland.

This is land that was fought over between English and Welsh for centuries, and the route passes close by two magnificent castles— Raglan Castle, built in 1435, with an unusual hexagonal French-style

On the road down from the Gospel Pass to Hay-on-Wye, Powys.

tower, and the late 12th-century White Castle in a very impressive setting—before dropping to the valley at Llanfihangel Crucorney. (For a note on Welsh place-names, see Chapter 15.)

Here begins one of the finest stretches of the whole route, through the Black Mountains. The road winds, gently at first, up the valley of the little Afon Honddu between steep ridges. Soon you will see, perched on the hillside to the east, the tiny medieval church of the village of Cwmyoy. This suffered a landslip soon after it was built but has remained leaning at a crazy angle for several hundred years since. Two steep little roads lead up to the village. The next landmark is Llanthony Priory, now ruined—closely followed by the last pub for some miles.

The road, though still up-and-down, begins to climb more now to the hamlet of Capel-y-ffin, while the hills beside the valley begin to close in. Beyond Capel-y-ffin, the road climbs out onto bare grassy hillside, uphill all the way with an average 10–12% grade to the pass at the top—the Bwlch-yr-Efengyl or "Gospel Pass," so named because in the days when those who wished to practice nonconformist worship were harassed, people would gather at this windswept spot to hear the gospel preached. The top of the pass is one of the highest roads in Wales at 542 m (1,778 ft.), and as you broach the top a tremendous view opens up over the middle Wye valley and the hills beyond.

There's a magnificent coast down over a vast lawn-like slope to the small town on Hay-on-Wye, with the rounded peaks at the end of the ridges standing high behind you. Hay-on-Wye's present claim to fame is as the secondhand book center of Britain. Enter the former movie theater at your peril: once you start browsing, night will fall before you emerge.

For a short distance from Hay-on-Wye, until you cross the river itself at the toll bridge at Whitney, the road is easy. Once over the river, however, the way becomes quite hilly once more, but on beautiful little lanes, through the small towns of Kington and Presteigne.

From Presteigne there's a choice of routes: if you have the energy, the climb up to the ridge along the border between England and Wales is well worth the effort. From the top, there are wonderful views down to the peaks of the Brecon Beacons, with the high peaks of Snowdonia visible to the northwest on a clear day. This is sheep country and you'll hear their plaintive bleats all around.

After Lingen the route follows the valleys of several small rivers and is much gentler, at least as far as Asterton. This hamlet lies under the flank of a high whaleback of a ridge, the Long Mynd, and the road wastes no time in getting to the top, by way of a 25% grade straight up the side of the hill. It's no shame to walk this one. The top of the Long Mynd is a great plateau covered with heather, vividly purple during late August and September. There are tremendous views back, and then, as you go over the top, ranges of hills open up in front of you to the east. On a fine day the top of the Long Mynd is one of the most exhilarating places we've ever been. The descent down the Burway to Church Stretton isn't as steep as the climb but has 15% grades in parts, so take care.

Soon after Church Stretton, you will be on a very old road, a narrow lane that follows the Roman road toward the Roman town of Viroconium (now the village of Wroxeter), near Shrewsbury. This lane shows one of the characteristics of Roman roads: that where terrain permits they are dead straight.

The route passes to the east of the town of Shrewsbury, along a pleasant series of narrow roads. At the crossing of the River Severn, at Atcham, there is a fine medieval bridge, now bypassed by the modern road but still usable by cyclists. This north Shropshire countryside is far more gentle and agricultural than the wilds of the Long Mynd. After the village of Northwood, for a short stretch of about 13 km (8 mi.) you are in Wales once more, before the quiet grazing country, almost park-like, of the Cheshire plain.

Chester on the River Dee was an important Roman military base. The Roman amphitheater, which originally had seating for 7,000, has been excavated. There are also Roman museums. The medieval city walls are well preserved, and it is possible to walk on them round the whole city. Chester has many black-and-white timbered buildings and another feature unique in Britain: the "Rows." Dating from the 13th century onward, these are raised covered galleries with two tiers of shops—forming, in effect, a medieval covered shopping mall.

Directions

1. Leave Bath city center N. by Broad Street (A4), then fork L. into Lansdown Road (uc. road), and continue to top of long hill.

2. About 1.5 km (1 mi.) after summit of climb, L. on uc. road to A420 at Wick.

3. L. on A420, then R. on uc. road to B4465 at Pucklechurch.

4. R. on B4465 over M4, then after about 1.5 km (1 mi.), S.O. (where B4465 goes R.) through Westerleigh to A432 on W. outskirts of Yate.

5. R. on A432, then L. on B4059 (which is subsumed into B4058 for a short distance) to Iron Acton.

6. R. on B4059 though Latteridge to junct. with B4427.

7. S.O. on B4427, passing over M5 to A38 at Rudgeway.

8. L. on A38, then R. on uc. road to Tockington, S.O. through Olveston to B4461.

9. L. on B4461 to rbt. junct. with A403 at Severn Bridge.

10. Take 3rd exit to service area and follow cycle signs for cycle route to Chepstow over bridge.

11. Continue on signed cycle route beside A466 after bridge, then continue on uc. service road to rbt. junct. with A48.

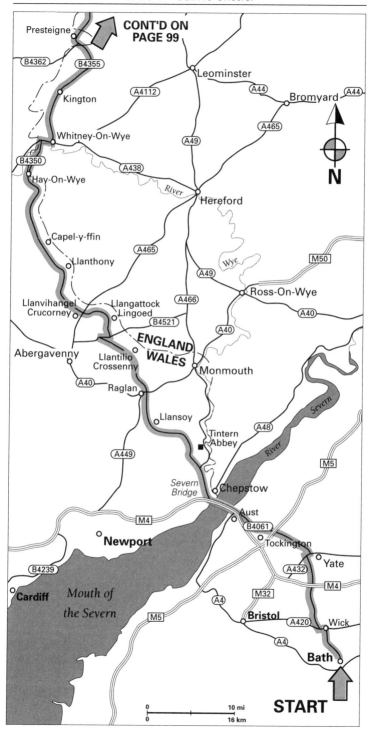

CONT'D ON PAGE 99

Presteigne

B4362 B4355

Kington

Whitney-On-Wye

B4350

Hay-On-Wye

Capel-y-ffin

Llanthony

Llanvihangel Crucorney

Llangattock Lingoed

Abergavenny

Llantilio Crossenny

Raglan

Llansoy

A449

Leominster

A4112

A44

Bromyard

A44

A465

A49

A438 *River*

Hereford

A465

Wye

M50

A49

Ross-On-Wye

A466

A40

ENGLAND

WALES

B4521

A40

Monmouth

Tintern Abbey

A48 *River* *Severn*

M5

M4

Severn Bridge

Chepstow

Aust

B4061

Newport

Tockington

Yate

B4239

A432

M4

Cardiff

Mouth of the Severn

A4

M32

M5

Bristol

A420

Wick

A4

Bath

N

0 — 10 mi
0 — 16 km

START

12. S.O. on A466 to St. Arvans, S.O. on uc. road (where A466 goes R.) to Trelleck Grange, L. to B4293 at Cobbler's Plain.

13. R. on B4293, then L. on uc. road through Llansoy.

14. After 4 km (2.5 mi.), R. at x-rds., then 1st. L. up hill to Kingcoed.

15. S.O. on uc. road to pass over A40.

16. L. at T-junct., then R., still on uc. roads, through Tregare.

17. R. through Penrhos to Llantilio Crossenny.

18. R. into village, then L. at church and S.O. on uc. road past White Castle to B4521.

19. L. on B4521 through Caggle Street and Llanvetherine, then R. on uc. roads and L. to A465 at Llanfihangel Crucorney.

20. Cross A465 L. and R. into village.

21. R. just before church, then L. through Llanthony and Capel-y-ffin over "Gospel Pass" (Bwlch-yr-Efengyl— 542 m/1778 ft.) then down to B4350 at Hay-on-Wye.

22. R. on B4350 through Hay and Clifford to cross River Wye at toll bridge to A438.

23. L. on A43, then 1st. R. on uc. road through Brilley to x-rds. at top of Brilley Mountain, R. through Hergest to Kington.

24. S.O. to rbt. junct. with A44 on far side of town.

25. S.O. on B4355 through Titley to Presteigne.

26. In town center, R. on uc. road across bridge over River Lugg, then S.O.* up hill by Stapleton to Birtley, then L. to A572 at Brampton Bryan. (* alternative less hilly route: R. after crossing River Lugg through Lower and Upper Kinsham and Lingen to Birtley and Brampton Bryan.)

27. S.O. across A572 on uc. road to cross River Teme, then L. to B4637.

28. R. on B4367 over rly. level crossing through Bucknell and by Bedstone to Hoptonheath, T-junct. with B4385.

29. L. on B4385 over rly. bridge and immediately R., still on B4385, to Purslow, junct. with B4368.

30. S.O. on uc. road to B4385 at Kempton.

31. L. on B4385, then after 3 km (2 mi.), R. on uc. road (where B4385 goes L.), and immediately L.

32. R. at 5-way x-rds. through Eyton to A489 at Plowden.

33. R. on A489, then 1st L. on uc. road to Asterton.

34. R. up very steep climb to top of Long Mynd (490 m/1,608 ft.) and follow moorland road to B4370 in Church Stretton.

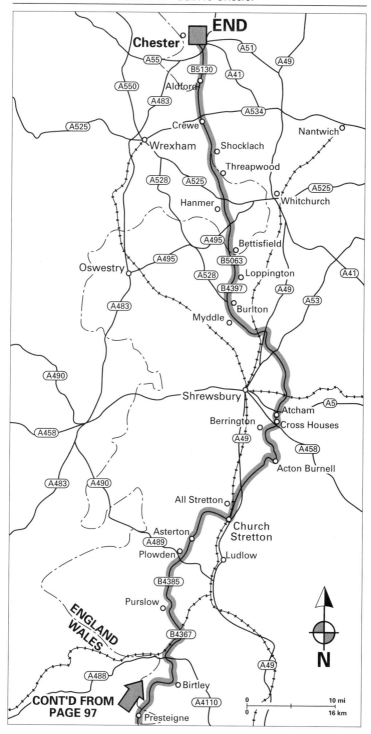

END

Chester

A55
A51
A49

B5130
A41

Aldford

A550

A483

A534

A525

Crewe
Nantwich

Wrexham
Shocklach

Threapwood

A528
A525

Hanmer
A525
Whitchurch

A495
Bettisfield

Oswestry
A495
B5063

A528
Loppington
A41

B4397
A49
A53

Burlton

A483

Myddle

A490

Shrewsbury
A5

Atcham

Berrington
Cross Houses

A458
A49

A483
A490
Acton Burnell

All Stretton

Asterton
Church Stretton

A489
Plowden
Ludlow

B4385

Purslow

ENGLAND
WALES
B4367
A49

A488
Birtley

CONT'D FROM
PAGE 97
A4110

Presteigne

0   10 mi
0   16 km

N

35. L. on B4370 through All Stretton; at far end of village, R. on uc. road over rly. bridge to A49.

36. L. and R. on uc. road across A49, then immediately L. on Roman Road through Hollyhurst and Frodesley to Acton Burnell.

37. L., still on uc. road, through Pitchford and Cantlop, then 1st R. through Berrington to A458.

38. R. on A458, 1st L. on uc. road to B4380 at Atcham.

39. R. on B4380 over River Severn, then L. on uc. road.

40. After about 1.5 km (1 mi.), R. over A5 to Upton Magna, L. into village.

41. In village center, R. on uc. road to B5062, S.O. on uc. road by Haughton to A53.

42. S.O., still on uc. road, through Astley to A49.

43. R. on A49 through Hadnall; at far end of village, L. on uc. road by Haston to B5476.

44. S.O. on uc. road across B5476, then across A528 through Harmer Hill to A528 at Myddle.

45. L. on A528 to Burlton, then R. on B4397 through Loppington to T-junct. with B5063.

46. L. on B5063 through Northwood; at far end of village, cross border into Wales and fork R. on uc. road through Bettisfield to A495.

47. R. on A495, then 1st L. through Arowry and Hanmer to A539.

48. R. and L. on uc. road across A539 through Little Arowry to A525.

49. S.O. on uc. roads across A525 through Tallarn Green and Threapwood to B5069.

50. L. on B5069, then R. on uc. roads through Shocklach and Crewe to A534.

51. S.O. on B5130 through Churton and Aldford to pass over A55 to join A41 to center of Chester.

CHAPTER 15

Route 12

Church Stretton to Holyhead

Total distance: 210 km (131 mi.)

Intermediate distances:

Church Stretton–Welshpool:
    37 km (23 mi.)
Welshpool–Bala:
    58 km (36 mi.)
Bala–Capel Curig:
    43 km (27 mi.)
Capel Curig–Menai Bridge:
    29 km (18 mi.)
Menai Bridge–Holyhead:
    43 km (27 mi.)

Terrain:

very hilly in parts,
rolling in Anglesey

Maps:

O.S. Travelmaster (1:250 000) sheet: 7

O.S. Landranger (1:50 000) sheets: 137, 136, 125, 124, 115, 114

Access:

By train: mainline rail station at Holyhead.

By bike: Church Stretton: Routes 1, 11, 19 (Tour A).

Summary:

This route links Routes 1 and 11 at Church Stretton with Holyhead, the port on the island of Anglesey that has connections for Dublin in the Irish Republic. Although a fairly direct connection, it takes in some of the best scenery of north Wales.

Description

The route is very hilly for the first part—and fairly hilly for the rest. It leaves Church Stretton by the way that Route 11 comes in: straight up the stiff grade of the Burway to the top of the Long Mynd. There is an exhilarating ride across the top of the wide ridge and a mainly gentler but winding descent on the other side to the hamlet of Bridges. Then it's up once more, toward the jagged outline of the Stiperstones ahead. These giant quartzite outcrops, like ragged teeth set in the heather-covered ridge, have fanciful names: the largest one is the Devil's Chair. There is another stiff grade to the top at 429 m (1,407 ft.) but with superb views of the patchwork of fields and hedgerows that are part of the charm of Shropshire.

This is far from the end of the climbing, for after the quick descent to the prettily named hamlet of The Bog, there's a series of quite hilly little lanes before the serious climb through woodland up the last of this series of ridges, Long Mountain. The route drops at

---

A bit about Welsh

Welsh has large groups of apparently unpronounceable letters— because some letter combinations have different meanings from their English ones. In particular, what look like double letters behave in fact as completely separate symbols. You can hardly expect to read off Welsh place-names like a native, but here is a very approximate pronunciation guide:

a   when short, (very approximately) as in "cat," but lighter, more like the French *à*
when long, a longer version of the same sound

b   as in English

c   always hard, as in "cat" again

ch   a separate letter, pronounced as in Scottish "loch"

d   as in English

dd   a separate letter, pronounced as *th* in "this" or "that"

e   when short, as in "yet"
when long, rather like the French *é*

f   as in "of"

ff   a separate letter, pronounced as *f* in "if"

g   always hard, as in "garden"

h   always sounded and is pronounced as in "hand"

i   has three sounds:
as a long vowel, pronounced as *ee* in "feed"
as a short vowel, pronounced as *i* in "pin"
as a consonant, pronounced as *y* in "yet"

ll   a separate letter with no real English equivalent; the nearest is said to be as the *tl* in "antler"

m   as in English

n   as in English—and the only single letter ever used doubled

ng   not generally regarded as a separate letter but a nasal form of *n*, pronounced as in "thing"

---

o   has two sounds:
short, as in "not"
long, roughly as au in "cause"

p   as in English

ph a separate letter, pronounced as in "phone"

r   trilled or rolled, rather as in Italian, or Scottish English

rh a separate letter with no real English equivalent—the nearest is as in "perhaps"

s   always as in "sun"

t   as in English

th a separate letter, pronounced as in "thanks"

u   generally, rather like the long and short versions of *i*

w   has three sounds:
as a long vowel, pronounced as *oo* in "cool"
as a short vowel, pronounced something like *oo* in "took"
as a consonant, pronounced as in "war"

y   has three vowel sounds:
two are rather like those for *u* (these are usually in the last syllable of a word), while the third is a sort of vague sound somewhat like *uh* in "uh-huh," and usually at the beginning.

There is no j, k, q, x or z in pure Welsh words.

Long vowels are sometimes indicated by a circumflex over the letter: â, ê, ô,î, û—but not always.

Anyhow, now you know how to say the place name "Eglwyswrw," which until a few moments ago you thought was rather short on vowels.

Another characteristic of Celtic languages is that the beginnings of words with certain initial letters (p, t, c, b, d, g, ll, m, rh in Welsh) change according to various quite complex grammatical rules. For example, the word for father, "tad," goes through the sequence "dad" (familiar enough), "nhad," "thad" in different grammatical circumstances. Once you're used to it, it seems natural and difficult to pronounce in any other way—but it's certainly confusing at first sight.

Nearly all Welsh place names are either straight descriptions of the place or a description plus a saint's name. The ubiquitous "llan," meaning a church enclosure, is usually used with the name of the saint, often an obscure Celtic one, to which the church is dedicated: Llandeilo is the "the church of Saint Teilo," Llanfihangel is "the church of Saint Michael," Llanbedr Pont Steffan is "the church of Saint Peter at Stephen's bridge."

last to the valley of the River Severn and the town of Welshpool, which has some fine Georgian buildings. Now that you are in Wales, the road signs become bilingual. Sometimes the Welsh versions of the names are immediately recognizable, sometimes not, as in Welshpool's Y Trallwng.

On the way into Welshpool you cross, not for the first time, the line of the earthwork known as Offa's Dyke, believed to date from the late 8th century and constructed on the order of Offa, king of the ancient kingdom of Mercia, to mark off his territory from Wales. Powis Castle, originally a medieval construction but with late 16th-century additions, is 4 km (2.5 mi.) southwest of Welshpool. There is a museum on the site.

The next part of the route is a series of delightful, if markedly up-and-down, lanes through a very green countryside of small fields, mostly used for grazing cattle and sheep. This is wonderful cycling country if you don't try to hurry. Obviously we're not the only ones to think so: one of the villages is named Llanfihangel-yng-Ngwynfa—"Saint Michael in Paradise."

Soon after comes the 19th-century dam that holds back the waters of the artificial LLyn Efyrnwy (Lake Vyrnwy), built in the 19th century to supply water to the English city of Liverpool. You can follow either the southwest or northeast sides of the lake. After the hills of the route so far, either road is refreshingly level. This is more than can be said for the next section, which strikes off north from Alltforgan over the Hirnant Pass (about 505 m/1,657 ft.) before the fine open run down to the little town of Bala.

After Bala, there's once more some quite earnest climbing in store over rather open moorland and rough grazing to reach the main A5 road, the old Holyhead Road of coaching days, at

---

Frequent elements of Welsh geographic names

aber = mouth (of a river)	glas = blue or green
afon = river	llan = church enclosure
bwlch = pass	llyn = lake
cae = field	melin = mill
castell = castle	mynydd = mountain
coed = wood	pont = bridge
coch = red	rhos = moorland or heath
croes = cross	rhyd = ford
dôl = meadow	tre(f) = settlement, village
eglwys = church	ty = house
ffordd = road	y = the, or of the
fforest = forest	yn = in

Pentrefoelas. On the other side of the A5, the road climbs over the moor before dropping to the valley of the Afon Conwy and the pleasant little market town of Llanrwst. Nearby Gwydyr Castle is a Tudor palace. Next comes a very pleasant forested stretch over to the cataract of Swallow Falls—spectacular when the river is high—and the A5 once more.

Although there's no real alternative to the main A5 road for the next 20 km (12 mi.) or so, the surroundings are spectacular, up the broad valley of the Nant Ffrancon. It was on the mountains that flank this road that early Everest expedition climbers trained, and at a former pub about 10 km (6 mi.) southwest of the village of Capel Curig that the detailed plans for the first succesful ascent in 1953 were made.

Around Bethesda and through to Bangor, the land is scarred with the remains of the slate quarries that made the area prosperous in the 18th and 19th centuries, when the blue-grey or greenish easily fashioned slate was the universal roofing material in the new in-dustrial towns. Bangor is the oldest seat of a bishop in Britain, ear-lier even than the better-known Canterbury. There has been a Bishop of Bangor (now Bangor and Dee) since the 6th century, and the cathedral of St. Deiniol dates from the 12th century. Nearby Penrhyn Castle had its origins at the same time but was virtually rebuilt in the 19th-century Victorian passion for improvement.

After the university town of Bangor, the route crosses the nar-row sea channel of the Menai Strait to the island of Anglesey, Ynys Môn in Welsh, by the Menai Suspension Bridge, the first major suspension bridge in the world, built by the engineer Thomas Tel-ford in 1826.

Anglesey and the mainland county of Gwynedd, which you have just left, make up one of the strongholds of the Welsh lan-guage. By comparison with the mainland, the landscape of Anglesey is gentle and rolling. Like the English county of Wiltshire, it is an area rich in prehistoric remains. The last few miles of the route cross to Holy Island, on which stands the port of Holyhead, Caer Gybi in Welsh.

Directions

1. Leave B4371 in center of Church Stretton W. by uc. road (Burway Rd.) up very steep hill—the Burway—to top of Long Mynd.

2. Just below summit, bear R. toward Ratlinghope down steep hill to T-junct.

3. L. and 1st R. to Bridges, R., L. and R. in Bridges to take uc. road up open hill to Stiperstones, passing stone outcrops on right.

4. Bear right through The Bog toward Pennerley; just before Pennerley, L. through Shelve to A488.

5. S.O. on uc. road across A488.

6. At T-junct. by P.H., L. on uc. road.

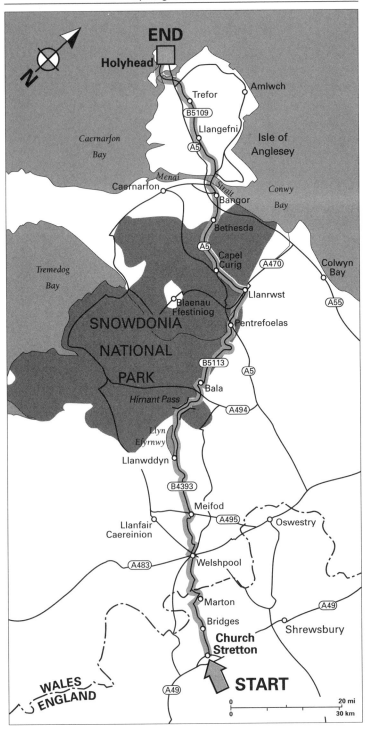

7. At next T-junct., L. again to Rorrington.

8. At far end of village, keep R., then turn R. to B4386 at Marton.

9. R. on B4386 through village; at end of village, L. on uc. road (effectively S.O. where B4386 goes R.).

10. After 1 km (0.6 mi.), L. to Trelystan, then S.O. still on uc. roads at top of long climb (Long Mountain) down hill to B4388.

11. R. on B4388, then L. on B4381 to Welshpool (Y Trallwng).

12. At A490/A458 in center of Welshpool, R., then 2nd L. by museum on uc. road to A490.

13. L. on A490, then immediately R. on uc. road through Groespluan.

14. After 1 km (0.6 mi.), R., and after 2 km (1.2 mi.), L. to B4392.

15. L. on B4392, then 1st R. on uc. road.

16. Near top of ridge, R., then S.O. at minor x-rds., then L. to A495 at Meifod.

17. R. and L. across A495, then L. on uc. roads for 9 km (5.5 mi.) to T-junct. with B4382.

18. R. on B4382 to Llanfihangel-yng-Ngwynfa.

19. L. on B4393, then keep R. on B4393 through Abertridw to dam.

20. R. or L. (both B4393) to follow L. or R. shore of reservoir Llyn Efyrnwy (Lake Vyrnwy).

21. At head of lake, N. on uc. road over Hirnant Pass to Rhos-y-Gwaliau.

22. At far end of settlement, L. to join B4391.

23. L. on B4391 to Bala.

24. In center of Bala, R. on A494, then L. on uc. road through Rhiwlas to B4501.

25. R. on B4501; after 3 km (2 mi.), L. on uc. road toward Ty Mawr Cwm.

26. Just before Ty Mawr Cwm, L., then R. and L. over ridge on uc. roads to A5 at Pentrefoelas.

27. S.O. across A5 on B5113 through Nebo to join A470 into Llanrwst.

28. After crossing over rly., L. on B5106; at T-junct, R. on B5106, then immediately L. on uc. road to A5 at Swallow Falls.

29. R. on A5 through Capel Curig and along valley toward Bethesda. There is no practical paved alternative to this main road for this stretch, although a "road used as public path"—untried by us—follows the W. bank of the Afon (river) Llugwy to a point 2 km (1.2 mi.) before Bethesda.

30. At Bethesda, L. on B4409 through Tregarth to T-junct. with B4366.

31. L. on B4366, then R. on uc. road under A55 toward Bangor.

32. After 3.5 km (2 mi.), L. on uc. road past hospital, then S.O. across A4087, still on uc. road, to T-junct. with A5122.

33. L. on A5122 to rbt., then R. across suspension bridge (A4080) over Menai Strait to Menai Bridge.

34. S.O. at two rbts. to join B5420.

35. S.O. across A5025 at rbt., still on B5420, through Penmynydd, Llangefni, Llynfaes and Bodedern to T-junct. with A6025 at Llanynghenedl.

36. L. on A6025, then R. on uc. road through Newlands Park to A5 at Dyffryn (Valley).

37. Cross A5 R. and L. on uc. road over rly., then R. on B4545 through Trearddur to Holyhead.

CHAPTER 16

Route 13

Cambridge to Chester

Including links to and from East Midlands and Manchester-Ringway airports

Total distance: 325 km (202 mi.)

Intermediate distances:

Cambridge–Oundle:
   71 km (44 mi.)
Oundle–Uppingham:
   24 km (15 mi.)
Uppingham–Melbourne:
   66 km (41 mi.)
Melbourne–Ashbourne:
   40 km (25 mi.)
Ashbourne–Goostrey:
   71 km (44 mi.)
Goostrey–Chester
   53 km (33 mi.)

Terrain:

Flat—in parts utterly flat—to begin with, then rolling hills, mostly with gentle grades, as far as Asbourne; very hilly in Peak District, then gentle to Chester.

Maps:

O.S. Travelmaster (1:250 000) sheets: 6 and 7

O.S. Landranger (1:50 000) sheets: 154, 142, 141, 130, 129, 119, 118, 117 (plus 108 for link to Manchester airport)

Goldeneye (1:126 720) sheet: Peak District

Access:

By train: Rail stations at Loughborough (2 km/1 mi S.W. of route), Crewe (10 km/6 mi S. of route).
By bike: Cambridge: Routes 2, 4, 7, 10; Chester: Routes 11 and 16.

Summary:

This route from the university city of Cambridge to the ancient and picturesque city of Chester cuts across the rural heartland of England, the Midlands. It leaves the flat country and low hills of the east to give the first taste of northern landscapes when it crosses the limestone country of the Peak National Park before dropping to the park-like Cheshire plain.

East Midlands Airport link joins/leaves near Long Whatton. Manchester Airport link leaves/joins at Goostrey.

Description

For a general description of Cambridge, see Route 2, Chapter 5.

This route and Route 14, described in Chapter 17, leave Cambridge by Castle Hill—a slight enough rise, but local residents proudly point out to visitors that there is nothing higher between it and the North Pole. The first part of the route gives a brief taste (and Route 14 rather more) of the dead flat Fenland area. This original marshland, flooded for much of the year, was progressively drained from the 17th century on, to form fertile black-soiled farmland. Small elevations formed scattered islands in the fen, and one of them—Ely, crowned with its dramatic 12th–13th century cathedral, built over one much earlier—dominates the horizon to the north. The route crosses the River Great Ouse at Earith, where one of the long straight "drains" that carry flood water to the sea stretches away to the northeast. The small town of St. Ives, which the route skirts, has an interesting bridge over the river with a small chapel built on it.

Once across the Great North Road—the original London-to-York road, now the A1—the route crosses gently rolling limestone country, the northern extension of the more famous Cotswold Hills. Here, in the Northamptonshire Uplands, there are still the compact and attractive limestone villages and towns, among them Oundle and Uppingham, both sites of famous "public" schools. An interesting feature of the villages is the way the color of the building stone changes from a creamy grey to a deep rich brown, often over a very short distance, as the iron content varies. The village of Lyddington, about 3 km (2 mi.) south of Uppingham, is a particularly fine red ironstone village with an interesting "Bede House"—converted from the bishop's palace in the 17th century to make a home for elderly residents.

After Uppingham there is a succession of attractive small lanes through very rolling country, a mixture of sheep grazing and cropping, to the valley of the River Soar, a small river that winds its way through lush grazing meadows. Climbing away from the valley, the next few miles bring you to the valley of the River Trent, one of England's largest rivers. The large village of Melbourne is well worth exploring, with the gardens of Melbourne Hall laid out in the style of the French palace of Versailles. Lord Melbourne (1779–1848) was Queen Victoria's first prime minister, and the city of Melbourne in Australia's Victoria was named for him. Another notable Derbyshire Melburnian was Thomas Cook—the inventor of the package tour.

Repton is another interesting large village, with yet another famous public school. The next few miles lead through quite open green cattle-grazing country to the the small town of Ashbourne, the gateway to the Peak National Park, England's first national park, created in 1945. This is mountain limestone country, and the villages and towns have a greyer, more solid and upland look than the golden stone of a few miles back.

Parts of the Peak District are very hilly, with some up and down grades—usually mercifully short—of over 20%. The route uses a short stretch of the Manifold Valley trail, one of the first bike-plus-pedestrian trails in Britain, following the bed of an old quarry railroad. This is a countryside of steep, often wooded, valleys, with fields on the ridges between them divided by dry-stone walls, built from local stone without mortar. Much of the enclosed upland is used for sheep grazing.

From Longnor the road begins to climb steadily, with an attractive miniature limestone gorge just after Gletton Bridge, and a couple of small passes to cross the jagged ridge of Axe Edge. This is open heather-covered moorland, a blaze of purple flowers in late August and September.

There's a fine downhill stretch from the Cat and Fiddle—one of the highest pubs in England at 515 m (1,690 ft.) above sea level—to the steep valley of Bottom-of-the-Oven, followed by a short, sharp climb through the forest and another downhill swoop past two pretty artificial lakes. The route crosses another of Britain's old canals, the Macclesfield Canal, by a swing bridge at Oakgrove.

The Cheshire plain, mostly very green cattle-grazing country with small hedged fields, is almost park-like and very gentle after the rigors of the Peak District. The park appearance is not entirely an illusion, for there are many large houses and estates; this was a favorite area for successful 19th-century industrialists to establish their homes. About 1 km (less than 1 mi.) north of the route, between Withington and Goostrey, there's a monument of a very different kind: the large dish of the Jodrell Bank radio telescope, one of the world's first radio astronomy centers. (This landmark dominates the Cheshire landscape and is easily visible from the Cat and Fiddle.) There is a visitor center and display where you can try your hand at steering a small radio telescope.

The final run in to Chester skirts Winsford and Northwich, towns that owed their existence to the underground salt deposits here, and then passes through another small forest remnant, Delamere Forest, before dropping to the valley of the River Dee on which Chester lies.

For a general description of Chester, see Route 11, Chapter 14.

Directions

1. Leave Cambridge city center N.W. by Bridge Street over Magdalene Bridge, then up Castle Street (A1307).

2. At top of Castle Hill, R. into Histon Road, B1049.

3. At crossing of northern bypass, A45, S.O. (2nd. exit) on B1049 to S. outskirts of Cottenham.

4. L. on uc. road through Rampton to B1050 at Willingham.

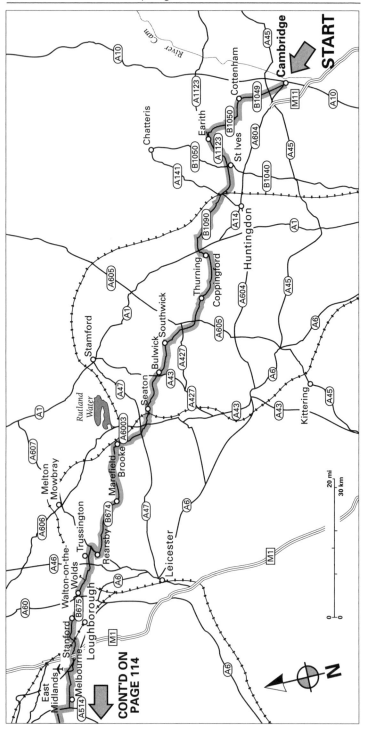

CONT'D ON
PAGE 114

5. R. on B1050 to A1123.

6. L. on A1123 through Earith, Needingworth to St. Ives.

7. R. on B1090, S.O. across A141 at rbt. by Kings Ripton and through Abbots Ripton to T-junct. with A1.

8. R. and L. on uc. road through Coppingford to x-rds., where R. on uc. road through Hamerton to B660 at Winwick.

9. S.O. on uc. road through Thurning and Barnwell to T-junct. with A605.

10. R. on A605, then fork L. on uc. road to A427 in Oundle.

11. R. on A427 through town center, then L. on uc. road past Oundle School by Glapthorn to Southwick.

12. L. on uc. road through Bulwick to A43.

13. L. and R. on uc. road through Laxton to Harringworth.

14. Under rly. viaduct, L. on B672, then R. on uc. road, then L. through Seaton to A6003 in Uppingham.

15. R. in Uppingham to rbt. junct. with A47.

16. Take second exit on uc. road through Ayston and by Ridlington to Brooke.

17. L. on uc. road through Braunston and Knossington, then L. to Owston.

18. In Owston, L. then R. through Marefield, then R. to B6047 at Twyford.

19. R. on B6047, then L. on B674 through Ashby Folville and by Gaddesby to A607 in Rearsby.

20. S.O. on uc. road into Rearsby village, then L. to Thrussington.

21. At far end of village, fork L. to A46.

22. R. and L. across A46 through Seagrave and Walton on the Wolds to B675.

23. R. and L. on uc. road, 1st R., then R. again to B676.

24. L. on B676 and 1st R. on very small "no through road."

25. At cycle gap at blocked-off end of road, S.O., crossing A60 with care, through Stanford on Soar and Normanton on Soar to A6006.

26. L. on A6006 through Zouch to A6.

27. L. on A6, then R. on B5324, then R. again on B5401 through Long Whatton; under M1 and over A42 through Diseworth to A453.

28. (Link to East Midlands Airport—R. on A453 for 1.5 km/1 mi.)

29. L. on A453 to Isley Walton, R. on uc. road to Melbourne.

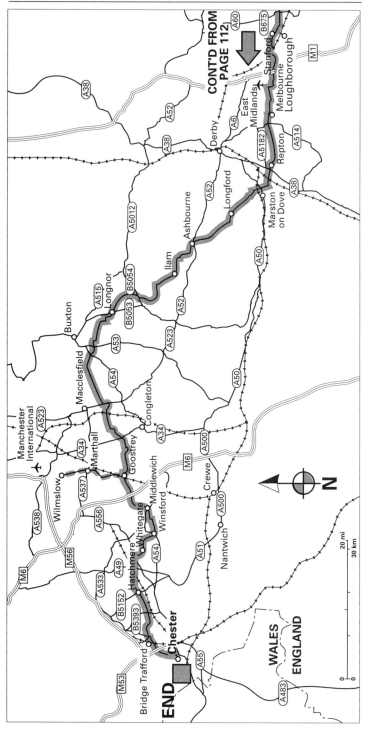

CONT'D FROM PAGE 112

30. At far end of village, R. on B587 to A514.

31. S.O. on A514, then 1st L. on uc. roads through Stanton, by Bridge and Ingleby, to Repton.

32. In village center, R. on B5008 to cross River Trent to A5132 in Willington.

33. L. on A5132 to pass over A38 to Hilton.

34. In Hilton, L. and R. on uc. road to pass under A516 through Sutton on the Hill, Longford, Rodsley and Wyaston to Ashbourne.

35. Follow signs on A515 to town center.

36. Leave Ashbourne N. on A515, then L. on hill on B5035.

37. R., still on B5035, then S.O. on uc. road where B5035 goes R., through Mappleton, then L., still on uc. road, through Thorpe to Ilam.

38. In Ilam, R. up hill, then follow uc. roads to Wetton, where R. to Wetton Mill.

39. S.O. on valley road, then S.O. at end of tunnel on paved cycle route to B3055 at Hulme End.

40. R. on B3055, then L. after bridge over River Manifold, through Sheen to Longnor.

41. In village, R. on B5053 to Gletton Bridge, then L. on minor road immediately after bridge over River Dove to follow moorland road to A53 at Axe Edge.

42. L. and R. on uc. road through miniature pass to A54.

43. L. and 1st R. on uc. road to A537.

44. L. on A537 past Cat and Fiddle inn at summit of climb (515 m/1,690 ft.).

45. After about 1 km (0.6 mi.), fork L. on uc. road to Bottom-of-the-Oven, L. at P.H., then R. and 2nd R. through forest and Langley to Sutton Lane Ends.

46. At x-rds. about 800 m (0.5 mi.) after village, L. to A523 at Oakgrove.

47. S.O. on uc. road over canal by Gawsworth to A536 at Warren.

48. L. on A536, then R. on uc. road to A34 at Marton.

49. S.O. on uc. road, then after 1 km (0.6 mi.), R., still on uc. roads, through Swettenham Heath to A535 at Twemlow Green.

50. S.O. across A535, then immediately R. through Goostrey.

51. S.O. across A50 and over M6 to B5081.

52. Link to/from Manchester Airport joins/leaves at Goostrey—see below.

53. L. on B5081 to A54, R. on A54 into Middlewich.

54. Just after town center, L. on A530 under Shropshire Union Canal, then R. on uc. road to rejoin A54.

55. L. on A54 over rly. bridge to Winsford.

56. Follow one-way system to leave N. on uc. road beside Weaver Navigation Canal to Whitegate.

57. L., still on uc. road, then at x-rds. after Foxwist Green, R. to cross A556 into Sandiway.

58. At x-rds., L. to A49 by Cuddington rly. stn.

59. S.O. across A49 on uc. roads through Norley to B5152 at Hatchmere.

60. S.O. across B5152 through Delamere Forest, and at x-rds. after passing under rly., R. to B5393.

61. S.O. on B5393, then L. on uc. road to B5132 at Bridge Trafford.

62. S.O. across B5132 to A56.

63. L. on A56 through Bridge Trafford, then R. at Mickle Trafford on uc. road signed "Cheshire Cycleway" into Chester.

Link to/from Manchester Airport:

1. Leave terminal buildings N., passing over motorway rbts. into Outwood Lane.

2. L. into Thorley Lane to recross motorway spur, then bear L. into Hasty Lane, which becomes Runger Lane, to rbt. junct. with A538.

3. L. on A538, which passes under airport runway.

4. 1.5 km (1 mi.) after underpass, R. on uc. road through Morley Green.

5. R. on uc. road, then L. to B5085 at Knolls Green.

6. R. on B5085, then L. on uc. road.

7. After about 1.5 km (1 mi.), at x-rds., R. on uc. road, then after a further 1.5 km (1 mi.), L. to A537 at Marthall.

8. S.O. across A537 on uc. roads through Blackden Heath to Goostrey to join main route.

CHAPTER 17

Route 14

Cambridge to York

With link to/from Hull, port for ferries to and from Holland and Germany

Total distance: 303 km (189 mi.)

Intermediate distances:

Cambridge–Stamford:
   95 km (59 mi.)
Stamford–Ancaster:
   48 km (30 mi.)
Ancaster–Lincoln:
   40 km (25 mi.)
Lincoln–Goole:
   80 km (50 mi.)
Goole–York:
   40 km (25 mi.)

Terrain: Quite easy

Maps:

O.S. Travelmaster (1:250 000) sheets: 5 and 6

O.S. Landranger (1:50 000) sheets: 154, 142, 141, 130, 121, 112, 107 (for Hull link), 106

Access:

By train: mainline rail station at Cambridge, Peterborough (8 km/5 mi. W. of route), Newark-on-Trent (12 km/7 mi. W. of route, and York.

By bike: Cambridge: Routes 2, 4, 10, 13; York: Route 15; Hull link leaves/joins near Elvington.

Summary:

This very gentle route links the university city of Cambridge with the historic city of York, traveling almost due north through eastern England.

Description

For a general description of Cambridge, see Route 2, Chapter 5.

Like Route 13, described in Chapter 16, this route begins by crossing part of the Fens, the reclaimed marshland that is now largely divided into geometrical fields of fertile black-soiled farmland.

The countryside is virtually dead flat—small areas are even below sea level—and everything is dominated by the sky. On a day with towering cumulus clouds it can be very impressive, but the wind can make the going quite hard if you're unlucky. The route crosses the River Great Ouse at Earith, where one of the long, straight artificial rivers that carry flood water to the sea—this one romantically named the Hundred Foot Drain—stretches away to the northeast. Few of the Fenland rivers are nowadays allowed to follow their original courses.

The Fenland villages and small towns are workmanlike rather than picturesque, but Ramsey Abbey is worth a look round. Shortly after this, the long straight road to Whittlesey and another from Thorney to Peakirk remind you of how few straight, flat roads there are in Britain. If you have time, the detour to Crowland, with its unique three-way bridge and abbey, (6 km/4 mi. northwest of Thorney) is worthwhile.

After Glinton, the route leaves the Fens for gentle limestone country through the attractive village of Barnack to the exquisite small golden-stone town of Stamford. Stamford was a prosperous 13th- and 14th-century wool town, the capital of Fenland, which was extensively damaged in the 15th-century Wars of the Roses and subsequently largely restored.

The route northward from Stamford follows the limestone country once more, much of it quite sparsely populated and with large arable fields, through to Ancaster. The "-caster" or "-chester" ending on a place-name indicates a former Roman settlement. Ancaster lies on Ermine Street, the Roman road from Castor, near Peterborough (Dvrobrivae to the Romans), to Lincoln and York. Our route, too, leads us to the cathedral city of Lincoln, but by a more winding route than the Romans took, through a succession of quiet villages.

Lincoln cathedral, high on its narrow limestone ridge— although actually only about 60 m (200 ft.) above sea level— dominates the skyline for quite some distance. There has been a cathedral here since the 11th century, but only the original west front remains, most being 13th century. The city still has the medieval pattern of steep, narrow streets, with some of the earliest buildings dating from the 12th century, and the limestone castle from 1080. Lincoln is also the home of the National Cycle Museum (call (01522) 545 091 for opening times and details).

From Lincoln the route drops gently to the plain of the River Trent, crossing from the east to the west bank at Gunness Bridge. The river is tidal here and at times a bore, or tidal wave—known here as the Aegir—sweeps up the river with the incoming tide; enquire locally for times (it is at its highest around full and new moon and when river flows are highest).

The route follows the small winding roads that meander through fields of wheat and sugar beet along the west bank of the Trent and the south bank of the Yorkshire River Ouse to the small port of Goole. Like the Fens, much of this originally marshy area was drained in the 17th century, a great deal of the work being carried out by the Dutch, particularly the engineer Vermuyden, who is commemorated in the canalized River Don, known as the Dutch River. From Goole, the route crosses the River Ouse by Boothferry Bridge, to reach the plain of York.

The last section follows small roads and lanes through mixed farming land to the city of York. The Roman city of Eboracvm on the site was the capital of the Roman province of Lower Britain. During the later occupation of this part of England by the Danes the city became Jorvik, from which the present name derives. In turn, the Normans sacked the Danish town, establishing their own stronghold. Clifford's Tower is the sole remnant of their 11th-century castle, but the medieval city walls remain largely intact. The maze of lanes and alleys that formed the medieval street pattern also survive. The great minster (cathedral) was built over the space of two-and-a-half centuries, from 1220 to 1470. York has a strong cycling tradition, with one of the largest everyday cycle usages in Britain and an extensive cycle route network.

Directions

1. Leave Cambridge N.W. over Magdalene Bridge into Castle Street.

2. After bridge at top of Castle Hill, R. into Histon Road, B1049.

3. At crossing of northern bypass, A45, S.O. (2nd. exit) on B1049 to S. outskirts of Cottenham.

4. L. on uc. road through Rampton to B1050 at Willingham.

5. R. on B1050 to A1123.

6. L. on A1123 to Earith, then R. on B1050 to Somersham.

7. L. on B1086, then fork R. on B1089 to join B1040.

8. S.O. on B1040 through Pidley to A141 at Warboys.

9. S.O. at rbt. to center of Warboys, then R., still on B1040, to Ramsey.

10. In Ramsey, L. to T-junct. with uc. road, R. on B1040 through Pondersbridge to Whittlesey.

11. R. on A605, then L. on B1040 to Thorney.

12. R. and L. across A47; after 600 m (0.4 mi.), L. on B1443.

13. R. and L. across A1073 to Peakirk and Glinton.

14. There are two alternative routes:

A. R. and L. in village center on uc. road where B1443 goes L., then cross A15 by footbridge to rejoin B1443.

B. L. on B1443 to rbt. junct. with A15, R. (3rd. exit) on A15 for 1 km (0.6 mi.), then L. on B1443 through Helpston, Bainton and Barnack to Stamford.

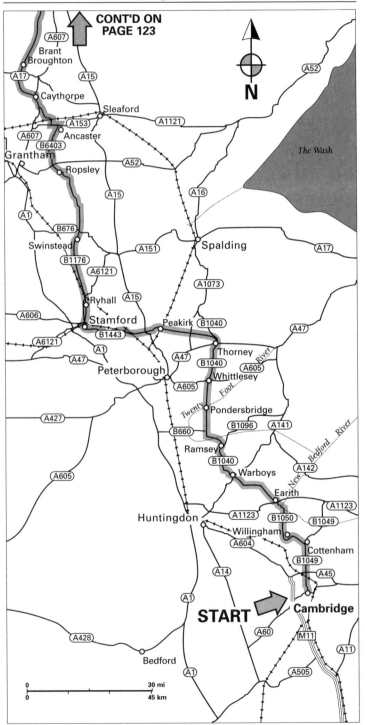

CONT'D ON
PAGE 123

N

The Wash

START

Cambridge

15. R. on A6121 to town center, R. on A6121, then L., still on A6121, to Ryhall.

16. After crossing River Gwash, L. on B1176 through Careby, Little Bytham and Creeton to Swinstead.

17. In Swinstead, R. on uc. road, S.O. across A151 to Irnham, L. just after village to Lenton.

18. L., still on uc. road, to Ingoldsby.

19. R. at T-junct. just after church, then R. to Ropsley.

20. At N. end of village, R. on uc. road, fork R. to cross A52 to B6403.

21. R. on B6403 to A153 at Ancaster.

22. L. on A153, then R. on uc. road through Sudbrook to A607.

23. S.O. on A607, then L. on uc. road into Caythorpe.

24. L. at church on uc. road to T-junct., R. through Stragglethorpe, S.O. across A17 to Brant Broughton.

25. At N. end of village, R. and L.

26. S.O., then L. on uc. road to A1434 at Bracebridge on S. outskirts of Lincoln.

27. R. on A1434 to city center.

28. (Southern link to Hull, port for Holland and Belgium, joins/leaves at Lincoln—see below.)

29. Leave Lincoln city center on Burton Road, B1369, to pass over A46, then through Burton to A1500.

30. L. on A1500 to Sturton-by-Stow, then R. on B1241 through Stow and Willingham-by-Stow, to Kexby.

31. Where B1241 goes L., S.O. on uc. road through Upton, Heapham and Springthorpe to A631.

32. L. on A631, then R. on uc. road into Corringham, L., then R. at T-junct., still on uc. road, through Pilham to B1205 at Blyton.

33. L. on B1205, R. on A151, then fork L. on uc. road through Laughton.

34. At W. end of village, R. on uc. road through forest to T-junct.

35. L. on uc. road to Susworth, then follow E. bank of River Trent through East Butterwick, passing under M180 to B1450 at Burringham.

36. S.O. on B1450 to A18, L. on A18 over Gunness Bridge, then immediately R. on B1392.

37. Follow B1392 through Arncotts, along W. bank of River Trent for about 9 km (5.5 mi.), then S.O. on uc. roads (where B1392 goes L.) through Garthtorpe, Adlingfleet, Ousefleet, Whitgift and Reedness to A161 at Swinefleet.

38. R. on A161 through Old Goole to cross Dutch River canals, then S.O. on uc. road through Goole.

39. At N. end of town, R. on A614 to pass over M62, then cross Boothferry Bridge over River Ouse.

40. Immediately after bridge, fork L. on B1228, then S.O. on uc. road where B1228 turns R., to A63.

41. L. on A63 for about 3 km (2 mi.), then R. on uc. road through Wressle and Breighton to A163 at Bubwith.

42. R. on A613, then L. on B1228 through Sutton upon Derwent and Elvington to A1079.

43. Northern link to Hull, port for Holland and Belgium, joins/leaves about 4 km (2.5 mi.) before Sutton upon Derwent—see below.

44. L. on A1079, S.O. at rbt. with A64 into York city center.

Northern link to/from Hull:

1. Leave center of Hull W. on A1150 (Anlaby Road), then at rbt. bear R. on B1231, then uc. road to Kirk Ella.

2. S.O. through West Ella to pass over A164 to T-junct.

3. R. to next T-junct., L. at next acute junct. under power lines on uc. road to Riplingham.

4. S.O. in village, then 2nd. L. to A1034 im South Cave.

5. L. and R. across A1034 through West End to B1230 at North Cave.

6. L. on B1230, then after 500 m (0.3 mi.), R. on uc. road, then L., through South Cliffe to North Cliffe.

7. L. on uc. road to A613, L. on A613 for 1 km (0.6 mi.), then R. on uc. road to Everingham.

8. Keep L. in village, then after 2.5 km (2 mi.), fork R. through Melbourne to join main route at B1228.

Southern link to/from Hull:

1. Leave center of Hull on A1150 (Anlaby Road) to N. end of Humber Bridge.

2. Follow cycle route signs (20% grade) to cycle path over bridge.

3. Cross bridge, and at S. end, follow cycle route signs to Far Ings Road, then follow B-road into Barton upon Humber.

4. L. on A1077, then R. on B1218.

5. After passing over A15, R. on uc. road to B1204 at Saxby All Saints.

6. L. on B1204 through Bonby and Worlaby to T-junct. with B1206.

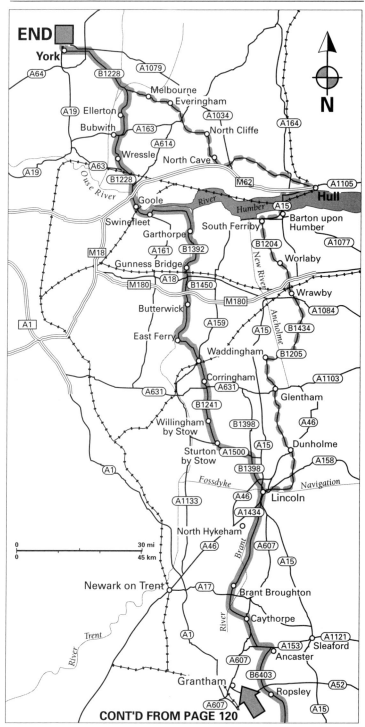

END
York
A64
B1228
A1079
A19 Ellerton
Melbourne
Everingham
A1034
A164
Bubwith
A163
North Cliffe
A614
Wressle
North Cave
A19
A63
Ouse River
B1228
M62
A1105
Goole
River
Hull
Humber
A15
Swinefleet
South Ferriby
Barton upon Humber
Garthorpe
B1204
A1077
M18
A161
B1392
Worlaby
Gunness Bridge
New River
M180
A18
B1450
Wrawby
M180
A1084
Butterwick
A159
Ancholme
A15
B1434
East Ferry
Waddingham
B1205
A1103
Corringham
A631
Glentham
A631
B1241
A46
Willingham by Stow
B1398
Sturton by Stow
A15
Dunholme
A1500
A158
B1398
A1
Fossdyke
A46
Navigation
A1133
Lincoln
A1434
North Hykeham
A46
A607
Brant
A15
Newark on Trent
A17
Brant Broughton
Caythorpe
A1121
Trent
A153
Sleaford
River
A607
Ancaster
River Trent
B6403
A52
Grantham
Ropsley
A607
A15

0   30 mi
0   45 km

N

CONT'D FROM PAGE 120

123

7. R. on B1206 over M180, then L. on uc. road through Wrawby to A18, where L. and R. on uc. road over rly. level crossing to A1084.

8. L. on A1084, then R. on B1434 through Howsham.

9. 1.5 km (1 mi.) after Howsham, R. on uc. road through North Kelsey to B1205 at South Kelsey.

10. R. on B1205 to Waddingham, then L. on uc. roads through Snitterby, Bishop Norton to A631 at Glentham.

11. R. and L. across A631, still on uc. roads through Normanby-by-Spital, Owmby-by-Spital to Spridlington.

12. R. and L. on uc. road to T-junct. at Welton, L., then R., still on uc. road, to A46 at Dunholme.

13. R. and L. on uc. road across A46 through Scothern and Sudbrooke to A158.

14. R. on A158, and after 1 km (0.6 mi.), L. on uc. road to Reepham.

15. R. then L. to Cherry Willingham, R. on uc. roads to Lincoln city center.

CHAPTER 18

Route 15

York to Edinburgh

With link to/from Newcastle upon Tyne, port for ferries to and from Norway

Total distance: 445 km (276 mi.)

Intermediate distances:

York–Stokesley:
    87 km (54 mi.)
Stokesley–Stanhope:
    87 km (54 mi.)
Stanhope–Corbridge:
    39 km (24 mi.)
Corbridge–Rothbury:
    47 km (29 mi.)
Rothbury–Bamburgh:
    53 km (33 mi.)
Bamburgh–Duns:
    58 km (36 mi.)
Duns–Edinburgh:
    74 km (46 mi.)

Maps:

O.S. Travelmaster (1:250 000) sheets: 4 and 5

O.S. Landranger (1:50 000) sheets: 105, 100, 93, 92, 87, 88 (for Newcastle-upon-Tyne link), 80, 81, 74, 75, 67, 66

Goldeneye (1:126 720) sheet: North Yorkshire Moors (covers part of route)

Terrain: A mixture of flat and very hilly

Access:

By train: mainline rail stations at York, Darlington (7 km/4 mi. W. of route), Durham (8 km/5 mi. N.E. of route), Newcastle upon Tyne (see link), Berwick-upon-Tweed, and Edinburgh.

By bike: York: Route 14; Edinburgh: Route 18; Newcastle upon Tyne link joins/leaves at Capheaton.

Summary:

This long—and in places hilly—route up through the eastern side of northern England into southern Scotland links the historic city of

York with Edinburgh, the capital of Scotland, passing through two national parks—North Yorkshire Moors and Northumbria.

Description

For a general description of York, see Chapter 17.

Although York lies in the almost flat Vale of York, after no more than a few miles of mixed cattle grazing and arable country the route climbs to the low ridge of the Howardian Hills. Just to the right of the route lies Castle Howard, a great house rather than a true castle, and built over the years 1700–1737 under the guidance of the architect Sir John Vanbrugh to replace the earlier Henderskelfe Castle, which had burnt down in 1639. Its recent fame lies from its use as the setting for the television production *Brideshead Revisited*; grounds and house are at times open to the public.

Beyond the Howardian Hills, the route passes into fertile Ryedale. Like Cheshire (Chapters 14 and 16), this is a countryside of frequent big houses set in parkland: a short side trip of about 3 km (2 mi.) west from Ness brings you to the largely 17th-century Nunnington Hall, beautifully set on the banks of the River Rye. Another treat is the picturesque village of Hutton-le-Hole, with its grey stone cottages set around a broad central open "green," a layout typical of many Yorkshire villages. The Ryedale Folk Museum here has a number of reconstructed local historic buildings.

You are now on the southern slopes of the North Yorkshire Moors, an upland plateau dissected by many steep river valleys, each with its own "dale" name—which usually has nothing to do with the name of the river. Farndale, which lies just west and below the route as it climbs to Blakey Ridge, is famous for its spring displays of daffodils. The Moors rise to a height of just under 450 m (1,490 ft.) and in late summer are covered in brilliant purple heather.

Dunstanburgh Castle, Northumberland, is located 6 km (4 mi.) east of Christon Bank.

In bad weather, though, the Moors can be very bleak indeed. The North Yorkshire Moors also have the dubious distinction, for cyclists, of harboring some of the steepest marked grades in Britain—30% and 33%. (You'll be relieved to hear that none as steep as this are on the route.)

If you have time, a hilly side trip of about 30 km (19 mi.) eastward brings you to the old whaling and fishing port of Whitby and the delightful village of Robin Hood's Bay nestling under the cliffs. Whitby is associated with Captain Cook, one of the first European explorers to survey Australia and New Zealand, in the late 18th century, and the museum of local history has Cook mementos. High on the cliff above the harbor is the gaunt ruin of the 13th-century Whitby Abbey; there has been an abbey here since 657.

After leaving the Moors, the route picks its way through the fringes of the industrial zones of the counties of Cleveland and Durham. The towns of Darlington, Stockton and Middlesbrough grew rapidly during the Industrial Revolution, at one time being centers of coal, iron and steel production. The first steam railroad in Britain ran between Stockton-on-Tees and Darlington. Although much diminished, some steel production continues, and the area is now one of the centers of the chemical industry. There are many relics of the Industrial Revolution, and the route passes one in Yarm: a railroad viaduct that lifts the tracks over the town and the River Tees and required 6 million bricks for its construction. Despite the nearness of industry, this is pleasantly green and rolling cycling country, with its gentleness a relief after the rigors of the North Yorkshire Moors.

Some sections of main road are unavoidable on the next stretch, up the valley of the River Wear through the town of Wolsingham to Stanhope. This is limestone and gritstone country again—the

The River Tweed, border between England and Scotland.

Durham Dales, a mixture of rough upland grazing and heather-covered moorland.

The moorland road leads down to the pretty village of Blanchland, with its stone-roofed cottages and 12th-century abbey, followed by some more climbing, through forest this time, to reach the little town of Corbridge on the River Tyne. To the Romans this was Corstopitvm, and about 5 km (3 mi.) north of the town, the route crosses the remains of Hadrian's Wall. The Roman emperor Hadrian ordered the wall be built in order to protect the Roman colonies to the south from the marauding Picts and Scots to the north. Construction began in A.D. 122. (The most spectacular parts of this impressive piece of engineering lie farther west and are covered in the description of the circular tour C, "Scottish Borders and the Roman Wall" in Chapter 25.)

The route now passes into the county of Northumberland, named from the old kingdom of Northumbria. Fortunately for the cyclist, Northumberland is one of England's largely undiscovered gems. Most of the roads are quiet, and there is a wealth of scenic and human interest.

For the first part the route is quite hilly. Just before the hamlet of Cambo the route passes Wallington Hall, a fine manor house built in 1688 on the site of a medieval castle. There is a spectacular drop to the large village of Rothbury, and an equally tough climb through forest on the way out. A side trip of about 12 km (7.5 mi.) northeast from the route at Edlingham takes you to the ancient town of Alnwick with its cobbled streets and castle (also visited on the "Borders and Roman Wall" tour). There's a castle at Edlingham too, dating from the 14th century.

The route then heads to the coast near Beadnell, passing through the attractive fishing village of Seahouses. From Seahouses there are boat trips to the nearby Farne Islands, a nature reserve and bird sanctuary, with large colonies of colorful puffins and grey seals.

The next village, Bamburgh, has an imposing, inhabited castle. The rock on which it is perched has been fortified since 547, but the building you see now dates in effect from an extensive restoration about a hundred years ago. In Bamburgh there's a small museum commemorating a local heroine, Grace Darling. She lived with her father, who was a lighthouse keeper on the Farne Islands, and played a heroic part in rescuing survivors during a storm from the shipwreck of the *Forfarshire* in 1838.

A further side trip from the route at Fenwick of about 12 km (7.5 mi.) leads eastward across a causeway that is submerged at high tide, to Holy Island with its ruined Lindisfarne Priory and spectacularly sited 16th-century Lindisfarne Castle. The twin villages of Ford and Etal (each with yet another castle—really manor houses fortified in the 14th century) are early examples of planned layout, dating from the early 19th century. The last castle, at least on the English section of the route, is at Norham on the River Tweed, which here forms the border between England and Scotland.

There is a pronounced southwest to northeast "grain" to the country just over the border, which brings a succession of small

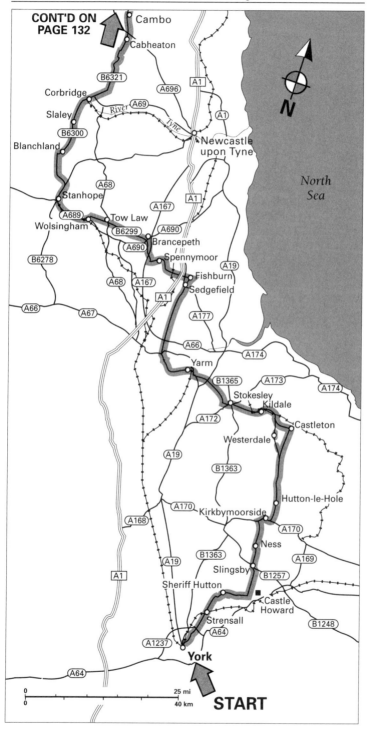

CONT'D ON PAGE 132

START

climbs and descents before the small town of Duns. Here begins a very lonely section of the route over the Lammermuir Hills, much of it open moorland, before the final run in to Edinburgh.

Edinburgh, Scotland's capital city, lay originally in the English kingdom of Northumbria and only finally became Scots in 1341. The old part of the city lay south of the castle, now visible in the cobbled streets of the Royal Mile and Grassmarket. The modern city layout is Georgian, the architects leaving the view from the main street, Princes Street, open toward the castle, perched high on its volcanic rock. The oldest part of the castle, St. Margaret's Chapel, dates from the 12th century, though most is much more recent. One of the more fanciful names for elegant and neoclassical Edinburgh is "the Athens of the North," and it has been an academic center since 1582, when the university was founded. The annual Edinburgh Festival of arts and performance in August attracts tens of thousands of visitors.

Directions

1. Leave York city center N.E. by B1363 (Gillygate, Clarence Street), then R. into Haxby Road (uc. road).

2. After 2 km (1.2 mi.), R. and then L. through New Earswick.

3. R. to Huntington, then L. to cross northern ring road, A1237 at Earswick rbt.

4. S.O. on uc. road through Strensall to Sherrif Hutton.

5. R. at x-rds. on uc. road through Bulmer.

6. At x-rds. 1.5 km (1 mi.) after Bulmer, L. past entrance to Castle Howard, S.O. across B1257 in Slingsby to East and West Ness.

7. At far end of village, bear R. to A170.

8. R. on A170 through Kirbymoorside, then fork L. on uc. road to Keldholme.

9. L. on uc. road through Hutton-le-Hole, then S.O. to climb Blakey Ridge to Rosedale Head.

10. At summit (418 m/1,371 ft.), bear L. through Westerdale, and then L. again after crossing rly. through Kildale and Easby to A173.

11. L. on A173, S.O. at rbt. (junct. with A172) on B1257, L. at 2nd rbt. in Stokesley on B1365.

12. At W. end of village, R. on uc. road and then R. again through Seamer and Hilton, passing over A19 to A1044 at High Leven.

13. L. on A1044 across River Leven, then fork R. on uc. road to A67 in Yarm.

14. R. on A67, then after crossing River Tees, L. on uc. road over rly. through Aislaby to A67 in Middleton St. George.

15. L. on A67, and after 1 km (0.6 mi.), R. on uc. road to pass under A66, through Sadberge, Great Stainton and Mordon to A689 at Bradbury.

16. L. on A689 to pass over A1(M), then immediately R. on uc. road to Ferryhill.

17. L. on uc. road to join B6287 and pass over A167 to Kirk Merrington.

18. R. on B6288, then bear L. on uc. road to pass over A688 through Spennymoor, crossing bridge over River Wear to A690.

19. R. on A690 and immediately L., still on uc. road, to B6299.

20. R. on B6299 to A68, S.O. on A68 to Tow Law, then L. on B6297 (effectively S.O. where A68 goes R.), joining B6296 to A689 in Wolsingham.

21. R. on A689 to Stanhope, R. on B6278 to climb to Stanhope Common.

22. At summit, bear L. on uc. road to B6306 at Blanchland.

23. S.O. on B6306 to junct. with B6307, R. on B6307 to L. and R. crossing of A695 to Corbridge (see note below for link to Newcastle upon Tyne).

24. In Corbridge, S.O. at rbt. on B6321 to pass over A69 to junct. with B6318.

25. L. on B6318 and immediately R. on uc. roads through Matfen, Ingoe and Capheaton (many T-juncts. and turns—follow signs) to junct. with A696.

26. (Link to Newcastle upon Tyne, port for Denmark, Norway and Sweden, joins/leaves near Matfen and Ingoe—see below.)

27. R. on A696, then L. on uc. road to join B6342.

28. S.O. on B6342 through Cambo to Rothbury.

29. In Rothbury, R. on B6344, then L. on B6341 to cross A697 to Edlingham.

30. In Edlingham, L. on uc. road to Bolton.

31. At T-junct. in Bolton, R. on uc. road to B6346.

32. R. on B6346, then L. on B6347 through South Charlton to junct. with A1.

33. L. on A1, then R. on B6347 again through Christon Bank to junct. with B1340.

34. S.O. on B1340 through Seahouses to Bamburgh.

35. In Bamburgh, continue S.O. on B1342 to Waren Mill, R. on uc. road through Elwick to A1.

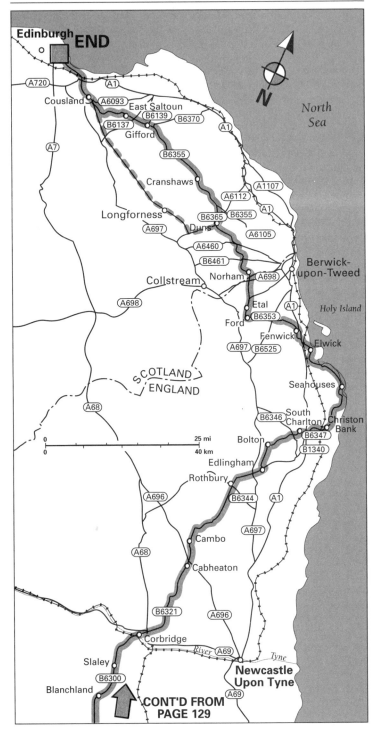

Edinburgh **END**

A720

A1

Cousland · A6093

East Saltoun

B6139

B6370

B6137

Gifford

A1

B6355

A7

Cranshaws

A1107

A6112

Longforness

B6365

B6355

A1

A697

Duns

A6105

A6460

B6461

Collstream

Norham

A698

Berwick-upon-Tweed

A698

Etal

A1

North Sea

Holy Island

Ford

B6353

Fenwick

Elwick

A697

B6525

SCOTLAND

ENGLAND

Seahouses

A68

South Charlton

B6346

Christon Bank

25 mi

40 km

Bolton

B6347

B1340

Edlingham

Rothbury

A696

B6344

A1

A697

Cambo

A68

Cabheaton

B6321

A696

Corbridge

Slaley

River A69

Tyne

Newcastle Upon Tyne

B6300

A69

Blanchland

CONT'D FROM PAGE 129

CONT'D FROM PAGE 129

36. R. on A1, then L. on uc. road through Buckton, L. at T-junct. to B6353 at Fenwick.

37. L. on B6353 through Lowick to Ford.

38. S.O. on B6354 (where B6353 goes L. over bridge) to Etal.

39. 1.5 km (1 mi.) after Etal, L. on uc. roads to cross A698 to junct. with B6470.

40. L. on B6470 to Norham to cross River Tweed into Scotland.

41. 1 km (0.6 mi.) after border, R. on uc. road, S.O. across B6461 to join B6347.

42. L. on B6347 through Whitsome; at end of village, R. on uc. road (effectively S.O. where B6347 goes L.) through Langrigg to B6460.

43. L. on B6460 to Sinclair's Hill, R. on uc. road to cross Blackadder Water to junct. with A6105.

44. L. on A6105 through Duns, and about 2 km (1.2 mi.) after town, R. on uc. road through Longformacus and over Lammermuir Hills to join B6355. (Alternatively, R. in Duns on A6112, then L. on B6355 over Lammermuir Hills.)

45. L. on B6355 through Gifford; cross B6368 to East Saltoun.

46. L. on uc. road through West Saltoun to B6371.

47. R. on B6371 to A6093, then L. on A6093.

48. After 1 km (0.6 mi.), R. on uc. road through Cousland to A6124.

49. R. on A6124, passing over A1 to Inveresk.

50. S.O. on A199 over River Esk (Bridge Street, North High Street, then Edinburgh Rd.).

51. Bear R. on B6415 (Musselburgh Rd., becoming Joppa Rd. and Portobello High Street).

52. At rbt., L. on A1140 (Portobello Rd., then A1, London Rd.) to Edinburgh city center.

Link to Newcastle upon Tyne:

1. A new, partly off-road cycle route, following the River Tyne to the main route at Corbridge, may be open by the time this book is published—check locally. Meanwhile, the route given here links to the main route near Capheaton. The first urban stretches include some busy roads.

2. Leave the Scandinavian Ferry Terminal N.W. by Coble Dene to Howdon Rd., A187.

3. L. on Howdon Rd. to Tyne Tunnel rbt.

4. S.O. on A187 (do not take tunnel road) over tunnel into Hadrian Rd., which becomes Buddle Street, Wallsend.

5. At rbt., L. into uc. road, Fisher Street, becoming White Street to A186, Walker Rd.

6. L. on Walker Road, then after crossing bridge over Ouse Burn, L. on Quayside, B6330, to pass under road bridges into Close and Swinnerburn Rd., passing under road and rly. bridges.

7. R., still on B6330, into Water Street to A695, Scotswood Rd.

8. L. on Scotswood Rd., then R. on uc. road, Park Rd., to T-junct. with Westmorland Rd.

9. L. on Westmorland Rd., then R. into Beech Grove Rd. to B6328, Elswick Road, becoming Adelaide Terrace.

10. R. into Condercum Rd., B6327, to West Rd., A186.

11. L. on West Rd. for 800 m (0.5 mi.), then R. on Two Ball Lonnen, B6326, to rbt. junct. with Stamfordham Rd., B6324.

12. L. on Stamfordham Rd. to pass over A1 to junct. with B6323.

13. S.O. on B6323, then S.O. on uc. road (where B6323 goes L.) to B6309 in Stamfordham.

14. R. on B6309, then L. on uc. road to Fenwick.

15. If going N., fork R. after village to join main route 3km (2 mi.) before Ingoe. If going S., S.O. to main route at Matfen.

CHAPTER 19

Route 16

Chester to Carlisle

With link to/from Heysham (port for ferries to/from Isle of Man and Northern Ireland)

Total distance: 281 km (175 mi.)

Intermediate distances:

Chester–Up Holland:
   61 km (38 mi.)
Up Holland–Preston:
   35 km (22 mi.)
Preston–Kirkby Lonsdale:
   76 km (47 mi.)
Kirkby Lonsdale–Penrith:
   69 km (43 mi.)
Penrith–Carlisle:
   40 km (25 mi.)

Maps:

O.S. Travelmaster (1:250 000) sheets: 5, just touches 7

O.S. Landranger (1:50 000) sheets: 117, 108, 102, 103, 97 (for Heysham link), 98, 90

Goldeneye (1:126 720) sheet: Lake District (part of route)

Terrain: Mainly easy to moderate, but with some hilly stretches, notably north of Preston

Access:

By train: Rail stations with InterCity service at Preston, Lancaster, Penright, Calrisle.

By bike: Chester: Routes 11 and 13: Carlisle: Routes 17 and 18. Heysham link joins/leaves at Dusop Bridge.

Summary:

This route leads from one historic city on the site of a Roman town, Chester, to another, Carlisle, following the western side of England and weaving a path, for much of the southern part, through urban and industrialized areas. Some lengths of main road cannot easily be avoided on this section, but there is the reward of fine upland and river valley scenery for the final four-fifths of the route.

Description

For a general description of Chester, see Route 11, Chapter 14.

The Cheshire Cycleway, which the route follows for a few miles, is one of a number of waymarked on-road cycle routes developed by individual counties. The route we are to follow also later crosses or follows parts of the Lancashire Cycleways (there are two, north and south) and the Cumbrian Cycleway.

Once clear of Bridge Trafford, there is a short stretch of Cheshire's park-like grazing country, with its green hedged fields, before the route drops to Frodsham (where there is an interesting preserved lift, or elevator, designed to lift barges bodily between canals at different levels), Runcorn and Widnes. The last two towns are separated by the River Mersey and the Manchester Ship Canal, an ambitious waterway opened in 1894 to allow seagoing ships to reach the inland city of Manchester, then the center of Britain's cotton industry. A new bridge carries the road high across both river and canal. Widnes—as you may smell—is a center of chemical manufacture.

After about 12 km (7.5 mi.) of mainly urban riding from Widnes, the route passes Knowsley Hall, a 17th- to 19th-century mansion, formerly the seat of the Earls of Derby, and set in over 1,000 hectares (2,500 acres) of parkland. Part of Knowsley Park is now a large safari park. From here, the route is for a time less built up, with gentle open countryside before the final few urban miles into the red sandstone town of Preston.

Preston is positioned astride the lowest practicable crossing on the River Ribble, making the town an important road and rail staging post. Preston was at one time a center of the cotton trade and industry, and one of the cradles of the Industrial Revolution. It was only potential local opposition to the expected loss of hand-craft employment that led Preston-born engineer Richard Arkwright to take his revolutionary cotton-spinning machine elsewhere for development.

Preston marks the end of the built-up section of the route, which now heads northeastward into the hills. The stone-built villages are a contrast to the lowland settlements earlier, and there is some fine riding on the undulating road following the valley of the River Hodder to Slaidburn.

There follows some real climbing over the open moorland crossing of the Forest of Bowland; despite the name there are now few trees here. The often bleak summit at Cross of Greet seems higher than its approximately 470 m (1,542 ft.) would suggest, but it is followed by a fine run down to High Bentham. To the northeast, the "Three Peaks" of Ingleborough, Whernside and Pen-y-ghent dominate the skyline. Their characteristic flat-topped outlines are caused by a capping of hard gritstone over limestone.

This area was settled by Scandinavians from Norway from about the 9th century, and the old Norse influence begins to show here: from here to the Scottish border and beyond, the hills are named as "fells"—very close to the modern Norwegian word *fjell*.

About 3 km (2 mi.) before High Bentham, to the left of the road is a prominent erratic boulder with the rather odd name of the Great Stone of Fourstones.

From Tunstall, about 10 km (6 mi.) farther on, the route follows the valley of the River Lune through the pleasant market town of Kirkby Lonsdale. The valley begins to close in with high fells to west and east as far as Tebay, where the route emerges into open country with stone-walled fields, through Orton to the quarrying village of Shap. In past days the village of Shap was the first sign of civilization after the bleak crossing of Shap Fell, over which the main road to the north, now the A6, climbed. Perhaps the local inhabitants were too eager in their quarrying activities: effectively the whole village was built from stone pillaged from the ruined 14th-century Shap Abbey.

Our route, though, is far less bleak than the daunting Shap Fell, and passes through the gentle grazing country of the valley of the River Lowther to the thriving town of Penrith, the largest settlement since leaving Preston. Penrith was another important river crossing, from at least Roman times; the name means "the main ford" (across the River Eamont) in the extinct Cumbrian Celtic language, which was closely related to Welsh.

This is the eastern fringe of England's Lake District National Park—a concentrated group of mountains and lakes that is a very popular tourist attraction, and one under pressure from its many summer visitors. Not all of it is crowded, however, and two pleasant out-and-home side trips of a few miles can give a taste of the quieter side of Lakeland.

The first is to follow the road for about 12 km (7 mi.) southwest from Bampton, between Shap and Penrith, to the head of the lake of Hawesawater. The second is about 15 km (10 mi.) southwest from Thorpe, near Penrith, through Pooley Bridge and along the southern shore of Ullswater. (It's one of the peculiarities of the Lake District that only one of the lakes—Bassenthwaite—is actually named a "lake": the rest are all "meres" or "waters.")

The final run in to Carlisle is through a succession of pleasant stone villages set in gentle upland farming country with some small forests. Carlisle, the "Border City," is another ancient strategic river crossing, the lowest crossing of the River Eden. Today it remains an important communication center. The Roman town of Evgwalivm on the same site was close to the western end of Hadrian's Wall (see circular tour C, "Scottish Border and the Roman Wall" in Chapter 25) and, following the Romans' departure, was successively raided by Picts, Vikings and Scots. It has an 11th-century castle, and its cathedral is one of England's smallest but claimed by many to be the most beautiful.

Directions

Note: From Frodsham to Up Holland, and again from Leyland to Preston, the route is largely urban and a little complex.

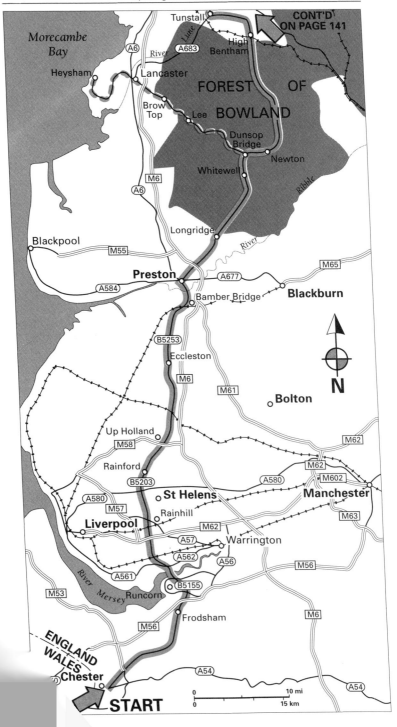

CONT'D ON PAGE 141

Morecambe Bay

Heysham

Tunstall

River Lune

A6

A683

High Bentham

Lancaster

FOREST OF BOWLAND

Brow Top

Lee

Dunsop Bridge

Newton

Whitewell

River Ribble

M6

A6

Longridge

Blackpool

M55

River

Preston

A584

A677

Bamber Bridge

Blackburn

M65

B5253

Eccleston

M6

M61

Bolton

Up Holland

M58

M62

Rainford

B5203

A580

M62

M602

St Helens

Manchester

A580

M57

Rainhill

Liverpool

M62

M63

A57

Warrington

A562

A56

M56

A561

River Mersey

Runcorn

B5155

M53

Frodsham

M6

M56

ENGLAND WALES

A54

A54

Chester

START

0   10 mi

0   15 km

N

1. Leave Chester city center N. by Northgate and Upper Northgate, then R. on A5116 (Birkenhead Rd.).

2. Just after rly. bridge, R. on uc. road through Newton to A41, S.O. on Cheshire Cycleway (signed) to join A56.

3. L. on A56 through Bridge Trafford.

4. After 2 km (1.2 mi.), bear R. just after rly. bridge on uc. road signed "Cheshire Cycleway."

5. S.O. across B5132 to pass under rly.

6. Take 2nd. L., then R. to T-junct. with B5393 at Buckoak.

7. L. on B5393, then 1st R. at Simmonds Hill on uc. roads to B5152 in Frodsham.

8. L. on B5152 to A56; R. on A56 to cross River Weaver and Weaver Navigation Canal.

9. Ignore 1st L. turn, A557, to Runcorn and M56 Junct. 12, and take 2nd L. to cross over M56, then L. into Beechwood Avenue (uc. road).

10. Pass under A557 onto Clifton Rd., S.O. across Heath Road into Moughland Lane.

11. After 800 m (0.5 mi.), R. to town center.

12. Pass under A533, S.O. across High Street into Church Street.

13. L. to join A533 (Queensway) across Runcorn Bridge over Manchester Ship Canal and River Mersey.

14. Take 2nd slip road L. off A533 down to rbt., L. into Ditton Road, then after 1 km (0.6 mi.), R. into Ditchfield Rd., pass under A562, then at x-rds. R. into Hale Rd.

15. Cross B5178 (Liverpool Road) S.O. on Prescot Rd., then Chapel Lane, to A5080 at Cronton.

16. After A5080, R. and L. in Cronton into Hale Lane to cross over M62.

17. At T-junct., L. on Mill Lane, which becomes Old Lane, Rainhill.

18. L. into Stoney Lane, then R. after hospital on Dragon Lane to A57, Warrington Rd.

19. R. on A57, then L. on B5201, Delph Lane.

20. At rbt., L., still on B5201 (Old Lane), to cross A58, St. Helens Rd.

21. S.O., still on B5201 (now Burrows Lane), then L. on B5203 (Gillars Lane, becoming Catchdale Moss Lane) to A580.

22. L. on A580, then 1st R., still on B5203 (now Blind Foot Rd., becoming Mossborough Rd.) to rbt. junct. with A570.

23. S.O., still on B5203, into Rainford.

24. Do not take B5205 turn, but take next R. on uc. road toward Up Holland (appears as Upholland on some maps).

25. After passing over M58, R. on uc. road to A577 at Up Holland.

26. R. on A577, then L. on uc. road through Roby Mill, crossing Leeds and Liverpool Canal and rly., to Appley Bridge.

27. L. on B5375 to A5209.

28. S.O. on uc. road, and after 800 m (0.5 mi.), R., then L. still on uc. roads to B5250 at Eccleston.

29. L. on B5250 to A581, R. and L., still on B5250, to rbt. at S. outskirts of Leyland.

30. At rbt. L., still on B5250, to rbt. junct. with A582. R. on A582, then L. at double rbts. on uc. road, R. across bridge over rly., to B5257.

31. S.O. on B5257 to rbt. junct. with A6.

32. S.O. on B5257 to B6258 at Bamber Bridge.

33. L. on B6258 to A675 and A6 (London Rd., becoming Stanley Street) to Preston town center.

34. Leave Preston town center on B6243 (Ribbleton Lane, becoming Ribbleton Avenue) to pass over M6, then through Grimsargh to rbt. with B5269 in Longridge.

35. R. on B5269, then L. (effectively S.O. where B5269 goes R.) on uc. roads along flank of Longridge Fell.

36. At T-junct. at foot of steep hill, L., then 1st. R. for 1.5 km (1 mi.) to T-junct.

37. R. over Doeford Bridge over River Hodder to follow river valley (more or less) through Whitewell to Dunsop Bridge.

38. (Link to Heysham, port for Isle of Man, leaves route here—see below.)

39. R. on uc. road to join B6478 at Newton, S.O. on B6478 to Slaidburn.

40. L. on uc. road in center of village (follow "Lancashire Cycleway" signs) over fell by Cross of Greet pass (summit about 470 m/1,542 ft.) to B6480 at High Bentham.

41. R. and L., still on uc. roads, S.O. at x-rds., then L. to A687 at Burton in Lonsdale.

42 L. on A687 to junct. with A683.

43. R. on A683 through Tunstall to A65 at Kirkby Lonsdale.

⸲ L. on A65 over bridge across River Lune, then R. on B6254 to Kearstwick, R. on uc. road following valley to B6256.

᾿n B6256 to A684.

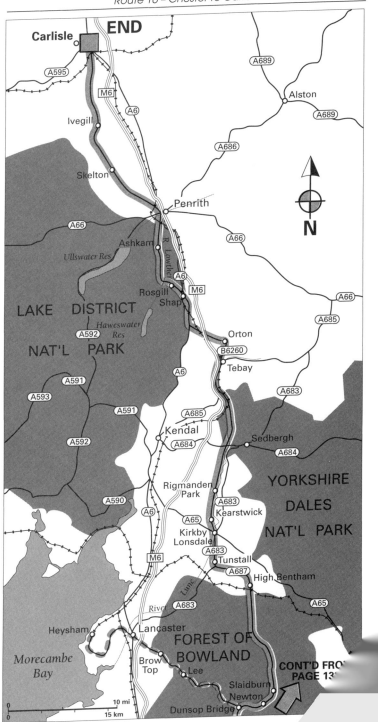

46. R. on A684, then L. on B6257, passing under M6 to A685.

47. R. on A685 to Tebay, S.O. at rbt. on B6260 to Orton, then L. on B6261 to pass under M6 (two separate bridges) to T-junct. with A6.

48. R. on A6 to Shap, then L. on uc. road through Rosgill, Bampton, Whale and Askham to B5320.

49. R. on B5230 to join A6 to center of Penrith.

50. Leave Penrith town center by B5288, cross over M6, then immediately R. on uc. roads through Newton Reigny and Skelton.

51. S.O. across B5305; after 6 km (4 mi.), R. through Ivegill, then L. on uc. roads (becoming Currock Road, then James Street and Viaduct) to Carlisle city center.

Link to Heysham:

1. At Dunsop Bridge, L. on uc. road through Sykes and over Trough of Bowland pass, then through Lee and Brow Top and under M6 to T-junct. with A6 in Lancaster.

2. R. on main road and follow one-way system over River Lune bridge, then L. on A589 under rly.

3. Fork L. on uc. road to join B5273, L. on B5273 and then L. on uc. road through Heaton.

4. Just past village, R. on uc. road to Middleton, R., still on uc. road, to A589.

5. L. on A589 to rly. stn. and harbor.

CHAPTER 20

Route 17

Carlisle to Stranraer

Total distance: 195 km (121 mi.)

Intermediate distances:

Carlisle–Dumfries:
   63 km (39 mi.)
Dumfries–Gatehouse of Fleet:
   56 km (35 mi.)
Gatehouse of Fleet–Stranraer:
   76 km (47 mi.)

Terrain: moderate

Maps:

O.S. Travelmaster
   (1:250 000) sheet: 4
O.S. Landranger (1:50 000)
   sheets: 82, 83, 84, 85

Access:

By train: mainline rail station at Carlisle.

By bike: Carlisle: Routes 16 and 18.

Summary:

This route through the southern Scottish region of Dumfries and Galloway leads from Carlisle to Stranraer and Cairnryan, ports for Belfast and Larne in Northern Ireland.

Description

For a general description of Carlisle, see Route 16, Chapter 19.
   For the first few miles out of Carlisle, a series of pleasant lanes through farming country and woodland give a quiet start to the route. However (at the time this book was being written), there is no alternative to about 5 km (3 mi.) of busy divided highway, the A74, to cross the River Esk and then the very small River Sark, which marks the border with Scotland. Roadbuilding in the area to continue the motorway M6 northward may eventually leave a quieter route for cyclists over this stretch.
   The first village in Scotland is Gretna. Gretna Green was famous—or notorious—as being in the 18th and 19th centuries the first place at which runaway eloping couples could become married under Scottish law, after an English law of 1754 banned clandestir

marriages. Scottish law merely required a declaration in front of witnesses and did not entail the several weeks' notice demanded in England. Further, the marriage did not require the services of a minister of religion, and the blacksmith at Gretna Green also achieved fame for conducting marriages as well as forging horseshoes. Although a Scottish law of 1856 brought in a three-week residence qualification, the Gretna blacksmith wasn't banned from conducting the ceremony until 1940.

From Gretna, the route turns west to follow quiet roads along the north side of the estuary, the Solway Firth, through quite gentle country, mostly grazing, with some woodland. The villages look somehow more solid than their counterparts south of the border: single-story stone cottages with storm porches against the westerly winds are typical of the border country. Annan is a bustling small town, while larger Dumfries is the regional capital. Between the two, Comlongon Castle lies about 5 km (3 mi.) northwest of the village of Ruthwell.

A quiet rolling road leads from Dumfries to the next town, Castle Douglas. There is no castle in Castle Douglas but at Threave, about 4 km (2.5 mi.) north of the next village on the route, Rhonehouse.

The route follows the southern side of the River Dee, crossing it just after Tongland to reach the next pleasant small town, Gatehouse of Fleet. Next comes a steady climb over the ridge to Creetown, where there is a gem rock museum. The region of Dumfries and Galloway is one of the most forested parts of Britain (itself one of the least forested countries in Europe), and the next part of the route—after the town of Newton Stewart—passes through long sections of mainly coniferous forest.

This can be lonely country, with fewer villages or even hamlets than on other parts of the route. There are two alternative routes after leaving the forest. The first and more northerly follows quiet roads through New Luce to Castle Kennedy (the castle is actually Lochinch, dating from 1867), and the other follows a southerly loop to Glenluce Abbey. The routes meet again in the solid but rather dour port of Stranraer.

Directions

1. From Carlisle center, N. on Lowther Street to cross river at Eden Bridge; continue N. on Scotland Road.

2. Part way up hill, bear L. on Etterby Street (uc. road), continue over rly. and past Cargo, to Rockliffe.

3. In Rockliffe, R., then 2nd. L. and 1st. R., still on uc. road, to join A74.

4. L. on A74 (beware heavy traffic for 3 km/2 mi.) to cross River Esk, then rly.

5. Take first major turning L., B721, to Gretna.

   L. on B721 through Eastriggs to Annan.

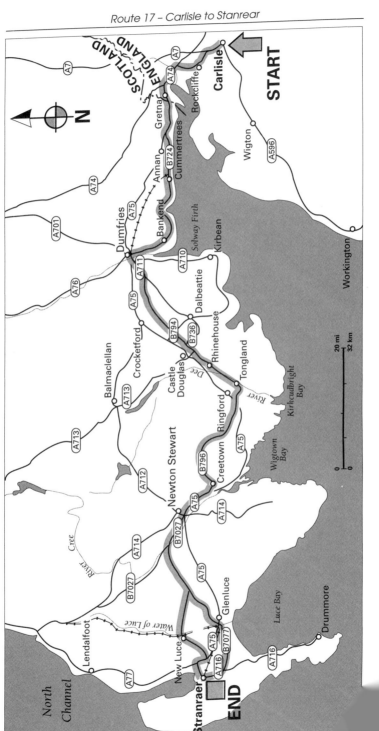

7. Cross River Annan, then at W. of town, L. on B724 through Cummertrees.

8. 5 km (3 mi.) after Cummertrees, L. on B725 to Bankend, where R. on uc. road to Dumfries.

9. In center of town, L. over River Nith on A711 through Cargenbridge.

10. At far end of village, R. on uc. road through Lochfoot and Milton to cross B794 at Haugh of Urr.

11. S.O., still on uc. road, to join A745 to center of Castle Douglas.

12. S.O. in center of Castle Douglas on A745, passing Carlingwark Loch on left, bear L. at S.W. end of loch, then after 1 km (0.6 mi.), bear L. on uc. road, then R. after 300 m (0.2 mi.) through Rhonehouse, following L. bank of River Dee to A711 at Tongland.

13. L. on A711, then R. on A762.

14. After 1 km (0.6 mi.), L. over bridge on uc. road, then S.O. at two minor crossroads to pass just S. of Twynholm, L. and R. crossing of A75, continue on uc. road to join B727.

15. R. into Gatehouse of Fleet, then at far end of settlement after crossing Big Water of Fleet, R. on B796 (which becomes uc. road after 10km/6 mi.) to Creetown.

16. R. in village to join A75; R. on A75.

17. Just after junction with A712, bear R. on B7027 to center of Newton Stewart.

18. In center of town, R. on A714 to Challoch, then L. on B7027 for 6 km (4 mi.) through Glenrazie to junction with uc. road at Glassoch Bridge.

19. L. on uc. road for 10 km (6 mi.) to Tarf Bridge (see alternative route below), then R. on minor uc. road to New Luce.

20. In New Luce, R. then L. to cross Water of Luce, L. on uc. road over rly. to Castle Kennedy.

21. R. on A75 to Stranraer.

Alternative route from this point with less of A75 but missing Castle Kennedy:

1. S.O. to Whitecairn, then R. to Glenluce Abbey, R. and L. on uc. road under rly. twice to join A75.

2. R. on A75, then L. on B7084.

3. R. on B7077 to Kilcrochet, R. on A716 to join A77 to Stranraer. (The alternative port of Cairnryan is approximately 12 km/7 mi. north of Stranraer, on the A77, Glasgow main road.)

CHAPTER 21

Route 18

Carlisle to Edinburgh

Total distance: 181 km (113 mi.)

Intermediate distances:

Carlisle–Langholm:
53 km (33 mi.)
Langholm–Innerleithen:
77 km (48 mi.)
Innerleithen–Edinburgh:
51 km (32 mi.)

Maps:

O.S. Travelmaster (1:250 000)
sheet: 4
O.S. Landranger (1:50 000)
sheets: 85, 86, 78, 79, 72, 73, 66

Terrain: hilly throughout

Access:

By train: mainline rail stations at Carlisle and Edinburgh.

By bike: Carlisle: Routes 16 and 17; Edinburgh, Route 15.

Summary:

This rather hilly route links the city of Carlisle on the Scottish-English border with Edinburgh, the capital city of Scotland.

Description

For a general description of Carlisle, see Route 16, Chapter 19.

The first part of the route is quite complicated through a network of small lanes and quite hilly, climbing away from the valley of the River Eden across the valleys of several small streams to reach the Scottish border at Pentonbridge over the Liddel Water.

The next small town, Langholm, in the valley of the River Esk, is the last settlement of any size on the route for over 65 km (40 mi.). The route follows the charming valley of the Esk, diverting from the B709 to stay by the river through Castle O'er. The "castles" of the name are two ancient earthwork hill forts. This is the start of a long forested section, which climbs to 334 m (1,096 ft.) before dropping to the valley of the Ettrick Water. This valley produced its own poet, James Hogg—known as "the Ettrick Shepherd"—who spanned the 18th and 19th centuries, writing in a version of the Scottish dialect.

147

There is a memorial at the site of his birthplace, 1 km (0.6 mi.) west of the hamlet of Ettrick.

From the Ettrick Water the road climbs again, to 359 m (1,179 ft.), mostly through open moorland to another valley—the Yarrow Water. A pleasant out-and-home side trip from the crossing at the Gordon Arms Hotel is to follow the A708 road west for about 8 km (5 mi.) to the two lochs (lakes) of St. Mary's Loch and the Loch of the Lowes. The direct route, however, goes straight on up a gentle climb, followed by a descent through Traquair to the small town of Innerleithen.

Traquair House is a chateau-style mansion, the original 10th-century building being completely rebuilt in 1642. It is said to have been continuously inhabited for over a thousand years, and 26 English and Scottish monarchs are claimed to have visited the house. It still houses its own 18th-century brewery. Innerleithen itself is famed for its woollens, and the first tweed mill opened here in 1790.

The last obstacle between Innerleithen and the run in to Edinburgh is the range of the open Moorfoot Hills, with the road rising to about 300 m (1,000 ft.). Then there's a swooping descent to Middleton and a short stretch of pleasantly wooded river valley country before you reach the suburbs of Edinburgh.

For a general description of Edinburgh, see Route 15, Chapter 18.

Directions

1. From Carlisle city center, N. on Lowther Street.

2. Cross River Eden by Eden Bridge, then R. into Brampton Road, B6264.

3. L. on uc. road through Houghton, then 4 km (2.5 mi.) after Houghton, L. to A6071 at Smithfield.

4. S.O. across A6071 on uc. road to Hethersgill, then L. to Boltonfellend.

5. At N. end of village, fork L. to B6318 at Crossings.

6. L. on B6318 through Catlowdy to cross Liddel Water at Pentonbridge.

7. Cross B6367, still on B6318, through Claygate to join A7.

8. R. on A7 into Langholm.

9. In Langholm, S.O. on B709 where A7 goes R.; follow B709 to Enzieholm Bridge.

10. L. on uc. road, then R. after 5 km (3 mi.), into forest past Castle O'er to rejoin B709 at Eskdalemuir.

11. S.O. on B709 through Ramsaycleugh and Ettrick to Tushielaw.

12. L., still on B709, to cross A708 at Gordon Arms Hotel.

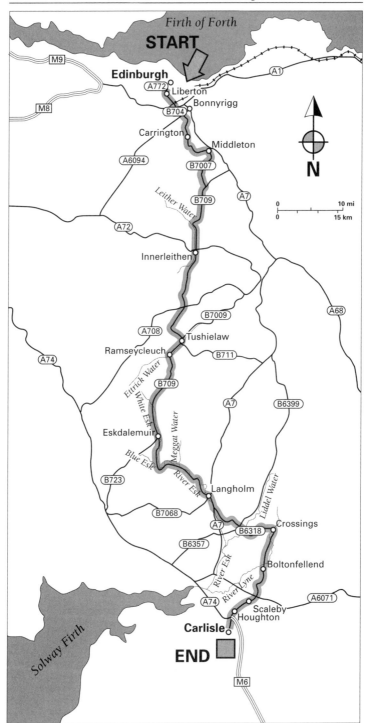

13. S.O. on B709 to A72 at Innerleithen.

14. R. and L. across A72, still on B709.

15. After about 20 km (12 mi.), L. on B7007, then after about 10 km (6 mi.), L. on uc. road to Middleton.

16. L. in Middleton on uc. road, bearing R. after bridge through Castleton to B6372.

17. L. on B6372 toward Temple, 1st R. on uc. road immediately after bridge to Carrington.

18. R. and L. in Carrington, still on uc. road, to B704.

19. L. on B704 (Cooper Rd.) to A6094 at Bonnyrigg.

20. S.O. across A6094 on B704 (High Street) to Lasswade.

21. L. on A768, R. into Lasswade Rd. (uc. road).

22. S.O. across A720, to A701 at Liberton.

23. Cross A701, R. and L., into Mayfield Rd. (uc. road), which becomes Causewayside, then Buccleuch Street, leading to Edinburgh city center.

CHAPTER 22

Introduction to Tours in Wilder Country

The five loop tours described in Chapters 23–27 introduce you to some of the best cycling country in Wales, northern England and Scotland. They are essentially scenic tours, much of them in wilder upland landscapes. All entail some riding in hilly or mountainous terrain.

We have used a rather different system of route directions for these tours. It is not possible, in the space available, to list every twist and turn. Neither can the sketch route maps be as detailed as for the earlier routes. So these route descriptions and sketch maps are intended to be used to allow you to follow the route on the British Ordnance Survey Travelmaster map (1:250 000, about 4 mi./in.). Larger-scale maps such as the O.S. Landranger (1:50 000) give more detail and more interest, but because, for example, the

Crossing the old Packhorse bridge at Stainforth, Yorkshire (on Tour B, Route 20)

Scottish Highlands tour would need 14 maps at about $7 each, adding about 1.3 kg (nearly 3 lb.) to your load and taking up two pannier bag pockets, you may well decide to stay with the Travelmaster for most of the way. In one or two places we suggest using the Landranger map for specific off-road sections.

The routes are specified as a series of place names, road numbers and road types. Each major town or intersection is followed by a distance and compass direction: this is the straight-line direction from the previously specified point, so that you can locate it on the map. If the next section of your route ends with, say, "¤ N.W. 15 km (9 mi.)," then you are looking for a point 15 km (about 9 mi.) N.W. of your current position. Note that the actual road distances are likely to be a good deal more. Because the Travelmaster is overprinted with a blue 10 km grid and the Landranger a 1 km grid, you may find it easier to use the metric distances to find your position, even if you usually think in miles.

Positions of some points are also given as a "grid reference" (G.R.). This is a metric grid of co-ordinates covering the whole country, allowing positions to be specified down to a precision of 100 meters (just over 100 yards) on the Landranger map. How this six-figure grid reference system works is explained on the legend panel of each Landranger map sheet.

The same system allows you to specify points down to a precision of 1 km on the Travelmaster map: just reduce the six co-ordinate figures given to four, by rounding down each of the three-figure groups. For example, the 100-meter reference 467 813 becomes kilometer reference 46 81, defining a kilometer square. To locate this square, find the vertical blue grid line numbered 4 (the "4" in the reference) along the bottom and top of the map, and the horizontal grid line numbered 8 (the "8" in the reference) along the sides of the map. Where these lines meet defines the bottom left-hand corner of the 10 km square in which square 46 81 lies. These 10 km squares repeat every 100 km—there's a system of letters to differentiate them—but you really should know where you are within 100 km at least. Now estimate $6/10$ of the way along the bottom of the square (the "6" in the reference), and then $1/10$ of the way up the square (the "1" in the reference). This gives the position of grid reference 46 81 to the nearest kilometer. If you're into co-ordinate geometry, then 46 is the x abscissa and 81 the y ordinate.

The routes are described in what we think is the better way to go round them, though obviously you could go in the reverse direction.

CHAPTER 23

Tour A (Route 19)

Circuit of the New Welsh Lakes

Total distance: 414 km (258 mi.)

Intermediate distances:

Church Stretton–Newtown:
    48 km (30 mi.)
Newtown–Machynlleth:
    66 km (41 mi.)
Machynlleth–Devil's Bridge:
    53 km (33 mi.)
Devil's Bridge–Pontrhydfendigaid:
    64 km (40 mi.)
Pontrhydfendigaid–Cynghordy:
    51 km (32 mi.)
Cycnghordy–Newbridge-on-Wye:
    40 km (25 mi.)
Newbridge-on-Wye–Anchor Inn:
    45 km (28 mi.)
Anchor Inn–Church Stretton:
    47 km (29 mi.)

Terrain: Quite hilly

Maps:

O.S. Travelmaster (1:250 000) sheet: 7

O.S. Landranger (1:50 000) sheets: 137, 136, 135, 146, 147, 160, 148

For following the off-road tracks on this tour, Landranger 1:50 000 sheets 135 and 147 are virtually essential.

Access:

By train: Church Stretton, Newtown, Caersws, Machynlleth, Cynghordy and Llangamarch Wells have local services on which bike capacity is likely to be limited.

By bike: Routes 1, 11, and 12 link at Church Stretton.

Note:

Villages and shops are few and far between in many areas along this route. Be sure to plan your accommodations carefully and keep well stocked with food.

Description

As the industrial cities of the English Midlands flourished and expanded in the 19th century, supplies of water to satisfy the needs of their growing populations and industry became inadequate. So, the governing corporations of the cities looked westward, eyeing the rain-rich uplands of central Wales. Before long, dams and artificial lakes had been built in the valley of the Elan near Rhaiadr, and Welsh water was being exported to England. Similar problems arose in the mid-20th century, and it was again to Wales that the water engineers looked, so more new reservoirs appeared: Claerwen to the west of the Elan valley, Llyn Clywedog near Llanidloes, Nant-y-moch to the east of Aberystwyth, and Llyn Brianne near Llandovery.

Now, thirty years later, most of the scars of construction have disappeared and the new lakes have settled into the landscape (although many Welsh people object to exporting their resources, free of charge, to England). All these new lakes have small roads running by them in superb cycling country. This tour links them up.

Like Route 12, this one begins by crossing the steep ridges west of Church Stretton on the Welsh border—a strenuous start amply rewarded by the views. There is something of a respite as the route follows the valley of the River Severn (Afon Hafren) to the first lake, LLyn Clywedog, set in coniferous forest.

The next section is superb in any season. After an unpromising start past disused slate quarries, the route—which was the ancient coach road to the small town of Machynlleth—climbs over a shoulder of the plateau to reveal an immense panorama, dominated by the peak of Cadair Idris.

There is a superb run down to Machynlleth and a gentle run toward the coast before the lonely road over the moors past the Nant-y-Moch Reservoir to Devils Bridge. Another long, lonely road

Beside the Claerwen Reservoir, Powys, mid Wales.

climbs inland to the head of the original reservoirs of the Elan valley, followed by a gentle run down past the tiers of dams.

The next section involves some not-too-difficult off-road riding on a gravel track round the Claerwen Reservoir. This is some of the most remote country south of the Scottish border and one of the few areas where rare birds such as the red kite may be seen.

At the end of the unpaved section at Pontrhydfendigaid ("the bridge of the blessed ford") there are two choices of route.

Long before the new Llyn Brianne drowned the lower part of the valley of the Tywy, this route from Strata Florida (Ystrad Fflur), with its ruined abbey, to the little town of Llandovery (Llanymddyfri) was a favorite cyclists' off-road route. The character has now changed with afforestation, but the challenge is still there. Not that the alternative paved route via Tregaron lacks challenge: there are many very steep grades. The new road that twists and plunges round the shores of Llyn Brianne is a delight, with the gentler delights of the lower valley to follow.

The return to Church Stretton follows a mostly forested route to Llangammarch Wells, and then crosses the valleys of the Irfon, Ithon and Wye before climbing to Kerry Hill, on the border between England and Wales. There's a fine run down to Clun, with a final leg to Church Stretton that follows one of the few routes into the town that doesn't cross a major ridge.

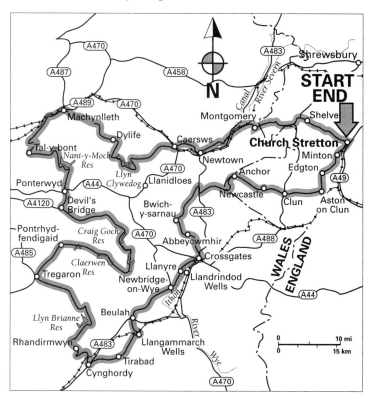

Directions

1. Leave Church Stretton W. on uc. road up Burway Hill, forking right at the top of the Long Mynd to Ratlinghope and Bridges. ¤ W.N.W. 6 km (4 mi.)

2. L. over River East Onny and R. on gated road, forking L. over the Stiperstones through Shelve to junct. with A488. ¤ W.N.W. 7 km (4 mi.)

3. (Route 12, to Holyhead, joins/leaves.)

4. L. on A488 for 2 km (1.5 mi.), then R. on uc. road at G.R. 319 979 through Priestweston to Chirbury.

5. R. on A490 for 300 m (0.2 mi.), then L. on B4386 to Montgomery (Trefaldwyn). ¤ W.S.W. 11 km (7 mi.)

6. R. on B4385, L. on B4385 at N. end of town to join B4386 to A483 at Abermule, G.R. 156 942. ¤ W.S.W. 6 km (4 mi.)

7. L. on A483 for 1.5 km (1 mi.), then R. on B4389 over River Severn and Shropshire Union Canal to junct. with B4568.

8. L. on B4568 along N. side of River Severn by Newtown (Y Drenewydd) to junct. with B4569 11.5 km (7 mi.) N. of Caersws at G.R. 038 932. ¤ W.S.W. 13 km (8 mi.)

9. L. on B4569, S.O. across A489 at Caersws to Trefeglwys.

10. S.O. on B4569 for 2 km (1.2 mi.) to fork at Cerist, G.R. 963 882 (not first fork at 963 885, 300 m/0.2 mi. earlier, to Van). ¤ S.W. 9 km (5.5 mi.)

11. R. on uc. road to B4518, L. on B4518, first R. on uc. road past Clywedog dam (G.R. 910 870) on very up-and-down road round W. side of Llyn Clywedog to T-junct. in forest at G.R. 867 893. ¤ just N. of W. 9 km (5.5 mi.)

12. R. through forest (L. turn is attractive route to the small town of Llanidloes) to rejoin B4518 at Staylittle.

13. L. on B4518 for 1.5 km (1 mi.), to junct. at G.R. 883 938. ¤ N.N.E. 5 km (3 mi.)

14. L. through Dylife on old coach road to Machynlleth. ¤ W.N.W. 15 km (9 mi.)

15. L. on A489, L. in Machynlleth on A487 to Ysgubor-y-coed or Furnace. ¤ S.W. 8.5 km (5.3 mi.)

16. L. on uc. road, and after 600 m (0.4 mi.) at G.R. 687 947, very sharp R. on gated road through Llwyngwyn.

17. At Gwar-cwm, G.R. 674 917, bear L. to join Tal-y-bont road at G.R. 678 902 (height marked 133 m/436 ft. on Landranger map). ¤ just W. of S. 5 km (3 mi.)

18. L. via forest and Nant-y-moch Reservoir to Ponterwyd. ¤ S.S.E. 11.5 km (7 mi.)

19. Leave Ponterwyd S. on A4120 to Devils Bridge.

20. L. on B4574 to Cwmystwyth. ¤ S.S.E. 8 km (5 mi.)

21. S.O. on old coach road to Pont-ar-Elan, G.R. 904 716. ¤ S.S.E. 11 km (7 mi.)

22. R. past reservoirs to bridge between Carreg Ddu and Caban Coch reservoirs, G.R. 910 639. ¤ S. 8 km (5 mi.)

23. R. over bridge and follow road on N. side of Caban Coch reservoir to E. side of Claerwen dam, G.R. 871 636. ¤ W. 4 km (3 mi.)

24. S.O. as road becomes track following N. shore of Claerwen reservoir, crossing Afon Claerwen (footbridge) and Afon Claerddu (stepping stones) to rejoin paved road at G.R. 794 680.

25. S.O. on road N. of "Teifi Pools" (Llynau Egnant, Hir, Teifi) to Ffair Rhos. ¤ W.N.W. 14 km (8.7 mi.)

26. L. on B4343 to Pontrhydfendigaid. ¤ S.W. 2 km (1.5 mi.)

There are now two possible routes to the Towy valley, one rough and quite time-consuming, the other longer and hilly but paved.

Alternative Route A:

1. 1. L. at Pontrhydfendigaid through Strata Florida. Road becomes track—mostly ridable—at G.R. 755 646, but with many fords, depth depending on season; multiplicity of forest roads can be confusing at one or two points.

2. Join paved road at G.R. 804 568, L. for 2 km (1.5 mi.), then R. on Llyn Brianne road to G.R. 805 537. ¤ S.E. 16 km (10 mi.) from Ffair Rhos.

Alternative Route B:

1. S.O. on B4343 for 9 km (5.5 mi.) to Tregaron; L. on uc. road via steep climbs and descents for 8.5 km (5.3 mi.) to G.R. 763 575.

2. R. at isolated phone booth for 9 km (5.6 mi.) past Soar-y-Mynydd chapel to join Llyn Brianne road at T-junct., G.R. 805 537. ¤ S.E. 16 km (10 mi.) from Ffair Rhos.

Continuation of combined route:

1. S.O. (from option 1) or R. (from option 2) following E. shore of Llyn Brianne to Rhandirmwyn. ¤ just W. of S. 11 km (7 mi.)

2. S.O. for 5 km (3 mi.) to G.R. 771 399, L. on uc. road to A483 at Cynghordy. ¤ S.S.E. 4.5 km (3 mi.)

3. R. on A483, first L. on uc. road to Tirabad, L. to Llangammarch Wells. ¤ E.N.E. 14.5 km (9 mi.)

4. L. over River Irfon and under rly. to Cefn Glancamddwr.

5. R. to join A483 to Beulah, R. on B4358 to Newbridge-on-Wye.
    ¤ N.E. 14 km (8.5 mi.)

6. R. and L. across A470 to rejoin B4358, then follow to A4081, then A4081 to Llanyre, G.R. 043 622.

7. L. on uc. roads to A44 at point marked as height 192 m (630 ft.) on Landranger map, G.R. 077 654.

8. R. on A44 to Crossgates. ¤ N.E. 10 km (6 mi.)

9. L. on A483 for 2.5 km (1.5 mi.), then L. on uc. road through Abbeycwmhir, then R. to Bwlch-y-Sarnau, G.R. 030 747.
    ¤ N.W. 11.5 km (7 mi.)

10. S.O. through Llaethdy to rejoin A483 at G.R. 086 824.

11. R. on A483 for 1.5 km (1 mi.), L. up steep climb on uc. roads to join B4355 at G.R. 120 827. ¤ N.E. 12 km (7 mi.)

12. R. on B4355 for 4 km (2.5 mi.), then L. on uc. road to join B4368, R. on B4368 to Anchor Inn. ¤ E.N.E. 6 km (4 mi.)

13. S.O. on B4368 to Clun. ¤ E.S.E. 13 km (8 mi.)

14. L. on A488 over River Clun, R. after 200 m (0.1 mi.) on B4368 through Clunton to Ashton-on-Clun. ¤ E. 9 km (5.5 mi.)

15. L. on uc. roads through Hopesay and Edgton to A489 at Horderley.

16. L. on A489 for 300 m (0.2 mi.), R. on B4370 to Cwm Head.
    ¤ N.N.E. 8 km (5 mi.)

17. L. on uc. roads through Hamperley and Minton to Little Stretton, where join B4370 to Church Stretton.
    ¤ N.N.E. 5.5 km (3.5 mi.)

CHAPTER 24

Tour B (Route 20)

"White and Red Roses"—Yorkshire and Lancashire

Total distance: 441 km (274 mi.)

Intermediate distances:

York–Bolton Abbey:
    72 km (45 mi.)
Bolton Abbey–Stainforth:
    66 km (41 mi.)
Stainforth–Slaidburn:
    37 km (23 mi.)
Slaidburn–Kirkby Lonsdale:
    55 km (34 mi.)
Kirkby Lonsdale–Kirkby Stephen:
    53 km (33 mi.)
Kirkby Stephen–Askrigg:
    47 km (29 mi.)
Askrigg–Ripon:
    58 km (36 mi.)
Ripon–York:
    53 km (33 mi.)

Terrain: Mostly hilly

Maps:

O.S. Travelmaster (1:250 000) sheet: 5

O.S. Landranger (1:50 000) sheets: 105, 104, 103, 112 (just), 97, 98, 99, 90, 91, 92

Goldeneye (1:126 720) sheet: Yorkshire Dales (covers much of route)

Access:

By train: Rail stations with InterCity services at York and Lancaster (5 km/3 mi. N. of Lee Bridge)

By bike: Routes 14 and 15 link at York. Route 19 crosses at Slaidburn. Either of these can be used as a link to Tour C, the Scottish Border and Roman Wall tour (Chapter 25).

Description

In the 15th century, before England was fully welded into one nation, the ducal houses of York and Lancaster in the north of England were often at loggerheads, culminating in 1455–1487 in the Wars of the Roses—so called because both houses had a rose as their emblem, white for York and red for Lancaster. This civil war extended far beyond the bounds of the respective counties and had far-reaching national and European repercussions. The battles are less bloody now, but there is still an underlying sporting, cultural and industrial rivalry between these ancient dukedoms that lie on either side of the Pennine range, the "backbone of England."

Some of Yorkshire's finest scenery is in the Dales, now a national park. These "dales" are long river valleys, penetrating deep into the limestone and gritstone of the Pennines. And if there are river valleys, then there must be ridges between them. The route starts gently enough, westward across the Vale of York, then into the lower reaches of Wharfedale, where the hilly sections begin.

The scenic part of the route begins near Bolton Abbey, with its 12th-century priory set beside the River Wharfe, of which part has served continuously as the parish church since about 1170. Nearby Bolton Hall is a 19th-century mansion. At Threshfield, the route leaves the valley to follow a short stretch of unpaved grassy track that then joins the ancient Mastiles Lane, a former "drove road"—a wide track between rough stone walls used for herding animals from place to place.

The next village, Malham, with its waterfall, rocky cliff known as Malham Cove, and Malham Tarn (lake), is a very popular tourist spot. The road climbs away past Malham Tarn to the next valley, Littondale, only to climb again to a fine moorland pass (460 m/1430 ft.) between Fountains Fell and Pen-y-ghent.

Down in the next valley, the next village on the route, Stainforth, boasts a fine arched packhorse bridge over the River Ribble, dating from the 17th century, when it lay on the main route from the Yorkshire town of Ripon (later on the route) to Lancaster. In the fall season, the nearby Stainforth Force waterfall is a favorite spot for watching salmon leap on their way upstream to their breeding grounds near the source of the river.

The next range of hills is the ancient Forest of Bowland—like so many "forests" on the map now high open moorland, bare of trees except for some recent planting. For good measure, the route crosses the range twice, first over the approximately 430 m (1,400 ft.) pass of Bowland Knotts, then down to the hospitable village of Slaidburn and back over the 300 m (1,000 ft.) "Trough of Bowland" down to the valley of the River Lune.

The route travels north and west of the Lune to Kirkby Lonsdale and then into the long open valley of Barbondale, finally dropping to the village of Dent, with its stony cobbled streets. Dentdale is a gentle climb beside the tumbling River Dent through grazing country, but the route then rears up the steep climb from Cowgill over the shoulder of Widdale Fell to Garsdale Head. At this remote spot, there's a rail station on the picturesque Settle-to-Carlisle line, which links the cities of Leeds and Carlisle.

The next section of the route passes two historic moorland inns that in horse-drawn traffic days were essential staging posts in the bleak trek over the moors—and are still very welcome to thirsty cyclists. The first is the Moorcock Inn at the road intersection at

Garsdale Head, and the second—after the run down to the pleasant little town of Kirkby Stephen, followed by a long climb—the Tan Hill Inn, at around 500 m (1,700 ft.) the highest pub in England. In a severe winter the snow can cut the Tan Hill Inn off to road traffic for months at a time.

At Tan Hill, the route passes back into Yorkshire after its excursion into Lancashire and Cunbria, and there's a superb run down West Stones Dale to one of the best-known of Yorkshire's dales, Swaledale, with its solid but attractive villages of Keld, Thwaite and Muker.

There's another tough climb in store over the moorland of Askrigg Common to reach the next dale, Wensleydale. Just to the north of the route, just before the village of Redmire, there is the imposing Bolton Castle, in a very fine parkland setting.

From Wensley, the "official" route follows a minor A-road, the A6108, for a few miles to Masham; there is a rather longer and more intricate alternative route on smaller roads to Masham that you can pick out on the map, to the northeast of the River Ure. The A-road, however, takes you past Middleham Castle and Jervaulx Abbey.

Middleham castle, now ruined, was once grand enough to be known as the "Windsor of the North" and was the capital of Wensleydale. It was for a time the home of King Richard III in the 15th century. Jervaulx Abbey was founded as a Cistercian monastery in 1156, surviving for 400 years; now it is a picturesque overgrown ruin.

The next small town, Ripon, is the largest settlement on the route since Kirkby Stephen and has a notable 12th-century Minster (cathedral), surrounded by narrow winding streets set about a medieval market square. About 6 km (4 mi.) southwest of Ripon is Fountains Abbey, the most extensive monastic ruin in Britain. It was founded in 1132 and is set in a magnificent deer park and 18th-century landscaped gardens.

By now the hills are behind you and the run in to York is along the plain of the now-placid River Ure as it joins with the Swale to become the River Ouse. The large village of Boroughbridge is built on the site of a Roman town, Isvrivm, which you can visit, about 1.5 km (1 mi.) southeast of the present village center.

Directions

1. Leave York N.W. on A59, Holgate Rd., fork L. at G.R. 587 514 on B1224 through Acomb and Rufforth to Long Marston.
   ¤ W. 10 km (6 mi.)

2. R. on uc. roads through Tockwith and Cowthorpe to pass over A1 at Ox Close House. ¤ just N. of W. 9.5 km (6 mi.)

3. S.O. on uc. road to junct. with B6164.

4. L. to North Deighton, R. to Spofforth on A661.

5. R. on uc. road at S. end of village, keeping R. to Follifoot.
   ¤ W. 6 km (4 mi.)

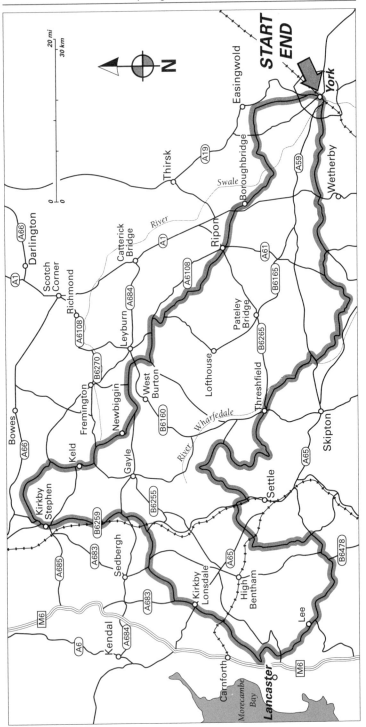

6. L. on uc. road to Spacey Houses.

7. Cross A61 R. and L. through Pannal, L. and L. through Daw Cross to Bunkers Hill.

8. R. by Brackenthwaite to junct. with B6161. ¤ just S. of W. 9 km (5.5 mi.)

9. L. on B6161 through Leathley to Leathley Bridge, R. on uc. road across River Washburn to B6451.

10. L. on B6451 to G.R. 200 460 at N. side of Otley Bridge. ¤ S.W. 7.5 km (4.5 mi.)

11. R. on uc. road and first L. by Weston, Askwith and Nesfield on N. side of River Wharfe, to junct. with A59 near Beamsley. ¤ N.N.W. 14 km (8.5 mi.)

12. Either R. on A59 for 1.5 km (1 mi.) then L. on uc. road, or L. on A59, R. on B6160. Both routes meet at Barden Bridge. ¤ N.N.W. 5 km (3 mi.)

13. N.W. on B6160 through Burnsall and Threshfield to fork at N.W. end of village at G.R. 988 638. ¤ N.W. 9 km (5.5 mi.)

14. Fork L. on uc. road, which becomes grassy track at G.R. 947 655.

15. S.O. on track to junct. with Mastiles Lane, L. to G.R. 930 655.

16. Fork L. by Goredale Bridge to Malham. ¤ W. 9 km (5.5 mi.)

17. R. at W. end of village by Malham Cove, passing W. of Malham Tarn on moorland road to Arncliffe. ¤ N.N.E. 9.5 km (6 mi.)

18. L. up Littondale through Litton to Halton Gill, L. over pass (436 m/1430 ft.) to Stainforth. ¤ W.S.W. 12 km (7 mi.)

19. R. on B6479 and L. after 200 m (0.1 mi.) over Stainforth Bridge by Stainforth Force (waterfall).

20. R at T-junct. to Swarth Moor, L. at T-junct. through Austwick, take 2nd L. turn in village to junct. with A65 at Harden Bridge. ¤ W. 6 km (4 mi.)

21. Cross A65 L. and R. on uc. roads for 5.5 km (3.5 mi.) to x-rds. at G.R. 726 666 (marked height 176 m/577 ft. on Landranger map).

22. L. (signed Slaidburn) over Bowland Knotts (summit about 420 m/1,380 ft.) to B6478.

23. R. on B6478 to Slaidburn. ¤ S. 14 km (8.5 mi.)

24. (Crosses Route 16, Chester to Carlisle)

25. S.O. on B6478 to Newton.

26. R. on uc. road to Dunsop Bridge, R. over Trough of Bowland, by Lee Bridge to x-rds. at G.R. 520 590. ¤ W.N.W. 20 km (12.5 mi.)

27. (S.O. to Lancaster, N.W. 5 km/3 mi., if desired)

28. R on uc. road through Quernmore to junct. with A683 at Caton.

29. L. on A683 for 400 m (0.3 mi.), first R. on uc. roads through Halton Green to T-junct. at G.R. 525 659. ◻ N. 6 km (4 mi.)

30. R. on uc. road to join B6254 through Arkholme and Whittington to Kirkby Lonsdale. ◻ N.E. 16 km (10 mi.)

31. R. on A65 over River Lune, first L. on A683 through Casterton, to G.R. 624 804. Fork R. on uc. road to Barbon. ◻ N.N.E. 4.5 km (3 mi.)

32. R. on uc. road up Barbondale to Gawthrop, R. into Dent. ◻ N.E. 10.5 km (6.5 mi.)

33. Leave Dent E. (choice of two roads) to Lea Yeat, Cowgill.

34. L. up very steep hill over fell road by Dent rly. stn. to Garsdale Head, junct. with A684. ◻ E.N.E. 9.5 km (6 mi.)

35. R. on A683 to Moorcock Inn, L. on B6259 to Kirkby Stephen. ◻ N.N.E. 20 km (12.5 mi.)

36. R. on A685 for 1 km (0.6 mi.), R. on uc. roads through Winton, Rookby and Oxenthwaite to Barras. ◻ E.N.E. 8 km (5 mi.)

37. R. on fell road to Tan Hill Inn, G.R. 896 067. ◻ S.E. 7.5 km (4.5 mi.)

38. R. down West Stones Dale to B6270. ◻ S. 5 km (3 mi.)

39. L. on B6270 through Keld, Thwaite and Muker.

40. 1.5 km (1 mi.) after Muker at G.R. 925 975, R. up very steep grade over Askrigg Common to Askrigg. ◻ S.E. 12 km (7 mi.)

41. L. and L. through Carperby and Redmire to Wensley, junct. with A684. ◻ E. 14.5 km (9 mi.)

42. R. on A684 for 700 m (0.4 mi.) over River Ure, first L. on uc. road through Agglethorpe to Coverham, L. to East Witton. ◻ S.E. 6.5 km (4 mi.)

43. S.O. on A6108 past Jervaulx Abbey, R. at S.W. end of park, where A6108 bears L., past Ellingstring and through Fearby to Masham.

44. R. on A6108 and second R. to Grewelthorpe. ◻ S.E. 13 km (8 mi.)

45. L. (choice of uc. roads) to Ripon. ◻ S.E. 10 km (6 mi.)

46. Leave Ripon E. on B6265 to pass over A1 through Boroughbridge for a further 6 km (4 mi.) to uc. road junct. (height marked 28 m/92 ft.) on Landranger map), G.R. 431 626. ◻ S.E. 14.5 km (9 mi.)

47. L. through Great Ouseburn, cross River Ouse at Aldwark Bridge, to Tollerton.

48. L. to cross A19 to Huby and Sutton-on-the-Forest. ◻ just N. of E. 15.5 km (9.5 mi.)

49. R. on B1363 to York. ◻ S.S.E. 13 km (8 mi.)

CHAPTER 25

Tour C (Route 21)

Scottish Border and the Roman Wall

Total distance: 447 km (278 mi.)

Intermediate distances:

Carlisle–Newcastleton:
    61 km (38 mi.)
Newcastleton–Bellingham:
    56 km (35 mi.)
Bellingham–Alnwick:
    89 km (55 mi.)
Alnwick–Morpeth:
    39 km (24 mi.)
Morpeth–Corbridge:
    43 km (27 mi.)
Corbridge–Middleton-in-Teesdale:
    51 km (32 mi.)
Middleton-in-Teesdale–
    Haydon Bridge:
    50 km (31 mi.)
Haydon Bridge–Carlisle:
    58 km (36 mi.)

Terrain: Quite hilly

Maps:

O.S. Travelmaster (1:250 000) sheets: 4 and 5

O.S. Landranger (1:50 000) sheets: 85, 86, 87, 79, 80, 81, 91, 92

Goldeneye (1:126 720) sheet: Lake District (small part of route only).

Access:

By train: Rail stations with InterCity services at Carlisle, Newcastle upon Tyne (22 km/14 mi. S. of Morpeth). Non-InterCity trains from Morpeth: bike space may be limited.

By bike: Routes 16, 17, and 18 link at Carlisle. Route 15 links at Corbridge and Blanchland and uses the same roads between these points.

Description

In A.D. 112, the Roman emperor Hadrian, troubled by the depradations of the Scots and Picts on Roman-held territories to the south, ordered the construction of a vast defensive wall across the country.

Building began in A.D. 122 and the immense defensive work—about 118 km (73 mi.) in length—followed the most easily defended line, often clinging spectacularly to crags and steep slopes to present its sternest face to the north. It was never breached until the Roman Empire crumbled in the 4th century.

Some of the finest stretches of the Wall survive, lower than their original height of some 4.5 m (15 ft.) but otherwise substantially intact after nearly 2,000 years. The modern cities of Carlisle—Lvgwalivm to the Romans—and Newcastle upon Tyne lie close to the western and eastern ends of this great wall. The Romans did eventually extend their conquest farther north, and there is a much less celebrated wall, the Antonine Wall, across the "waist" of Scotland, but Hadrian's Wall remains the great northern boundary of that immense vanished empire.

The route begins by following the line of the Wall, of which there is here little trace, then striking northward through rolling farmland, only to recross the line to the little town of Brampton. About 4 km (2.5 mi.) northeast of Brampton lies Lanercost Abbey, and shortly after this the route passes through the village of Bewcastle. A few miles later, there is the first taste of what is to be a feature of the first half of the route, the enormous (by British standards) Kielder Forest. At the edge of this section of forest comes the border between England and Scotland. The next small town, Newcastleton, is the last settlement of any size until Bellingham, some 60 km (40 mi.) farther on, so stock up here if you need to.

After the hamlet of Saughtree, the route climbs back into England through forest to the village of Kielder, at the head of the artificial lake of Kielder Water, constructed in the 1970s. The road route follows the western side of Kielder Water; if you have time or

Hadrian's Wall, following the crests of the crags near Steel Rigg, Cumbria.

a zest for a more adventurous route, there is an unpaved bike route to the east of the Water and bike trails in the forest.

Down the valley of the River Kielder, Bellingham is a bustling stone-built village and, although relatively small, very much the commercial center of the surrounding area. After the long ride through the forest, this is open farming country again. From here the route becomes quite undulating as the road climbs and falls across the many small streams flowing toward the coast, finally dropping to the much deeper valley of the River Coquet. This is a renowned salmon-fishing river, and during the autumn you can sometimes see salmon jumping the rapids and waterfalls above Alwinton.

From Alwinton, the route skirts the base of the Cheviot Hills, running above the valley with tremendous views of the hills of Harwood Forest and Rothbury Forest to the southeast. The next town on the route, Alnwick, is the largest settlement since Carlisle. Its cobbled streets, intricate alleyways and castle—dating from the 12th century, long ruined but then extensively restored in the 18th and 19th centuries—well repay exploration.

There's another 12th-century castle at the next village, Warkworth, and a 14th-century Hermitage, with a small chapel cut out of the solid rock, which can only be reached by boat. Warkworth also has an unusual old bridge with a tower at one end, and some attractive old terraces of buildings. The large fishing village of Amble, with its fine views north and south along the strands of Alnmouth Bay and Druridge Bay, lies 2 km (1.5 mi.) southeast of the route.

The next town on the route is Morpeth, the administrative capital of the county of Northumberland. It, too, boasts a castle—of which only a gatehouse remains—and abbey. The route passes another ruined castle at Mitford—at one time a rival to Morpeth—on the way out of the town, and yet another a few miles farther on, at Belsay.

Before long, the route crosses the line of Hadrian's Wall once more. Visible here is the "vallum," the second defensive line of an earth mound and ditch to the south of the Wall. The route then drops to the valley of the River Tyne and the modern village of Corbridge, on the site of Roman Corstopitvm. Corstopitvm was originally a Roman cavalry depot but was modified in A.D. 140 to act as a base for operations against Scotland. There is a museum at the site. The route crosses the river by the Old Tyne Bridge, built in 1674 and the only bridge on the whole river to survive a great flood in 1771.

The next section of the route is, frankly, quite tough cycling. The road follows, in reverse, the route described in Chapter 18 to Stanhope in Weardale, the valley of the River Wear. Then there is another tough climb over the moorland of Bollihope Common before the long run down to Middleton-in-Teesdale. The climbing isn't over yet, for the next section, back over to Weardale, goes over one of the two highest through roads in England, the 627 m (2,057 ft.) climb of Harthope Common.

For the record, the other claimant also is above St. John's Chapel, on the road to Alston. It's only fair, too, to point out that if

you want to avoid these two severe climbs, there is a shortcut directly up Weardale, on a minor road south of the River Wear, from Stanhope to St. John's Chapel, at the foot of Harthope Common. This
misses Teesdale altogether.

From St. John's Chapel, a moorland road leads to Allenheads, at
the head of the valley of the River East Allen. This was formerly rich
lead-mining country, and there are many remains of the 17th- and
18th-century workings on the way down the valley.

A short climb over the moor brings you to the River South Tyne
at the village of Haydon Bridge, and from here a 6 km (4 mi.) ride
leads to the old Roman road that runs just south of Hadrian's Wall.
Although classified only as a B-class road, this can be quite busy
with tourist traffic in summer, and as a straight but very up-and-
down Roman road it can be dispiriting, particularly into a head-
wind—but it is virtually the only way of reaching the most
spectacular parts of the Wall.

The museum at the Roman fort of Vercovicium—now known as
Housesteads—gives a very clear and dramatic presentation of
Roman life in the area. There are numerous other small museums
and excavations along or near to the line of the Wall—some quite un-
expected, such as a small Mithraic temple right beside the B6318.

*The Cheviot Hills, which straddle the border between Scotland and
England.*

You can, however, really only appreciate the drama of the Wall on foot, and one of the most imposing stretches can be reached easily from Steele Rigg, near the Twice Brewed Inn. Here the Wall clings to high crags above the waters of Crag Lough.

After all this 2,000-year-old activity, the 12th-century castle at Greenhead seems modern by comparison. Like many buldings along the line of the Wall, it doubtless incorporates stone plundered from the original Hadrian's Wall, which was looked on by succeeding generations as a useful source of ready-shaped building stone. The final run in to Carlisle is back by Lanercost Priory once again, but then follows a southerly loop past Talkin Tarn.

Directions

1. Leave Carlisle N. on A6, then R. after crossing River Eden on B6264.

2. After 1.5 km (1 mi.), L. on uc. road through Houghton to pass over M6 through Scaleby to T-junct. with A6071.

3. R. on A6071 through Newtown to Brampton. ◻ E.N.E. 12 km (7.5 mi.).

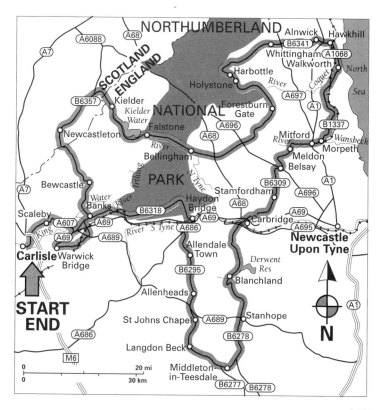

4. S.O. on A6071 for 1 km (0.6 mi.), then L. on uc. roads via Bridge End, Lanercost and Banks to junct. with B6318 at G.R. 550 675 ¤ N.N.E. 7 km (4.5 mi.)

5. S.O. on uc. road to Bewcastle, L. to junct. with B6318.

6. R. on B6318 for 300 m (0.2 mi.), then S.O. on uc. road, where B6318 bears L., through Blackpool Gate, and Kershope Forest to Newcastleton. ¤ N.N.W. 21 km (13 mi.)

7. R. on B6357 to Saughtree. ¤ N.E. 13 km (8 mi.)

8. R. on uc. road through Kielder Forest along W. side of Kielder Water (alternative unpaved cycle route signed along E. side of Kielder Water) to junct. at G.R. 721 869, just short of Stannersburn. ¤ S.E. 19 km (12 mi.)

9. L. to Falstone, R. through Lanehead to Bellingham. ¤ E.S.E. 13.5 km (8.5 mi.)

10. S.O. on B6320, then R. in Bellingham village on uc. road through Redesmouth, cross A68 at G.R. 908 819.

11. S.O. on uc. road past Sweethope Lough (lake) to cross A696 at Knowesgate.

12. S.O. on uc. road to junct. with B6342, 2 km (1.5 mi.) N. of Cambo. ¤ just N. of E. 19 km (12 mi.)

13. L. on B6342 to junct. at G.R. 060 977, 1.5 km (1 mi.) after Forestburn Gate. ¤ N.N.E. 10 km (6 mi.)

14. S.O. on uc. road where B6342 bears R., to Great Tosson, L. through Allerdene and Little Tosson to join B6341 for 700 m (0.4 mi.).

15. R. on uc. road through Holystone and Harbottle to Alwinton Bridge. ¤ W.N.W. 16 km (10 mi.)

16. R. through Netherton to Whittingham; R. at T-junct. in village to junct. with A697. ¤ E.N.E. 17.5 km (11 mi.)

17. S.O. on uc. roads to B6341; L. on B6341 to Alnwick. ¤ E. 10 km (6 mi.)

18. Leave Alnwick S. on B6346 to rbt. junct. with A1068.

19. L. on A1068 through Hipsburn to Warkworth. ¤ S.E. 9 km (5.5 mi.) (alternative uc. roads)

20. Leave Warkworth S. on A1068, then after 500 m (0.3 mi.), S.O. on uc. road where A1068 bears L., by Morwick Hall to Acklington.

21. R. on B6345 to junct. at G.R. 205 996. ¤ S.S.W. 8 km (5 mi.) L. on uc. road through Chevington Moor to Ulgham.

22. R. on B1337 through Longhirst to join A197 to Morpeth. ¤ S. 13 km (8 mi.)

23. Leave Morpeth W. on A197, then L. on B6343 to pass under A1 through Mitford to Dyke Neuk. ¤ W. 8 km (5 mi.)

24. L. on uc. roads through Meldon, R. and R. to Bolam, L. and L. to junct. at G.R. 098 795, just before Belsay. ¤ S.S.W. 6.5 km (4 mi.)

25. R. on uc. road to cross A696 obliquely onto B6309 through Stamfordham.

26. S.O. across B6318, still on B6309, to junct. 1 km (0.6 mi.) after B6318 at G.R. 059 675. ¤ S.S.W. 12.5 km (7.5 mi.)

27. S.O. on uc. road (where B6309 goes L.) to join B6321, passing over A69 into Corbridge, cross River Tyne.

28. (Route 15, York to Edinburgh, joins/leaves here.)

29. Bear L. past rly. stn., cross A695 L. and R., then follow uc. road S. up Prospect Hill, then via uc. roads to Slaley, junct. with B6306. ¤ S.W. 13 km (8 mi.)

30. L. on B6306 to Blanchland. ¤ S. 7.5 km (4.5 mi.)

31. S.O. on uc. road over River Derwent, bear L. over Edmundbyers Common to join B6278, to Stanhope. ¤ S.S.E. 11 km (7 mi.)

32. R. on A689, then fork L. over River Wear on B6278 over Bollihope Common to junct. at G.R. 992 288. ¤ S. 10 km (6 mi.)

33. R. on uc. road to Middleton-in-Teesdale, R. on B6271 by Newbiggin, Forest in Teesdale and Langdon Beck to junct. at G.R. 849 317, 800 m (.5 mi.) after Langdon Beck. ¤ N.N.W. 14.5 km (9 mi.)

34. R. over Harthope Moor (equal highest through road in England, 627 m/2057 ft.) to St. John's Chapel.

35. L. on A689 to junct. with B6295. ¤ N. 9 km (5.5 mi.)

36. R on B6295 through Allenheads and Allendale Town. ¤ N. 20 km (12.5 mi.)

37. Follow B6303 through Catton, then R. on B6304.

38. L. on B6295 to Langley, junct. with A686. ¤ N. 13 km (8 mi.)

39. R. on A686, L. on uc. road past cemetery to cross River South Tyne by old bridge at Haydon Bridge.

40. S.O. past church and rly. stn. on uc. road to junct. with B6318. ¤ N. 9 km (5.5 mi.)

41. L. on B6318 (optional out-and-home detours to N. to Roman Wall) to Greenhead (road busy in summer). ¤ W.S.W. 17 km (10.5 mi.)

42. R. on B6318 through Gilsland to Kiln Hill. ¤ W.N.W. 4.5 km (3 mi.)

43. L. on uc. road along line of Hadrian's Wall to Banks.

45. L. to Lanercost, L. up hill after Lanercost Bridge to cross A69 to Fralam Hall, Beck, junct. with A689. ¤ S.W. 8 km (5 mi.)

46. S.O. on A689, R. after 300 m (0.2 mi.) on uc. roads through Kirkhouse Farlam and Talkin to Warwick Bridge, junct. with A69. ¤ W.S.W. 9.5 km (6 mi.)

47. S.O. across A69 to Newby East, L. to Low Crosby.

48. L. on A689 to Carlisle. ¤ W. 8 km (5 mi.)

CHAPTER 26

Tour D (Route 22)

Argyll and the Trossachs

Total distance: 445 km (277 mi.)

Intermediate distances:

Stirling–Rowardennan:
    53 km (33 mi.)
Rowardennan–Strachur:
    48 km (30 mi.)
Strachur–Strachur:
    66 km (41 mi.) (detour via
    Tighnabruach adds
    32 km/20 mi.)
Strachur–Cladich:
    45 km (28 mi.)
Cladich–Kilmore:
    77 km (48 mi.)(to Oban add
    5 km/3 mi.)
Kilmore–Crianlarich:
    61 km (38 mi.)
Crianlarich–Callander:
    68 km (42 mi.)
Callander–Stirling:
    27 km (17 mi.)

Terrain: Hilly to mountainous

Maps:

O.S. Travelmaster (1:250 000) sheet: 4

O.S. Landranger (1:50 000) sheets 49, 50, 57, 56, 55, 63, 62

Access:

By train: Rail stations with InterCity services at Stirling. Other rail stations (cycle capacity may be very limited) at Tarbet (2 km/1.2 mi. N.E. of Arrochar), Oban, Connel, Taynuilt, Lochawe, Dalmally, Tyndrum, Crianlarich, Ardlui.

By air: Edinburgh Airport (near Cramond Bridge on Edinburgh-to- Stirling link).

By bike: Links from Stirling to Edinburgh (Routes 15 and 18) and with Northwest Highlands route (Tour E, Route 23).

Description

This route takes in some of the most attractive coastal scenery of southwest Scotland. Less popular with tourists than parts of the Highlands, the generally quiet roads make this excellent cycling country.

The city of Stirling has been an important communication center for centuries: until the 1930s it was the lowest bridge crossing of the great River Forth. Its strategic position made it the site of two defeats of English forces by the Scots, in 1297 by William Wallace at Stirling Bridge, and in 1314 by Robert the Bruce at Bannockburn, a little to the south of the city. The Bruce's victory assured Scottish independence for nearly 300 years, until the two countries became effectively united by a series of royal marriages. The present castle, which dominates the skyline of the city, dates from the 15th and 16th centuries, though such an obvious strategic point had been fortified from a much earlier date.

The central "waist" of Scotland, where Scotland's main cities, Glasgow and the capital Edinburgh, are situated, is—unlike the rest of the country—relatively flat. It is a broad rift valley lying between two long-stable geological faults. There are some ranges of moderate hills, and the route begins by passing through one of them, the rolling Campsie Fells, and then following the valley of the Endrick Water as it flows down to romantic Loch Lomond.

After the large village of Drymen, about 5 km (3 mi.) of wooded road brings you to the shore of the loch, but the little road is far from a flat lakeside promenade, rising and weaving over headlands and through woodland of birch and oak to the ferry across the loch at Rowardennan.

This may not be the true Highlands, but the hills to the west of the loch rise well over 700 m (2,300 ft.), so you'll be glad to learn that

The "Bridge over the Atlantic," which crosses the salty, but hardly oceanic, waters of Seil Sound, south of Oban.

the route follows a little pass, Glen Douglas, between them down to Loch Long. Note, by the way, that Scottish place names do not distinguish between freshwater lochs, which are lakes, and "sea-lochs," which are inlets of the sea, often like small fjords; Loch Long is one such sea-loch.

The next village or small town, Arrochar, is typical of many on this part of the route, with its grey and rather stern stone buildings dating mainly from the 19th century, when the opening up of the country by rail made this a favorite area for health resorts and country retreats. There's a stiff climb up from Arrochar (with, unfortunately, no easy way of avoiding the main A83 road), and you'll understand at the 245 m (803 ft.) summit why the road is known as the Rest and Be Thankful. Less obvious is why the valley leading down to Loch Fyne, another sea-loch, should be burdened with the name Hell's Glen.

The next stretch of the route, beside the shores of Loch Fyne, is a delight—a colorful mix of sea, wooded hills, gentle agriculture on the small patches of flat land, and the sparkling sea loch. Unfortunately, there is no longer a ferry across the loch at Otter Ferry, and the route has to follow a loop—very pleasant, but a loop nonetheless—through forested country, round the heads of sea-lochs Loch Riddon and Loch Striddon and then beside the inland Loch Eck back to Strachur.

There is a length of main road round to the white walls of the little town of Inveraray, with its 18th-century castle—built like many of these Scottish castles as a dwelling as much as a fortification.

From Strachur, a rolling road leads over to Claddach and the shores of the inland Loch Awe. This is a very long, narrow loch, some 30 km (20 mi.) from end to end, and the route follows the southeastern side, close to the shore by Fincharn to Ford at the southwestern tip of the loch.

After Ford, another delightful road leads through forest with glimpses of the loch below along the northwest side of Loch Awe, and then climbs away by a very fine but quite tough road beside Loch Avich, followed by a very winding descent to Kilmelford.

The quite hilly road north meets the seashore at several points. From Kilinver, a side trip of about 11 km (7 mi.) leads to the craft village of Easdale on Seil Island, including a crossing of the "Bridge over the Atlantic"—a handsome curved stone bridge across the scarcely oceanic but nevertheless salty waters of Seil Sound.

A further side trip of about 6 km (4 mi.) from Kilmore leads north to the seaside resort of Oban, while the main route heads inland along very quiet roads to Taynuilt. From here, unfortunately, there is no real road alternative to the main A85 road (and, later, the A82) through the Pass of Brander—beside Loch Awe once again—then through Glen Lochy and Strath Fillan to Crianlarich.

These main roads can be busy in July and August but are generally fairly quiet at most other times. (It is possible to take the train—limited cycle accommodation and £3 fee at the time of writing—from Taynuilt to Crianlarich or Ardlui, beside Loch Lomond; enquire locally.) Prominent Kilchurn Castle near Dalmally, on its

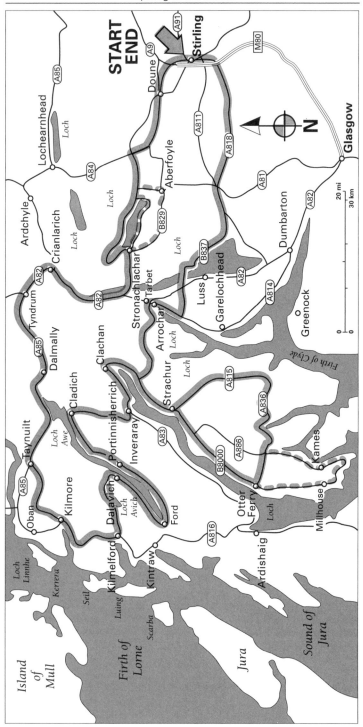

sea-girt promontory, was a 15th-century fortress, abandoned like so many after the 1745 uprising.

From the little staging post of Crianlarich, another 15 km (10 mi.) or so of the A82 bring you beside the west shore of Loch Lomond to Inveruglas and the ferry across the loch. The short journey past Loch Arklet leads to Loch Katrine, where there is a fine car-free cycle route round the head and north shore of the loch to the Trossachs Hotel. The Trossachs is a very attractive area of forest and loch scenery, with a number of forest bike trails.

The final leg back to Stirling follows the north shore of Loch Vennachar and then climbs over to the valley of the River Teith (with a possible side trip of less than 0.5 km/0.3 mi. to the center of the busy small town of Callander). A little south of the route, about 13 km (8 mi.) southeast of Callander, is the castle at Doune, a 15th-century building traditionally given to queens of Scotland as a marriage gift.

Directions

Note that this route makes use of ferries that do not operate every day of the week or out of the summer season. Use phone numbers given to check.

1. Leave Stirling S.W. on uc. road through Torbrex, crossing M9 at G.R. 784 921 through North Third to junct. with B818 by Carron Valley Reservoir; R. on B818 to Fintry. ¤ S.S.W. 20 km (12.5 mi.)

2. S.O. on B818, then R. on uc. roads to A875 at Balfron.

3. L. on A875, then immediately R. (effectively S.O. where A875 goes L.) on uc. road to Balfron Stn. (no rly.).

4. Cross A81 S.O. on uc. road to A811, L. on A811 to Drymen. ¤ just N. of W. 14 km (8.5 mi.)

5. R. on B837, becoming uc. road at Balmaha along E. shore of Loch Lomond to Rowardennan Pier. ¤ N.W. 15 km (9.5 mi.)

6. Take ferry (Easter to September, not Sundays—call (0136) 087 273) to Inverbeg.

7. Cross A82 on uc. road up Glen Douglas to join A814. ¤ W. 10 km (6 mi.)

8. R. on A814 to Arrochar, L. on A83 to Rest and Be Thankful. ¤ N.W. 8 km (5 mi.)

9. L. on B828, R. on B839 to A815, L. on A815 to Strachur. ¤ W.S.W. 15 km (9.5 mi.)

10. R. on A886 for 6 km (4 mi.), then R. on B8000 to Otter Ferry. ¤ S.W. 24 km (15 mi.)

11. L. on B8000, fork L. after 1 km (0.6 mi.) on uc. road to join A886.

12. R. on A886, then L. on B836 through Clachaig to A815 at Dalinlongart. ¤ E. 22 km (13.5 mi.)

13. (Alternatively, continue on B8000 through Kilfinan to Millhouse, S.O. on uc. roads via Ardlamont Point to Tighnabruaich, return on A8003 to T-junct. with A886. R. on A886 for 2 km (1.2 mi.), then L. on B836 as main route to Dalinlongart.)

14. L. on A815 beside Loch Eck to Strachur.
    ¤ W.N.W. 20 km (12.5 mi.)

15. R. on A815 to Glen Kinglas, L. on A83 to Inveraray.
    ¤ N. 8 km (5 mi.)

16. R. on A819 to Cladich. ¤ N. 14 km (8.5 mi.)

17. L. on B840 by S. and E. shore of Loch Awe to Ford.
    ¤ S.W. 30 km (18.5 mi.)

18. R. on uc. road on N.W. shore of Loch Awe through Dalavich to Barnaline Lodge. ¤ N.E. 15 km (9.5 mi.)

19. L. on uc. road just after River Avich bridge to Kilmelford.
    ¤ W. 13 km (8 mi.)

20. R. on A816 to Kilmore. ¤ just E. of N. 13 km (8 mi.)

21. (Continue S.O. on A816 if you want to visit Oban. To rejoin main route, leave Oban E. on uc. road past golf course.)

22. R. on uc. road; after 500 m (0.3 mi.), L. past Loch Neil to junct. at G.R. 890 292 (link to Northwest Highlands tour leaves/joins).

23. R. on uc. road through Glen Lonan to A85 at Taynuilt.
    ¤ E.N.E. 14 km (9 mi.)

24. R. on A85 through Dalmally to Tyndrum. ¤ E. 33 km (20.5 mi.)

25. R. on A82 through Crianlarich to Inveruglas.
    ¤ S. 22 km (13.5 mi.)

26. Take ferry (seasonal service: enquire locally) across Loch Lomond to Inversnaid.

27. Follow uc. road to Stronalachar. ¤ E. 8 km (5 mi.)

28. L. to follow cycleway round the head of Loch Katrine to Trossachs Hotel. ¤ E. 12 km (7.5 mi.)

Alternate routes:

A Take ferry (one per day, May to September, not Sundays—call (01877) 30 342) to Trossachs Pier, then S.O. to Trossachs Hotel.

B R. on B829 to Aberfoyle, then L. on A821 over Duke's Pass to Trossachs Hotel.

C Follow signed Glasgow-Killin cycleway (strenuous, indifferent surface in places) from Aberfoyle through Queen Elizabeth Forest, then beside Loch Vennachar to rejoin main route just after it leaves A821.)

Continuation of route

1. Follow A821 through Brig o' Turk; 1.5 km (1 mi.) after foot of Loch Vennachar, R. on uc. road to A81.

2. R. on A81 over Braes of Greenock. ¤ just S. of E. 12.5 km (7.5 mi.)

3. S.O. on B822; after 200 m (0.1 mi.), L. on B8032 to T-junct. with A84.

4. L. on A84 over bridge to Doune. ¤ E.S.E. 10 km (6 mi.)

5. R. on A820; after 1.5 km (1 mi., R. on B824 to junct. with A9/M9.

6. S.O. on A9 at roundabout for 2 km (1.2 mi.), then R. in Bridge of Allan on B823 to Stirling. ¤ S.E. 11 km (7 mi.)

Edinburgh-to-Stirling link:

To combine this tour with one of the routes that end in Edinburgh (Routes 15 and 18), follow these directions from Edinburgh.

1. Leave Edinburgh W. on A90.

2. 2 km (1.2 mi.) after Cramond Bridge, take slip road L. on B924 under River Forth rly. and road bridges to Queensferry, 15 km (9.5 mi.) ¤ W.N.W. of Edinburgh city center.

3. R. on A904 for 5 km (3 mi.), then L. on uc. road under M9 to T-junct. with B9080.

4. R. on B9080 to rbt. junct. with A803 in Linlithgow. ¤ W. 11 km (7 mi.)

5. L. on A803 through Linlithgow Bridge, L. on B825 and immediately R. on uc. road through Whitecross to B805 at Maddiston.

6. R. on B805, then L. on uc. road to California.

7. R on B8028 to outskrts of Falkirk. ¤ just N. of W. 12 km (7.5 mi.)

8. L. on B803, then fork R. opposite hospital on uc. road to South Drum.

9. R. to B816 at High Bonnybridge.

10. S.O. on B816 to A803 in Bonnybridge.

11. L. on A803, then R. on A872 under M876. ¤ W.N.W. 8 km (5 mi.)

12. After 3.5 km (2 mi.), L. on B818 under M80 to Carron Bridge. ¤ W.N.W. 7 km (4.5 mi.)

13. To join main Argyll and Trossachs tour route, S.O. on B818 to Fintry.

14. To Stirling, R. on uc. road to pass over M9 to A872 close by Bannockburn battle monument. L. on A872, then L. on B8051 to center of Stirling. ¤ N.N.E. 12 km (7.5 mi.)

Link to Northwest Highlands tour (Tour E, Route 23, Chapter 27):

1. S.O. (N.) at junct. at G.R. 890 292, 4 km (2.5 mi.) E. of Oban, to A828 at Connel.

2. R. on A828 over bridge through Benderloch and Barcaldine. ¤ N.E. 17 km (10.5 mi.)

3. 3 km (2 mi.) after Barcaldine, take path over old rly. bridge to cross Loch Creran.

4. L. on A828 to rbt. junct. with A82. ¤ N.E. 17 km (10.5 mi.)

5. R. on A82 over Ballachulish Bridge to join Northwest Highlands tour route at Corran Ferry. ¤ N.W. 6 km (3.5 mi.)

CHAPTER 27

Tour E (Route 23)

Northwest Highlands of Scotland

Total distance: 774 km (480 mi.)

Intermediate distances:

Inverness–Bonar Bridge:
  68 km (42 mi.)
Bonar Bridge–Skiag Bridge:
  68 km (42 mi.)
Skiag Bridge–Lochinver:
  43 km (27 mi.)
Lochinver–Ullapool:
  47 km (29 mi.)
Ullapool–Aultbea:
  71 km (44 mi.)
Aultbea–Kinlochewe:
  55 km (34 mi.)
Kinlochewe–Applecross:
  58 km (36 mi.)
Applecross–Kyle of Lochalsh:
  56 km (35 mi.)
Kyle of Lochalsh–Armadale:
  39 km (24 mi.)
Ferry to Mallaig, then
Mallaig–Strontian:
  76 km (47 mi.)
Strontian–Corran:
  26 km (16 mi.)

Corran–Banavie:
  56 km (35 mi.)
Banavie–Fort Augustus:
  53 km (33 mi.)
Fort Augustus–Inverness:
  58 km (36 mi.)

Terrain:

Everything from flat to mountainous; some steep grades on coastal roads and the Bealach-na-Ba, otherwise most grades steady but often quite long.

Maps:

O.S. Travelmaster (1:250 000) sheet: 2

O.S. Landranger (1:50 000) sheets: 15, 16, 19, 20, 21, 24, 25, 26, 32, 33, 34, 35, 40, 41

Access:

By train: Rail stations with InterCity services at Inverness, Fort William (at time of writing). Other rail stations (cycle capacity may be limited and some small stations are unstaffed and unable to make cycle reservations): Bonar Bridge, Invershin, Strathcarron, Stromeferry, Kyle of Lochalsh, Mallaig, Arisaig, Lochailort, Locheilside, Corpach, Banavie.

By air: Inverness Airport

By bike: Links from Argyll and Trossachs tour at Corran (Tour D, Route 22).

Description

This tour takes you through some of the grandest of Scotland's scenery, where—for probably the first time in Britain—you will meet remoteness and grandeur on the scale of continental Europe or even parts of North America and Australia. There can be long gaps between sources of food and supplies, so stock up at every opportunity. Because of the high latitude—the northernmost point of the trip is about 58° 20′ N., roughly level with Juneau, Alaska—it's highly rewarding to visit the area from mid-May to mid-June when the midsummer days are long and nightfall is postponed to 11 P.M.

From about mid- or late July to perhaps late September, the dreaded Scottish "midges"—minute black flies with a very irritating but otherwise harmless bite, who are seemingly able to penetrate most materials—can make outdoor life in the Highlands, and particularly camping, less pleasant than it ought to be.

The first part of this route has been revolutionized over recent years by bridge-building, some of it supported by funds from the European Commission. So now, if you're heading from Inverness, "the capital of the Highlands," for the far northwest, you can ride high over the waters of the Moray Firth on the impressive new Kessock Bridge, and rather lower on the one over the Cromarty Firth.

The main A9 road is the principal link with the northernmost parts of Scotland and cannot easily be avoided in places, but in others the new road has left the old ones quieter than ever, and the route follows these wherever possible.

The first section, across the peninsula of the Black Isle, traverses rolling agricultural country, but once you are over the Cromarty Firth, the rugged forest and moorland uplands of the Highlands begin.

"Firth," by the way, is the Scots term for a river estuary. A "strath," which we'll encounter later, is a broad river valley. A "kyle," also to be met later, is a strait or narrow sea passage.

On the quite hilly road from Alness to Bonar Bridge, you'll encounter at Aultnamain one of the most welcome features of Scottish Highland touring: an isolated hotel serving drinks and food to travelers, just at the point where you want one.

Beyond Bonar Bridge begins one of the more lonely stretches of the route, up Strath Oykel, now quite extensively forested, with clearings of rough grazing. As you progress farther northwest, the distinctive outlines of two mountains, Suilven and Canisp, increasingly dominate the skyline. They are part of a line of rugged volcanic peaks (safely extinct for 30 million years) that shape the landscape here. The geology of the area is in fact very complex, and the Loch Assynt area is a favored one for college field trips. Much of this area is now a large nature reserve. The route passes the impressive ruin of Ardvreck Castle, built in 1591.

From Skiag Bridge, another of the peaks, Quinag, dominates the view. The next section of road round the base of Quinag, to the little settlement of Drumbeg, is one of the hardest we've ever met, with a succession of up and down 25% grades, but it is very rewarding if you don't try to hurry, with its open uplands, wooded valleys and lochs and sea inlets. This area was one of the last parts of Britain to be covered in glaciers during the Ice Age some 10,000 years ago, and the landscape shows the characteristic glacial mix of small lochs and small rounded hills.

The next town of any consequence is the small fishing port of Lochinver, and it is here that one of the most delightful stretches of the route begins, following a winding, twisting, climbing and plunging little road through a landscape of dwarf oak and birch woods, mountain views, tumbling streams and sea inlets.

The road inland from the end of this "Mad Little Road of Ross," as it's been called, is spectacular in a different way, with lochside scenery and the almost symmetrical cone of Stac Pollaidh to the left of the road. Some 15 km (10 mi.) of main road lead to Ullapool, much the largest town on the northwest coast and nowadays something of an international rendezvous for fishing fleets, as well as a principal port for ferries to the outlying Western Isles. Ullapool lies beside Loch Broom, a sea-loch, and there are fine views of the town as you climb away to the head of the loch. Although this is a trunk road, traffic is relatively light, while the next stretch of A-class road down to Little Loch Broom and Gruinard Bay is positively quiet.

This is crofting country—the traditional form of subsistence farming, with each family living in its simple croft cottage, surrounded by enough land to support it. This leads to a very even spread of habitation: there may be no more than two or three of the typical one-story whitewashed houses per square mile, but every square mile will have its quota of crofts. Much of the settlement on the outer islands and indeed in the west of Ireland is very similar. This traditional pattern of life was uprooted in the 17th, 18th and to some extent 19th centuries when crofters were displaced by their landlords to make way for large sporting (i.e., shooting) estates. Crofting is now officially backed by the Crofting Commission, which supervises the letting of crofts.

The warming influence of the North Atlantic current is unexpectedly demonstrated in one of the next settlements, Poolewe, where there is a tropical garden, open to visitors and complete with palm trees.

Soon after the small village of Gairloch, the road climbs away inland to follow the southwestern shore of the inland Loch Maree, dominated by the molar-tooth shape of Slioch mountain on the opposite shore. From Kinlochewe, just beyond the head of the loch, a rather featureless road heads west, past the Beinn Eighe nature reserve into Glen Torridon, and from here on, a switchback road leads to the picturesque village of Shieldaig.

Until quite recently the next part of the route round the seaward side of the peninsula was no more than a path, but now some 30 km (20 mi.) of narrow and superbly scenic road lead round to Applecross. The open little road offers superb sea views across to the rugged Cuillin mountains on the island of Skye.

Applecross lies at the head of a sheltered sandy bay, and marks the start of the climb of the 626 m (2,054 ft.) Bealach-na-Ba, "the pass of the cattle." The road twists and winds across the treeless rocky landscape, with immense views back toward Skye from just before the top. Then comes the surprise as you pass the summit and look down into the great cleft of the pass's eastern approach, with the road hairpinning away down to sea level. Take care, because it is quite steep in parts—20% or so.

From the sea arm of Loch Kishorn at the foot of the Bealach-na-Ba, a short climb leads over to the head of Loch Carron and another switchback road beside the loch, and then through woods and surprising domestic-looking rhododendrons to the little port and rail terminus of Kyle of Lochalsh.

The traditional way to the island of Skye has always been by a short ferry crossing from Kyle of Lochalsh to Kyleakin, but at the time of writing, a road bridge linking the island to the mainland was nearing completion and seems likely to close another ferry—and to alter the way of life of the island.

The route crosses to Skye—which would well repay a much longer visit if you have time—and then heads south to the small ferry port of Armadale. The route directions suggest a worthwhile side trip across the peninsula to Tokavaig and Torskavaig, from where there are fine views of the rugged 1,000 m (3,000 ft.-plus) Cuillin mountains. The half-hour ferry trip from Armadale brings you to the mainland fishing port of Mallaig—the largest place on the route since Ullapool.

From Mallaig, the route follows the rugged and remote Moidart and Ardgour peninsula, with a superb mix of forest, sea-loch and mountain scenery. On this section of the route, once more, sources of food and supplies are very infrequent.

The route eventually emerges on the shores of the long sea-arm of Loch Linnhe and follows its northwest shore on a magnificent road round to Loch Eil (the westward extension of Loch Linnhe). Provided the weather is clear, which is probably more common in winter than summer, there are excellent views of Scotland's (and Britain's) highest mountain, Ben Nevis, 1,344 m (4,406 ft.).

After some of the roads we've been on, this is gentle, level riding, westward beside the southern shore of Loch Eil and then eastward along its northen side.

At the village of Banavie, about 5 km (3 mi.) before the town of Fort William, the route turns left to follow the line of one of Scotland's engineering landmarks, the Caledonian Canal. This canal, on which work began in 1803 by the great pioneering engineer Thomas Telford, was an ambitious scheme to link the North Sea with western waters and avoid the long and often stormy sea journey round the northern tip of Scotland, by joining the freshwater lochs along the length of the Great Glen, the rift valley which links Inverness and Fort William.

Our route keeps to the west of the canal and inland Loch Lochy to follow a new cycle route on a gravel forest track high above the lake through to Laggan. About a year before the time of writing, this cycle route was being extended, so it is worth checking whether you can avoid some or all of the A82 trunk road to Fort Augustus.

Fort Augustus was one of three military settlments built along this valley—the others were Fort William and Fort George at Inverness, which was blown up in 1746—by the English to subdue the Scots in the 18th century. At the same time, a set of military roads, often referred to as "General Wade's Military Roads," named for the army commander from 1726–1737, was laid down to enable the garrisons to travel quickly to trouble spots. Ironically, their main use was to enable rebel forces in the 1745 "Bonnie Prince Charlie" uprising to move rapidly across the country. The route follows part of the line of one of these roads across open country to the southeast of Loch Ness, before turning down to the lochside road for the final run in to Inverness.

Directions

Note that this route makes use of ferries that do not operate every day of the week or out of the summer season. Use phone numbers given to check.

1. Leave Inverness rly. stn. R. on Academy Street, which becomes Chapel Street, to rbt. junct. with A82.

2. R. on A82 to rbt. junct. with A9. L. on A9 over Kessock Bridge.

3. Take path (steps) down to North Kessock either immediately after end of bridge or 1.5 km (1 mi.) after bridge, then L. on uc. road to North Kessock.

4. R. on uc. road along N. side of Beauly Firth to Redcastle. ¤ N.W. 9.5 km (6 mi.)

5. R. on uc. road to A832 at Newton, S.O. on uc. road to A835.

6. L. on A835 for 4 km (2.5 mi.), R. on B9169 to Easter Kinkell.

7. L. on uc. road, then R. after 1.5 km (1 mi.) to B9163.

8. S.O. on B9163 to A9. ¤ N. 11.5 km (7 mi.)

9. L. on A9 over bridge to cross Cromarty Firth, then L. on uc. road under rly. through Evanton to B9176. ¤ N.N.E. 9 km (5.5 mi.)

10. L. on B9176 to A836 at Fearn Lodge. ¤ N. 20 km (12.5 mi.)

11. L. on A836 through Bonar Bridge to Invershin.

12. L. on A837 up Strath Oykel to junct. with A835 at Ledmore. ¤ N.W. 49 km (30.5 mi.)

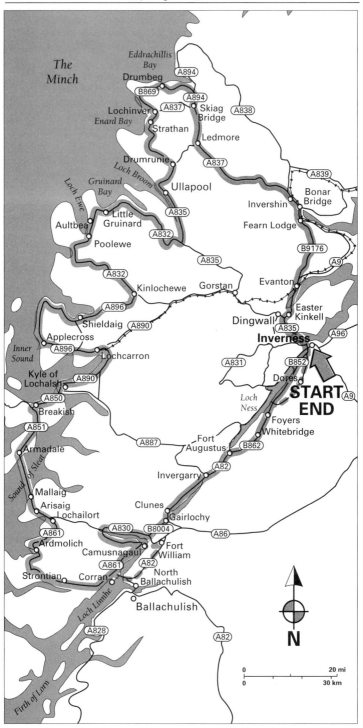

13. R. on A837 through Inchnadamph to Skiag Bridge.

14. R. on A894 to junct. with B869. ¤ N.N.W. 20 km (12.5 mi.)

15. L. on B869 on very up-and-down road—one of the hardest we know—through Drumbeg and Stoer to rejoin A837 near Lochinver. ¤ W. 13.5 km (8.5 mi.)

16. R. on A837 through Lochinver, and at S. end of village, S.O. on uc. road through Strathan and Inverkirkaig to junct. at G.R. 063 113. ¤ S.S.W. 13 km (8 mi.)

17. L. on uc. road to join A835 at Drumrunie, R. on A835 to Ullapool. ¤ S.S.W. 19 km (12 mi.)

18. Continue on A835 to junct. with A832; R. on A832 to Dundonnell. ¤ S. 8.5 km (5.5 mi.) (Seasonal, infrequent or on-demand ferry—call (01854) 83 230—operates across Loch Broom to Aultnaharrie, Allt na h-Airbhe on Landranger map; very steep and rough ascent to join uc. road to Dundonnell.)

19. Continue on A832 by Gruinard Bay and Aultbea to Poolewe. ¤ just S. of W. 27 km (17 mi.)

20. Continue on A832 beside Loch Maree to Kinlochewe. ¤ S.S.E. 26 km (16 mi.)

21. R. on A896 to Shieldaig. ¤ W.S.W. 23 km (14.5 mi.)

22. 1 km (0.6 mi.) S. of Shieldaig, R. on uc. road following coast to Applecross, L. to summit of Bealach-na-Ba. ¤ S.S.W. 12 km (7.5 mi.)

23. Descend pass to Tornapress, R. on A896 to Lochcarron. ¤ E. 14 km (8.5 mi.)

24. L., still on A896, to junct. with A890; R. over bridge on A890 to Achmore. ¤ S.S.W. 7.5 km (4.5 mi.)

25. R. after bridge on uc. roads through Duirinish to Kyle of Lochalsh. ¤ S.S.W. 12 km (7.5 mi.)

26. Take ferry, or cross new bridge when open, to Kyleakin on Skye.

27. Continue on A850 through Breakish to junct. with A851, L. on A851 to Armadale (optional detour N.W. to Tokavaig). ¤ S.W. 25 km (15.5 mi.) Note: this is just a lightning visit to Skye. There are many more very rewarding roads farther N. and W. on the island.

28. Take ferry from Armadale to Mallaig (Monday, Wednesday, Saturday—call (01687) 2403). ¤ S.S.E. 9 km (5.5 mi.)

29. Follow A830 S. to Arisaig and then E. to Lochailort. ¤ S.E. 18 km (11 mi.)

30. R. on A861 through Kinlochmoidart to Salen. ¤ S.S.W. 15 km (9.5 mi.)

31. L. on A861 through Strontian to Ardgour. ¤ E. 34 km (21 mi.)

32. (For quick route to Fort William, take ferry to Corran, L. on A82 to Fort William. ¤ N.E. 14 km/8.5 mi.)

33. S.O. on A861 along W. side of Loch Linnhe to Camusnagaul. ¤ N.E. 13 km (8 mi.)

34. Either take ferry to Fort William, except Sundays—call (01463) 234 121—or S.O. on A861 along S. side of Loch Eil to junct. with A830. ¤ W.N.W. 14 km (8.5 mi.)

35. R. on A830 to Banavie. ¤ just S. of E. 16 km (10 mi.)

36. For Fort William, S.O. on A830 to A82, R. to Fort William. ¤ S. 4 km (2.5 mi.)

37. To return to Inverness, L. in Banavie on B8004 to Gairlochy, S.O. on B8005 to Clunes. ¤ N.E. 15 km (9.5 mi.)

38. R. on gravel forest trail signed as cycle route along N.W. shore of Loch Lochy to join paved road to A82 at North Laggan.

39. L. on A82 through Invergarry to Fort Augustus. ¤ N.E. 27 km (17 mi.)

40. (New cycle route avoiding all or part of A82 between North Laggan and Fort Augustus may be open: check when in area.)

41. In Fort Augustus, R. on B862 to Whitebridge.

42. L. on B852 through Foyers along S.E. shore of Loch Ness to Dores, then L. on B862 to Inverness.

43. Alternatively, follow upper "General Wade's Military Road" (uc. road) from Inverfarigaig, on shore of Loch Ness 4 km (2.5 mi.) beyond Foyers, to Inverness. ¤ N.E. 47 km (29 mi.)

CHAPTER 28

Suggested Combinations of Routes

The possible combinations of the 18 point-to-point routes described in Chapters 4–21 and the 5 tours (Chapters 23–27) are almost endless. In most cases, starting and finishing points can be modified. Also, most routes can be done in the reverse order, although we think the order quoted is better.

1. Circular tour of southern England

From London-Heathrow Airport:

Route 1 to Oxford, Route 10 to Bath, Route 5 in reverse to Overton, Route 9 to just south of Oxford, Route 1 in reverse to Heathrow Airport.

2. Circular tour of central England

From London-Heathrow Airport:

Route 2 to Cambridge, Route 13 to Chester, Route 11 in reverse to Bath, Route 10 in reverse to Oxford, Route 1 in reverse to Heathrow Airport. A circular tour taking in midland England, including the Peak National Park, two Roman cities, the Welsh border country and a taste of Wales, and some of southern England's archeological sites.

3. Linear tour across England and Wales to Ireland

From Dover, Folkestone, the Channel Tunnel, Gatwick Airport:

Route 5 to Bath, Route 11 to Church Stretton, Route 12 to Holyhead. A flying visit to southern England, the Welsh border country and north Wales en route for Ireland.

or:

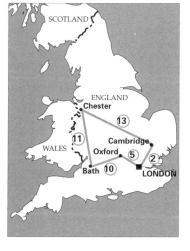

Route 5 to Overton, Route 9 to Oxford, Route 1 to Church Stretton, Route 12 to Holyhead. An even more flying visit to southern England, the Welsh border country and north Wales en route for Ireland.

4. Linear tour from Southampton or Portsmouth to Holyhead

Route 9 to Oxford, Route 1 to Church Stretton, Route 12 to Holyhead. Another link from France to Ireland, showing you some fine parts of England and Wales on the way.

5. From Stranraer to Harwich or Felixstowe

Route 17 in reverse to Carlisle, Route 18 to Edinburgh, Route 15 in reverse to York, Route 14 in reverse to Cambridge, Route 4 in reverse to Harwich. A route from Ireland to the European continent taking in fine forest country, Scotland's capital city, historic castles and coastal sites, three national parks (Northumberland, Yorkshire Dales, North Yorkshire Moors) and the gentle countryside of eastern England.

or:

Route 17 in reverse to Carlisle, southern leg of Borders and Roman Wall route to Blanchland, Route 15 in reverse to York, Route 14 and link in reverse to Hull. A shorter link, omitting Edinburgh but giving a chance to visit the Roman Wall.

6. From Harwich or Felixstowe to Stranraer

Route 4 to Cambridge, Route 14 to York, White and Red Roses tour to Lancaster (Heysham link

for the Isle of Man), Route 16 to
Carlisle, Route 17 to Stranraer. An
even more direct link showing off
some fine scenery in England's
backbone, the Pennines.

7. From London-Gatwick Airport to Wales

Link, then Route 5 in reverse to
Dallington, Route 7 to
Cambridge, Route 10 to Oxford,
Route 1 to Church Stretton, Tour
of the New Welsh lakes, Route 11
in reverse to Bath, Route 5 in
reverse and link to Gatwick Airport. Two university cities,
Shakespeare country, some of the
best of the Welsh border country
and central Wales on incredibly
quiet roads, with a return via the
elegant Roman and Georgian city
of Bath and some archeological
centers.

8. American Heritage, from London-Heathrow Airport

Route 2 (via Jordans) to
Cambridge, Route 10 (via
Sulgrave Manor loop) to Oxford,
Route 1 to Church Stretton, Route
11 in reverse to Bath, Route 10 in
reverse to Oxford, Route 1 in
reverse to London-Heathrow Airport. Some American links, plus
Shakespeare country and Bath,
the Roman and Georgian city that
everybody wants to see.

9. Roman cities, from London-Gatwick Airport

Link and Route 5 to Bath, Route
11 to Chester, Route 16 to Carlisle,
Borders and the Roman Wall tour
to Corbridge, Route 15 in reverse
to York, Route 14 in reverse to
Cambridge, Route 7 in reverse to
Dallington, Route 5 then link to
London-Gatwick Airport. Roman
cities and Roman relics from

2,000 years ago, plus a remarkable variety of England's scenery.

10. From Southampton or Portsmouth to the north of Scotland

Route 9 to Oxford, Route 10 in reverse to Cambridge, Route 14 to York, Route 15 to Edinburgh, link to Argyll and the Trossachs and Northwest Highlands tours. Return by rail from Inverness. The Grand Tour: southern England, two great university cities, York, three national parks (Northumberland, Yorkshire Dales, North Yorkshire Moors), the gentle countryside of eastern England, the elegance of Scotland's capital city and some of Scotland's finest mountain and coast scenery.

or:

Route 5 from Dover, Folkestone, the Channel Tunnel or London-Gatwick Airport to Overton, then Route 9 to Oxford, continuing as above.

11. From Harwich or Felixstowe to the north of Scotland

Route 4 to Cambridge, (or link from London-Stansted Airport, then Route 7 to Cambridge), Route 14 to York, Route 15 to Edinburgh, link to Argyll and the Trossachs and Northwest Highlands tours returning to Edinburgh, Route 18 in reverse to Carlisle, Route 16 in reverse to Chester, Route 11 in reverse to Church Stretton, Route 1 in reverse to Oxford, Route 10 in reverse to Cambridge, Route 4 in reverse to Harwich (link to London-Stansted Airport). Another version of the Grand Tour.

CHAPTER 29

Coping with Britain

The chapters of this last part of the book are those that are of interest only to foreign visitors. They contain all the relevant information for cyclists, as well as some basic general travel information.

Language, Accents and Dialects

It is not only visitors to Britain who find some of the vast range of British regional accents and dialects difficult. Even many English southerners claim to find it impossible to understand speakers with strong northern, Scottish or Welsh accents.

There are also two true separate Celtic languages spoken in Britain. In the extreme northwest of Scotland, particularly on some of the westernmost islands known as the Outer Hebrides or Western Isles, Gàidhlig, a Gaelic language related to Irish, is in everyday use; in some areas of Wales, again mainly in the west and north, the Welsh language Cymraeg is widely spoken—Wales is officially bilingual, as you will note from the road signs. English is widely understood, though you may sometimes find people reluctant to use it. When they do speak English, however, the combination of a millenia-old oral storytelling tradition (as there is in Ireland) and natural Celtic speech patterns and rhythms gives them a remarkable articulacy and fluency.

Most accents and dialects in other parts of the country are really part of Britain's living historical heritage. They stem at least in part from the varying degrees of influence that the invading Angles, Saxons, Jutes, Danes and Normans had on particular areas.

The accent of the counties of Norfolk and Suffolk, northeast of London and known as East Anglia, still carries the up-and-down rhythms of Danish speech, while many words in the dialect of northeastern England around Newcastle upon Tyne are virtually pure Old Norse. The speech of Yorkshire, again in northern England, has relics of Old Low German. Lowland (southern) Scots, "Lallans," has hundreds of its own words from a range of sources.

Less marked than they used to be, but still there nonetheless, are the differences of accent marking differences of social class. "BBC English," sometimes known as Standard Received Pronunciation, is still largely middle-class. Some members of the upper social classes retain traces of that combination of clipped consonants and slight drawl that makes British movies from the 1940s and 1950s seem so dated now, but its use is declining. So, too, is the notion that the possession of a regional accent denotes lower- or working-class origins; nowadays academics, for example, may speak with almost any accent. (Oddly enough, a genteel Scottish accent from Edinburgh was always acceptable, even considered an asset, particularly for medical men and engineers.)

Finally, don't forget that everybody assumes that it is they who speak "normal" English. As a visitor, the one with the quaint accent will be you.

Asking Your Way Around

The pronunciation of place names can be a trap. Americans are conspicuous as soon as they ask for "Lye-sess-ter Square" (it should be pronounced "Lesst'r") or "Bir-ming-ham" (say "Birming'm"). Space does not allow the inclusion of a U.K.-U.S. glossary of place names, but we can provides some hints here.

☐ The vowels in -er, -don, -ton, -ford, -mouth and -ham on the ends of place names are almost suppressed—the sound is a short "uh," as in "uh-huh."

☐ The stress is usually on the first syllable, but it is on the second syllable in many Scottish place names.

☐ In county names, if in England, -shire is pronounced "sheer," if in Scotland, it is pronounced "-shyre."

☐ Some other pronunciation examples include Thames ("Temz"), Norwich ("Norrich"), Worcester ("Wuster"), and Salisbury ("Sawlsbree").

The Rules of the Road

In Britain, we ride and drive on the left side of the road. It's not difficult to get used to, and as long as there is other traffic to remind you, you will have no problems. The times when memory lapses are possible are: after leaving a one-way street, particularly if you have been using the right-hand side of it; after making a right turn at an intersection, when you can forget to go completely across the road; and after leaving a stop such as a shop or café that happens to be on the right-hand side of the road. Traffic circles (U.K. = roundabouts)—of which there are many, including "mini-roundabouts"—may also give you cause to stop and think for a moment.

In British law a bicycle is treated as a road vehicle, and a cyclist has to obey traffic regulations, as does any other vehicle. Cyclists are expected to obey traffic light signals and one-way street instructions. Bicycles are ridden on the main paved part of the road and, except in special "contraflow" lanes (below), in the same direction as the rest of the traffic. They may not legally be ridden on the sidewalk unless it has been assigned "shared-use" status, marked by a circular blue sign with figures of a pedestrian and child together with a bicycle—side-by-side with a dividing line if the path is marked out half for walkers and half for bikes, one above the other if both share the same area.

Other special cycle routes are shown by a similar circular blue sign with a bike symbol; a rectangular version of the same sign denotes a recommended bike route that is shared with local traffic. Unless there is a sign forbidding cycling—circular with a red border, white background and black bike symbol—you may still use the main part of the road even if there is a bike path or shared-use path. A few roads have special bike lanes marked; once again these are not mandatory (just as well, since drivers often treat them as parking lanes) and even the not-too-cynical have been known to observe that their main usefulness is that the bike symbols painted on the road remind other traffic that there are bicycles around.

Particularly in cities, some lanes may be marked for use by buses plus bikes, or buses and bikes plus taxis. These generally are respected and often useful. Some one-way streets have "contraflow" cycle lanes going against the main direction of traffic; these, too, can be useful since they can avoid long detours, possibly in heavy traffic.

The most useful cycle facilities are exemptions and special crossings. Increasingly cars are being deterred from using residential roads by "traffic-calming" measures, which can include road closures and "no-entry" markings. Cyclists are often exempt from these. Roads usable by cyclists in this way but not by cars are usually indicated by a small notice below the no-entry or no-through-road sign marked "Except . . . "plus a bike symbol.

Special cycle crossing facilities include cyclists' traffic signals (sometimes combined with pedestrian ones) and cyclists' or shared-use bridges over busy roads, railroads or waterways. These,too, often open up for bike use a network of quiet roads.

Otherwise, bicycles may be ridden on any road not marked with the "no-cycling" sign described above, except "motorways." These (mostly) freeways are for motor traffic only and numbered "M" (for motorway)—e.g., M4, M62 or A1(M)—and clearly marked with blue signs. There is also a prominent board at every motorway junction listing the classes of traffic (such as horse-drawn carts, herds of animals and farm vehicles as well as bikes) that are not allowed on them.

On otherwise all-purpose roads, "no cycling" signs are usually placed on high-speed flyovers and the like, where there will always be some alternative for bikes. Most of the major motorway bridges over major rivers have bike paths alongside, reached from nearby all-traffic roads.

The road signing system follows the basic principle that circular signs give orders (white with a red surround in general for prohibitions, white on blue for positive instructions), triangles (white with a red surround) warn, and rectangular signs give information.

The pictorial warning signs are now virtually uniform throughout Europe and are largely self-explanatory. The red eight-sided "Stop" sign is used, while the "Give Way" sign has precisely the same meaning as the American "Yield." Note that in Britain (unlike some American states) you may not make a nearside turn (to the left in Britain) on a red light unless there is a lit green filter arrow or a separate traffic lane bypassing the signal.

The only hand signals used by cyclists are to indicate left and right turns. In both cases you hold the appropriate arm out horizontally from the shoulder, with the palm of the hand facing forward.

Cycling and the Law

As the law now stands in Britain you must as a cyclist:

☐ Have efficient brakes.

☐ When riding (and even in theory when walking your bike), observe traffic signs and signals and obey the directions of a police officer, a traffic warden directing traffic or a school-crossing patrol. You must not cross the stop line at traffic lights when the light is red, but note that some signals now have advanced stop lines to allow cyclists to position themselves ahead of other traffic.

☐ Give way to ambulances, fire engines, and mountain or cave rescue, coastguard or police vehicles with sirens sounding and blue lights flashing.

☐ Give precedence to pedestrians on "zebra" or light-controlled pedestrian crossings. Zebra crossings have black and white rectangles marked on the road and a flashing orange globe on a post on either side of the road.

☐ When riding between sunset and sunrise, carry a front lamp showing a white light, a red rear light and a red rear reflector. Pedal reflectors are required on some machines. The requirements for the lights and reflector are quite complex, but visitors from abroad are unlikely to be penalized for having the wrong markings on their lights. Note that flashing lights may not be fixed to the bicycle in Britain. Lamps and so on need not be fitted when you are riding in daylight.

You may not:

☐ Ride "dangerously," without "due care and attention" or without "reasonable consideration" for other road users.

☐ Ride under the influence of alcohol or a drug, although there is no statutory limit on blood alcohol concentration nor any compulsion to submit samples for test.

☐ Hold onto a motor vehicle or trailer in motion.

☐ Carry a passenger unless your bicycle is "constructed or adapted for the carriage of more than one person."

☐ Stop, except in an emergency to avoid an accident, on a pedestrian crossing, or leave a bicycle where it may cause danger or obstruction.

☐ Ride on a "footpath (footway, U.S. = sidewalk) by the side of any road or set apart for the use of foot-passengers" except to cross it for access.

☐ Ride along a road designated as a motorway or on a road or path showing the appropriate no-cycling signs.

You are allowed:

☐ In the dark to wheel your bicycle while on foot as near as possible to the left-hand edge of the road without lights, or to stop temporarily with lamps unlit.

☐ To ride in bus lanes where they are marked with a cycle as well as bus symbol.

☐ To ride on a path marked with a blue pedestrian-plus-bike sign indicating that it is for shared use.

☐ To ride (in England and Wales) on a bridleway or long-distance trail with bridleway status—with the obligation to give way to pedestrians and riders of horses if necessary.

Money Matters

The currency unit of Britain is the pound sterling, indicated by the symbol £. Nowadays it's divided into 100 pence; you may still find people calling them "new pence" although the change from the old 12-pennies-to-the-shilling was made in 1971. Most people just call them "p."

There are seven coins:

☐ two bronze-colored—1p and 2p (though they may not be with us much longer)

☐ two round and silvery with milled edges—5p and 10p

☐ two silvery and seven-sided with plain edges—20p and 50p

☐ a brassy milled-edge £1 coin with four national design variations

You may find coins referred to as "pieces"—as in "this machine accepts 20p and 50p pieces." Slot machines—notably phones and rail ticket machines—use coins from 10p upwards, although some non-standard phones in pubs or restaurants do not accept 50p or £1 coins.

Denominations over £1 are covered by bills (U.K. = banknotes, or just "notes"), £5, £10 and £20 being the commonest and most generally acceptable. In Scotland, several banks also issue £1 notes. These should be accepted in England as well, but if you have problems a bank will change them. If your home bank has given you £50 or £100 notes and you're stopping at budget accommodations, it can be worth changing them for £20 or smaller at a bank or "bureau de change" (money exchange) early on in your trip. Many small stores, campgrounds, youth hostels or B&Bs may be unwilling to accept large-value notes—and even if they are, may not have enough cash to give you your change.

Credit cards are widely used in shops and for travel, less commonly at campgrounds and private B&Bs. The major cards are Access, affiliated with Mastercharge/Mastercard, and Visa. Charge cards such as Amex and Diner's are less commonly accepted, except by large restaurants, hotels, travel companies and of course banks. It's worth noting that if you are buying British items such as books or maps by mail order from Britain before your trip, the credit card is much the easiest method of payment. Not only is the U.K. sterling price automatically converted, but the exchange is made at the commercial rate rather than at the tourist rate.

Outside the most American-frequented spots, U.S. dollar bills and travelers' checks in any currency are changed only by banks or "bureaux de change."

Banking hours are expanding, with some open from 9:30 A.M. to 5:30 P.M., Monday to Friday; 4:45 P.M. or even 3:30 P.M. are commoner closing times, however. In Scotland, banks may stay open later but close from 1 to 2 P.M. for lunch. Bank branches at airports or in major stores are often open for longer hours. Many banks have "through-the-wall" cash machines that accept a variety of cards, including Visa and Mastercard. Different banks handle different combinations of cards.

Weights and Measures

Americans will be relieved to know that, for all the European "harmonization" measures, road distances in Britain are still signed in miles, altitudes (except on some maps) in feet, and weights often in pounds and ounces.

For the record, the exact conversions are:

1 mi.	=	1.6013 km
1 ft.	=	0.305 meters or 305 mm
1 pound (lb.)	=	454 g
1 ounce (oz.)	=	28.35 g

You will never need to convert to this degree of accuracy.

Packaged products are usually in metric packs nowadays, but for practical purposes, 250 g is ½ lb. and 500 g, 1 lb. Many liquids, such as drinks, are now supplied in fractions or multiples of a liter (spelled "litre" in Britain). Milk (usually) and long drinks in pubs are still in pints—but the British pint (568 ml), quart (1,135 ml) and gallon (4.54 l) are about 20% larger than the U.S. versions.

One final oddity is that personal weights, if not metric, are generally quoted in "stones," a historic unit of 14 lb. If you say you weigh 160 lb. you'll probably be met with a blank stare or a hurried mental calculation; to a Briton it's "11 st. 6 lb." or just "11 stone 6."

Public Holidays

British national public holidays are traditionally known as "bank holidays"—and you certainly won't find banks open. Most large shops will be closed on bank holidays, and there may be modified rail services. Some smaller food shops may open but for a shorter period than usual. Bank holidays are more or less uniform in England and Wales, but Scotland has both different national holidays and a series of area public holidays.

In England and Wales, the dates of the holidays not celebrated in the U.S. include: the first Monday in May (which may be replaced by an autumn holiday from 1996); the Monday following the last Sunday in May ("Spring Bank Holiday"); the last Monday in August ("August Bank Holiday"), and 26 December ("Boxing Day").

In Scotland there are fewer national holidays and more local or area ones—you'll have to enquire at tourist information offices when you're there to find out if any will affect your plans. The national holidays are 1 and 2 January, in most places the first Monday in August, and 25 December, Christmas Day. Some stores and banks may also be closed on some of the English holiday dates.

One other type of holiday that can affect you, particularly in villages and small towns, is the "early closing" day. These date from some of the earliest 19th-century laws to protect shop workers from exploitation. To compensate them for working on Saturday afternoons, shops were legally required to close on one other afternoon each week. The day varies from place to place—usually a Wednesday or Thursday—but on that afternoon many or most of the shops in that town or village will be shut. The handbooks of the youth hostels associations indicate early closing days in towns and villages near hostels; the *CTC Handbook* lists them for bike shops. Early closing days are gradually disappearing.

The British Sunday

Although more happens now on a British Sunday than once did, usually the only shops you'll find open are a few small food stores and newspaper and candy ("sweet") shops—and then often only for the morning. Recent relaxing of English Sunday trading laws may gradually see more and larger stores open on Sundays.

Pub Sunday opening hours are shorter, and fewer cafés and restaurants are open, at least during the day. In some areas of Wales, pubs do not open at all on Sundays; the area where this operates is fixed by a local referendum every few years.

In parts of the country with a strong nonconformist church tradition—particularly Wales and rural Scotland—complete Sunday closing of stores and services is more widespread.

There is a more restricted rail and bus service on Sundays and some services do not run at all. In addition, railroad engineering is usually carried out on Saturday nights and up to 4 P.M. on Sundays. Trains may be replaced at quite short notice by buses—which don't carry bikes—while the work is being done. Check at the rail station before traveling.

Telephones

British phones are one of two types: card-operated or coin-operated. Booths ("kiosks") for card-operated phones are marked "Cardphone." Phonecards may be bought from bookstalls, newspaper shops, post offices and often from other shops, too.

Public coin phones usually accept 10p, 20p, 50p and £1 coins; some pay phones in pubs, hotels and restaurants may not accept 50p and £1 coins. Coin-operated phones return unused coins, making it better to use several small coins unless you are certain the call will be long enough to use up a larger one. Some coin phones will also accept Phonecards and credit cards.

For all phones, insert the coins or card immediately after lifting the handset and before dialing. Except for "Freephone" (toll-free) numbers and emergencies (below), all calls, including local ones, are charged.

British phone numbers consist of an area code, often known as the STD (Subscriber Trunk Dialling) code, which is generally printed in parentheses, plus the individual number. For local calls merely dial the number; for all other calls, dial the area code followed by the number. If you don't know whether or not it's a local call, dial the code plus the number—it'll still work.

The British dialing tone is a low-pitched hum; the ringing tone is a medium-pitch double beep or ring, repeated at two-second intervals; the busy signal (U.K. = "engaged" tone) is a continuous series of similarly pitched longish beeps; "number unobtainable" is a higher-pitched continuous tone.

International calls may be dialed direct from most phones. Dial 00 to access the international network, then dial the country code (1 for the United States and Canada, 61 for Australia, 64 for New Zealand) followed by the area code and the number you require. To call a British number from another country, dial as needed to access the international network (00 in most of the European Union), then 44 for the United Kingdom, followed by the U.K. area code without the initial 0, followed by the number required.

Home Country Direct calls on U.S. charge cards can be made by initially calling the appropriate toll-free U.K. number for the particular card. These are listed in Section 3—International Codes—of the U.K. phone book.

Emergency Services

The free emergency number is 999. The six emergency services that may be called are police, ambulance, fire, coastguard, mountain rescue and cave rescue. If you or a member of your party are involved in a road accident, ask first for the police, who will make arrangements for an ambulance if necessary. Initially services are free, though charges for rescue may be payable later; these should normally be covered by your travel insurance.

CHAPTER 30

Accommodations and Eating Out

In this chapter, we will take a look at the everyday problems of life as a tourist in Britain, particularly the way they affect you as a cyclist. Compared to a motorist, you are more limited in your ability to go long distances to reach hotels, restaurants and shops, but compared to those using public transportation or hiking, you are more flexible.

Overnight Stops

Let's be honest from the start: by the standards of continental Europe and North America, hotels, even mid-range ones, can be expensive in Britain. That's not to say you won't find exceptions, but hotels offering bed and breakfast without evening meal for less than £30 (say US $45) per person are rare—and many are much more. Motels too can be quite costly, with two-person rooms usually in the £35–45 (US $50–70) range. Both hotels and motels are often geared to business travelers and may have concessionary rates on (U.K. = at) weekends. All accommodations are more expensive near London— say within 80 km (50 mi.)—and to lesser extent near other large cities.

As a result, there is a well-developed second tier of accommodations: guest houses and private "bed and breakfast"(B&B). Price ranges can overlap—some guest houses in particular are more expensive than the cheaper hotels—but a guest-house bed with breakfast is usually around £20–25 (US $30–35). There isn't any exact definition of a guest house. Most are like small hotels but with fewer

You can tell a pub by its colorful signboard and usually traditional name. Many pubs serve food as well as drinks, and some have gardens where you can eat your picnic—but always ask first.

formal public rooms, and possibly fewer bedrooms with en-suite bathrooms—although this is becoming less and less the case. Guest houses may also offer an evening meal, but the choice of menu, if any, is likely to be much less than in a hotel restaurant, and the meal will probably be served at a specific and usually early hour. Many guest houses are geared to stays longer than one night.

The tradition of bed-and-breakfast in private homes grew up with the growth of touring cycling early this century. At one time, one of the main attractions of membership in the British national cycling association, the Cyclists' Touring Club (CTC), was being entitled to receive the *CTC Handbook*—at that time almost the only nationwide listing of B&Bs, all the entries having been recommended by fellow cyclists. Now B&B houses are much more common and there are many sources of listings.

A B&B offers just that—a bed and a cooked breakfast in a private house. This may lack some of the trappings of a hotel, but many now offer en-suite showers or exclusive use of a guest bathroom. The range of buildings is enormous, from ordinary town houses to centuries-old cottages and farms deep in the country. They are a marvelous way of meeting ordinary people, many of whom will be able to tell you all about the local places of interest. Some may be able to provide an evening meal, while others will recommend a nearby pub or restaurant.

Most B&Bs, especially if they are on local council listings, are subject to some degree of official inspection to ensure that they meet the necessary standards. Prices once again vary, ranging from about £10–25 (US $15–35) per person per night, with about £13–16 (US $20–25) the commonest band. Some pubs (below) also offer bed and breakfast, but they can vary widely.

There are several sources of listings of hotels, guest houses and B&Bs. Area tourist boards (see Appendix 1) all produce lists, as do many county and district councils. These will all be available from the boards or at local Tourist Information Centers. Most towns and large villages have a public library, and you will find accommodation guides in the reference section. They may also have free leaflets covering the immediate neighborhood. The CTC (see Appendix 1) still publishes the *CTC Handbook* for its members at intervals, though with more general information and less emphasis solely on B&Bs than it once had. Many local Tourist Information Centers operate a phone book-ahead system known as BABA ("Book-a-bed-ahead"): you can call in the morning and they'll book you a bed for the night in another area through other Tourist Information Centers, or they will phone local addresses on their list to book you a place. There is usually a small charge for this. If you haven't booked ahead it's advisable to start looking fairly early, say around 4:30–5 P.M. Most local Tourist Information Centers, especially small ones, close at 5:30 or 6 P.M.

Youth Hostels

There are two youth hostel associations in Britain—the YHA, or Youth Hostel Association (for England and Wales), and the SYHA, or Scotish Youth Hostel Association. Their addresses can be found in the Appendix.

There are about 250 hostels in England and Wales, and nearly 80 more in Scotland. Naturally they are concentrated in the tourist areas, but although there are now gaps in parts of the country, there is usually a hostel within a day's bike-riding distance. Hostel buildings range from farms and converted lighthouse-keepers' cottages to manor houses and even castles. Youth hostels can be used by members of the hostel association of any country affiliated with the International Youth Hostels Federation (IYHF), or you can buy an International Guest Pass in Britain. If you plan to spend more than two or three nights at hostels, it's best to join the youth hostel association of your own country before you leave home.

Many YHA hostels (as opposed to most SYHA ones) are nowadays geared to use by groups—often school parties during the week—and many now offer an evening meal plus bed-and-breakfast package (including the use of a sheet sleeping bag, which you used to have to bring with you). Hostel charges now depend on the grading of the hostel (no less than nine divisions in English ones). At the top end, prices are now higher than for a moderately priced B&B.

There are in addition a number of independent hostels. They tend to be simpler than YHA ones, mainly offering self-catering facilities only, and you have to bring your own sheet sleeping bag. In Scotland a number of hotels have low-price bunkhouse annexes, much used by climbers. Unfortunately, there does not appear to be a complete and up-to-date listing of English and Welsh independent hostels. The best listing, for CTC members, is probably the *CTC Handbook*—otherwise enquire at local Tourist Information Centers. The address for a list of independent hostels in Scotland is included in the Appendix.

More primitive are "camping barns"—partially converted stone barns offering a roof, water supply, sanitation and usually a communal sleeping area. Some are more lavishly equipped, but you usually have to bring your own camping-style sleeping bag, knives, forks, etc., and possibly cooking stove and pots—everything but the tent, in fact. Some camping barns are under the aegis of the YHA, some are administered by national parks, and others are independent. The YHA and the national park authorities have listings for those under their administration; otherwise enquire at local Tourist Information Centers.

Camping

Campgrounds ("campsites") are fairly numerous but far from evenly spread. Some will accommodate only camping trailers (UK = caravans), but most will find space for a small tent. Campgrounds are shown on the maps we recommend—with a small tent symbol in blue for tents only, tent-plus-trailer symbols if mixed, and trailer symbol alone if for caravans only. Many are signed at turnoffs from major roads by signs with similar symbols. As in much of Europe, many have a large number of semi-permanent trailers; it's not very pleasant camping overshadowed by large trailers, occupied or unoccupied. On the other hand, some "caravan parks" may rent out trailers by the night—a godsend if it's been raining for a week.

Camping in Britain is relatively unsophisticated, and the quality of sanitary facilities varies widely—from little more than basics to well-equipped shower and laundry blocks. Prices vary from about £2.50 (US $4) upward; some charge per person, some per tent and others by a combination of the two. Local Tourist Information Centers should have details of nearby camping facilities, while the most comprehensive listing is given in the members-only handbook of the Camping Club of Great Britain and Ireland, quite a few of whose grounds are also open to members only. There are commercial listings of campgrounds. Once again, a local library will usually have these in its reference section.

If you can't find an official campground, you can always ask at a farm if you can camp in the corner of a field or orchard. Your chances are probably better at smaller farms and at ones with grazing meadows than at those that obviously concentrate on cereals or root crops.

Wild camping is possible in some parts, although the legal position is unclear (except where there are official "no camping" signs, such as in many forest, seaside and tourist areas). In theory every square inch of Britain is owned by someone, and it's wise to ask—if there is anybody to ask. Don't pitch on obviously cultivated land, nor too near to habitation or to the road. Do not pollute streams and rivers, and take all your trash away with you. Don't light fires on land with trees or other vegetation.

Fuel for camping stoves is best bought from camping shops; there is usually one in any moderate-sized town or more frequently in tourist areas. The commonest fuels for lightweight stoves are small cylinders of butane, or butane laced with propane for better performance in cold weather. Epi Gas and the French Camping Gaz brands are the commonest, with either pierceable disposable cartridges or more recent resealable ones. Many campgrounds have small stores that may include butane cartridges in their stocks.

Fuel for Coleman-type gasoline stoves is fairly easily obtainable from camping shops. Unleaded gasoline (U.K. = petrol) should be available from filling stations, but most pumps can only deliver a minimum quantity of 2 liters.

Kerosene for pumped pressure stoves is generally known as "paraffin" and may be available from gas stations or hardware stores. Alcohol for Trangia and similar stoves is known as "methylated spirits" and is usually available from hardware stores or sometimes the hardware section of supermarkets. It has a percentage of methyl alcohol in it to make it (theoretically) undrinkable and a violet dye to make it both conspicuous and bitter-tasting.

If you need alcohol fuel desperately, a rather expensive solution is to buy "surgical spirit" from a pharmacy (often in UK = chemist). Note that none of these fuels, even in sealed unused cartridges, may be carried in airline baggage.

The English Pub (and, largely, the Welsh one, too)

The pub—short for "public house"—has a long history going back over a thousand years and more of taverns, inns and alehouses. The pub has a special place in English affections since, with the village store, it has long been a social center and meeting-place for the community.

Most pubs sell food, either light meals served at the bar or more elaborate ones in separate dining rooms. The "bar-snack" meals can be substantial and represent very good value—and because pubs are so widespread and so numerous they can be very useful for the traveling cyclist. Many also serve morning coffee and tea.

But pubs have their peculiarities. All have to be officially licensed, and their opening hours are quite strictly controlled. Typical opening hours are 11 A.M. to 3 P.M. and 6 P.M. to 10:30 or 11 P.M., Monday through Saturday, and 12 noon to 3 P.M. and 7 P.M. to 10:30 P.M. on Sundays. However, pub keepers ("landlords" or "landladies") have some choice in how they allocate their hours; quite a few now have all-day licenses, from 11 A.M. to 11 P.M. This means that there is at least some chance of getting a drink when you'd really like one—in the heat of the late afternoon. Many pubs now display their opening hours. Note, though, that if the front door is shut and locked then the pub's shut; no amount of knocking on the door will open it. Children under 14 years old are not allowed in pubs except to the parts where meals are served, and under-18s are not allowed to buy or consume alcoholic drinks. Penalties for infringement can be quite heavy both for buyer and seller.

You should also be aware that British beers are more alcoholic than American brews, and apple cider should not be confused with what is served up in the U.S. under that name: it can be pretty potent stuff, even if it tastes mild.

Service in pubs for drinks and food is at the bar, and normally you pay when you order, except in restaurant-style dining rooms where you may expect table service. Meals ordered at the bar may take a little time to prepare, and these are often brought to your table.

There are fewer pubs in Scotland but much the same facilities are offered by hotel barrooms. These are often separate from the main hotel—the entrance may be at the side or back.

Restaurants and Cafés

Most small towns will have some sort of restaurant, often nowadays Indian or Chinese. Many of these also offer meals to go (UK = takeaways). Americans may find portions smaller than at home, and you will generally have to ask for such items as bread and water. Most restaurants have a license to sell wines or other alcoholic drinks with meals; occasionally you may find one in the Australian tradition where you are invited to bring your own bottle. They'll supply the glasses, sometimes even free. An average not-too-sophisticated small restaurant will offer a three-course meal for around £10–15 (US $15–20) without drink. Cafés often supply simple meals, usually fairly basic ones, as well as serve tea, coffee, hot chocolate or cold drinks.

Cafés and restaurants tend to be in towns, but there are some out-of-town possibilities (apart from pubs) of at least a cup of tea and a cake, particularly on Sundays. Most garden centers and many craft centers have a small cafeteria; some National Trust stately homes that are open to the public have refreshment rooms; in summer, village halls may be taken over by fund-raisers for the local church restoration fund or other worthy local causes that offer afternoon teas (tea, sandwiches and cakes) or run coffee stalls to make a small profit for their funds. These functions are rarely advertised except by a small notice on a discreet parish billboard or a chalked up direction arrow—but they can make an interesting and thirst-quenching afternoon stop, many of them in out-of-the way rural spots.

Shops

Most villages have a small store, often doubling as the village post office. Stocks and variety of foods vary. Most will have basics such as sliced bread, cookies ("biscuits"), milk, other dairy products and canned foods and drinks. Some have a reasonable variety of fresh fruit and vegetables.

In general, however, you will find fresh meat only in a butcher's shop and unsliced bread with more variety at a baker's, and there may be more choice of fruit and vegetables at a greengrocer's or fruiterer's. Typical opening hours for village shops are 8:30 or 9 A.M. to 5:30 or 6 P.M., although some are open longer. Some close for lunch from 1 to 2 P.M.—and remember the possibility of early closing days. Some are open also on Sunday mornings, until noon, 12:30 or 1 P.M.

There are also several chains of supermarkets, of varying size, some on the edges of towns, some nearer the centers. Opening hours vary, but on weekdays 9 A.M. to 7 or 8 P.M. are typical.

CHAPTER 31

Traveling with Your Bike

This chapter deals both with getting to Britain with your bike and transporting it within the country. Note that in Britain, although the 12-hour clock is universally used in ordinary conversation and writing, all times for air, sea, rail and road travel are given using the 24-hour clock. For example, 18:30 is 6:30 P.M.—not 8:30 P.M. Dates written down as series of numbers are different from the convention used in the U.S.—Christmas Day 1996 would be 25/12/96 in Britain, not 12/25/96.

Traveling to Britain

By air

Many airlines fly direct to British airports. The largest and busiest British airport is one of five London airports, London-Heathrow (see Routes 1, 2 and 3). Not only is it large and busy but it is not very bicycle-friendly. Situated in the suburbs to the west of London, about 20 km (12 mi.) from the city center, it is very much geared to car, taxi or subway travel. Even getting out of the three northern terminals (one of these, Terminal 3, is the usual arrival terminal for long-haul flights) onto the general road system is not easy for cyclists, since the main access tunnels are closed to them. Sometimes a separate tunnel is available for cyclists' use, sometimes you have to take a special shuttle bus and bike transporter.

Many long-haul operators fly instead to London-Gatwick (Routes 5 and 6), about 40 km (25 mi.) south of central London. This airport has excellent rail connections to the city center (and to some other parts of Britain as well) or, since Gatwick is close to open country, it's a good airport to begin cycling from. Of London's other three airports, City Airport is served mainly by small turbo-prop aircraft connections to European business centers, and London-Luton by holiday charters, mostly to European destinations. Quite the bicycle-friendliest of London's airports is London-Stansted (Routes 4, 7 and 8), 50 km (30 mi.) northeast of the capital. You can ride straight away from the front of the terminal building into the quiet roads of the countryside of the county of Essex.

It may be heresy to say it, but our considered view is that plunging jet-lagged and travel-weary on a bicycle into London's traffic is not the best introduction to a strange city—particularly one whose inhabitants insist on driving on what may be to you the wrong side of the road. For those who must, we provide Routes 3, 6 and 8, but these are merely the best choices from a very poor selection. Once you know it a little, central London is fine on a bike, provided you have somewhere secure to park it; it's the 20–30 km (13–20 mi.) of busy suburban road that are unpleasant and hazardous.

Should you have a choice, the best times for travel in and around London by bike are early on Saturday and Sunday mornings. The most rewarding part of London to explore by bicycle is the riverside part of the financial center, the true City of London, and the riverside route westward from there to Westminster, the home of "Big Ben" and the Houses of Parliament. The best time is early on a Sunday morning.

If you do wish to visit or explore central London, we'd suggest making your base for a few days in a small town say 30 km (20 mi.) out and traveling in by rail or subway (Underground). From these small towns you can buy an "off-peak" (after 9:30 A.M.) one-day "Travelcard," which covers the round trip to the center plus any number of Underground or bus trips in the capital. You can judge after the first trip or two whether it's worth taking your bike in the next time. (Bikes travel free on off-peak services on British Rail suburban lines around London; on London Underground services there are restrictions and charges.)

If you arrive at Heathrow Airport, we would suggest making your base in Windsor (which is worth a visit in its own right); from Gatwick Airport, Crawley, Horley, Horsham, Redhill or Reigate; or from Stansted Airport, Bishop's Stortford or Saffron Walden. There are convenient youth hostels at Windsor (and another quite near at the Quaker village of Jordans, which has connections with William Penn) and at Saffron Walden; the nearest hostels to Gatwick are at Brighton or a simple one, Tanner's Hatch, near Dorking.

But London isn't Britain, and it is equally possible to fly to other airports that are more cycle-friendly. Birmingham Airport (Route 1) links easily to the Shakespeare country, and Manchester's Ringway Airport (Route 13) is convenient for northern England and Wales. The Scottish airports at Glasgow and Edinburgh (Routes 15 and 18) also make good starting points. Fares may be cheaper to these airports than to London-Heathrow. We've indicated links to some of these other airports when a route goes near them.

Most airlines on long-haul transatlantic routes require you to box your bike for shipment. Some provide boxes (one or two even free), others require you to provide your own box—many people get a used bike box from their local bike shop. Other airlines will accept bicycles in large bags, or in nothing at all. In all cases a certain amount of dismantling is needed. In general the rule is to carry out as little dismantling as the airline will allow.

The following list is in diminishing order of desirability—work down the list only as far as you have to. If you are riding to the airport, make sure that items you need to remove or unscrew are not frozen—if necessary, free them with WD-40 or similar penetrating oil.

☐ Remove computer, pump, and all bags, bottles and lights (except alternator-powered systems).

☐ Always remove the pedals. These add to the width of the packed bicycle and can get tangled with other parts of the bike or other baggage. Don't forget that the right pedal has a left-hand thread: to unscrew it you turn it in the opposite direction to normal. Most pedals have flats on the spindle for which you need a thin 15 mm open-ended wrench.

☐ Loosen the handlebar stem wedge nut and turn the handlebars parallel with the frame. With drop bars, loosen the binder bolt on the handlebar stem and turn the bars so that the brake levers point down. Usually you will find that one side of the handlebar fits round the frame top tube.

☐ If necessary, remove the seat and seat post by undoing the binder bolt at the top of the frame seat tube. First mark (with electrical tape is easiest) the seat post at the point where it goes into the frame so that you can be sure of replacing it at the correct height. Do not just lower the seat: not only does that score the seat post but it will also destroy any clue as to its correct position.

☐ If you need to remove wheels, see if you can manage by removing the front one only. Strap this wheel to the frame (with suitable padding between) using cycle pedal toe straps. Prepare beforehand a small block of 25 x 25 mm (1 x 1 in.) wood, 100 mm (4 in.) long, to act as a protective spacer between the fork ends. (Some bike shops sell a plastic gizmo that performs the same function.)

☐ If you remove the front wheel you may also need to remove low-rider pannier racks as well.

☐ Many airlines still ask you to deflate the tires. This is completely illogical; however, the flight loader has the last say on whether your bike travels or not, so you have to comply.

Within Europe, many airlines will accept a bicycle with the minimum of dismantling; removing loose fittings and pedals is often enough. Nearly all damage to bicycles when traveling by air occurs during ground handling and loading. At smaller airports, bikes are usually loaded and delivered to the baggage hall by hand. This is another argument in favor of avoiding London-Heathrow when traveling with a bicycle.

When waiting to reclaim your bike at a large airport, find out where "out of gauge" items (those which won't pass through the port to the usual baggage carousel) will be delivered. Some airports (Heathrow, again, among them) have a lethal "out of gauge" roller conveyor in which bikes can get caught up.

The standard free baggage allowance on transatlantic flights is two pieces of baggage with certain size and weight limits. The bike, boxed or not, counts as one. For the second piece, we have found it worthwhile to bundle the remaining bike bags and loose items such as camping mats, bike pumps and bottles, etc. into a light rip-stop nylon bag. Within Europe and on most other flights, the standard allowance for economy-class passengers is 20 kg (about 44 lb.). In dozens of flights over thirty years we have only once been charged the excess baggage fee, although we have carried well over 20 kg on many cycle-camping trips.

It is possible to store a bicycle box or bag at most airports so that you can pick it up again when you leave. Ask at the enquiry desk for long-term baggage storage.

By sea

If you're combining your British trip with a visit to Ireland or to continental Europe, it may well be easiest to cross to or from Britain by sea. Nothing could be simpler. On any of the car ferries, you just check in, wheel your bike on to the car deck when told to by the loading crew, take off of it what you need for the voyage, secure the bike lightly to a suitable anchorage (an elastic strap is ideal) and go upstairs to the passenger section of the ferry. (Note that there is usually no access to the car deck during the crossing, so take whatever cash, travel documents and passport, clothing, etc., you need with you.) Many cross-Channel services allow bikes to travel free; others make a (usually small) charge.

By rail

There are two ways to travel with your bicycle through the new Channel Tunnel. The first is on "le Shuttle," the rail "ferry" connecting the two tunnel terminals near Folkestone and Calais. Eurotunnel, the tunnel operating company, has a bus and trailer service for bikes, which conveys them and their riders between signposted assembly points near to the two terminals. Peak-hour services are expected to run at least every half-hour.

The second route is via the "Eurostar" high-speed passenger train service connecting the London-Waterloo international terminal to Paris-Gare du Nord and Brussels-Midi. The latest information is that up to eight bicycles can be carried on each train. Reservations are necessary and there is a fee.

Traveling in Britain with a Bicycle

By air

Because distances are so short, it is usually only worth considering air travel within Britain for the longer journeys, such as from London to Scotland, or to destinations that would otherwise call for a ferry trip, such as the Isle of Man or some of the Scottish islands. Air travel within Britain with a bicycle is broadly similar to international travel. The normal baggage allowance, however, is only 15 kg (33 lb.), and some airlines make a separate charge for bicycles; enquire which rules apply when making a reservation. Boxing or dismantling beyond removing the pedals is usually unnecessary. It is desirable to arrive at the airport about 30 min. before the advertised check-in time to allow time to prepare the bicycle.

By rail

Rail travel with a bike ought to be simple—but it often isn't. Over most of the British railway network you have to reserve a place for a bike on a specific train and pay a fee (at the time of writing, £3—about $4.50—irrespective of distance). At most station ticket offices, you can make the computer reservation for your bicycle when you buy your travel ticket. On a few lines there are complete bans on taking bikes, and on nearly all there are restrictions.

On nearly all services without separate luggage compartments, there are peak-hour trains (usually up to 9:30 or 10 A.M. and from 4:30 to 6:30 or 7 P.M.) on which you can't take bikes at all, and there are nearly always limits on the number of bicycles—sometimes only one per train, making travel difficult for even a cycling couple, let alone a family or group. These trains run mainly on shorter local routes, although some are on local cross-country express services.

In general, longer-distance InterCity trains, which do have separate luggage space, are more accommodating. These trains run on the main routes radiating north and west from London, and on cross-country routes from southwest England to northeast England and Edinburgh in Scotland, and from south and southeast England to northwest England and Glasgow, also in Scotland.

You need to book a space for a bicycle and pay the fee, preferably at least half an hour before the train leaves. It is best to book even earlier on popular routes at peak travel times—on Saturdays and Sundays in July and August and at Bank Holiday weekends. If your proposed itinerary involves changing trains, the single cycle fee covers the whole journey. When traveling via or from London, note that there are no less than 15 main-line terminal stations in London. InterCity trains leave from the following:

Euston: west Midlands, northwest England and Scotland
St. Pancras: east Midlands
Kings Cross: northeast England and Scotland
Liverpool Street: eastern England north of London
Victoria: Gatwick Airport
Paddington: west and southwest England, south Wales

The overnight sleeper services from London Kings Cross to Scotland (including the far northern cities of Inverness and Aberdeen) and from London Paddington to the extreme southwest of England are well worth considering. The Scottish trains have ample baggage space; a reservation is required but there is no bicycle fee on the Scottish services.

At the time of writing, bicycles could be taken free of charge and without reservation on off-peak trains in the extreme southeast of England and for about a 80 km (50 mi.) radius round London; on the InterCity Gatwick Express linking London-Gatwick airport with the city center (which has an enormous baggage car); on services around Manchester, Liverpool, Sheffield, Glasgow, Birmingham and Leeds; and on one or two other local lines.

Bicycles may also be taken in off-peak hours on some London Underground trains, notably those that serve surface stations. Enquire locally. You are required to pay a child fare for your bike.

There are two classes of rail travel in Britain, Standard and First. First Class fares are about 50% higher than Standard Class, but the differential is in practice much wider because there are substantial discounts on Standard Class round-trip (U.K. = return) fares if you travel outside peak hours. It is even cheaper on days other than Fridays, or—on InterCity—if you book ahead. Ask for Apex, Super-saver, or Saver tickets. Standard Class travel is quite comfortable, and in any case many trains not on the InterCity network have no First Class accommodation.

On most long-distance services, seat reservations are free. If you plan much rail travel in Britain, it may be worth checking before you leave your home country whether you are eligible for any of the con-cessionary rail passes such as the BritRail pass. These can not be pur-chased after you have arrived in Britain.

If the bicycle is to travel in a separate baggage compartment, remove any detachable accessories such as bags, pumps, bottles, computer and lights, and secure the bike so that it cannot fall over (but without locking it to anything). Hooked elastic straps are very handy for this. On trains without separate compartments, you may have to remove any bulky baggage just to fit the bicycle in.

Ferries

In addition to the ferry services to nearby countries, there are many ferries crossing river estuaries or linking offshore islands to the main-land and each other. Most make some charge for carrying bicycles. The most comprehensive listing is given in the *CTC Handbook*, avail-able to members.

On car ferry services, such as many of those from Scotland to the various islands, a reservation is not required. Similarly, most roll-on, roll-off estuary or sea-loch crossings in Scotland also require no reservation. On some of the small, essentially foot-passenger ferries, some of which do not have a regular timetable but make a crossing on demand, it is necessary to make prior arrangements. Enquire lo-cally or see the *CTC Handbook* for contact phone numbers.

Buses

British buses do not in general carry bicycles, and those services that do are generally local and seasonal. There is no national listing; en-quire locally.

Renting a Bicycle

Most cycle rental schemes in Britain are linked either to a holiday package or to a cycle trail center. Some hirers, usually in larger cities, are geared to longer-term cycle hire. The CTC (see Appendix 1) can supply a listing of cycle hirers; send a self-addressed envelope ac-companied by four international reply coupons (or simply stamped if you live in the U.K.). However, the situation is fluid, so it is worth enquiring locally at Tourist Information Centers. Cycle rental is not cheap (about the same as the cost of renting a small car in the U.S.), particularly if you wish to hire a mountain bike.

CHAPTER 32

Bikes and Components

Bike Shops

British bike shops are much like bike shops anywhere else in the world: dens of colorful bikes, bike components and clothing. Bike shop opening hours are usually 9 A.M. to 5:30 or 6 P.M.—and don't forget the possibility of those early closing days.

Traditionally, British touring cyclists have always carried out a great deal of their own maintenance. We have never met, for example, a British cyclist who would expect a shop to dismantle a bike for air travel or reassemble it afterwards. However, virtually all bike shops will carry out repairs and component replacements. As with most hardware, British prices are often roughly 30% higher than those in America.

Bike shops are listed in the Yellow Pages phone book perfectly logically under "cycle shops" or occasionally "cycle [accessory] retailers." Tourist Information Centers ought also to be able to give you addresses of local bike shops.

Fittings and Sizes

There are no great differences in sizing of components for American, Australian and British bikes—which are likely in any case to be (with the possible exception of the frame) largely Japanese, Taiwanese or European.

The most likely problems may be in tire and wheel sizes: in Britain there are five sizes of tire calling themselves "26-inch," for example. There are now international ISO standards for wheel and tire nomenclature: the ISO designations should be molded on the tire wall, and are based on the "bead seat diameter" of the rim and tire. This is (to within a millimeter or so) the actual diameter of the small shoulders on the inside of the rim on which the tire bead sits when inflated. These are 630 mm for "27-inch" tires, 622 mm for "700C" tires, and 559 mm for "26-inch mountain bike" tires. All of these are easily obtainable in Britain. The other element in the ISO designation is the nominal width of the inflated tire in millimeters. Different manufacturers appear to interpret this width measurement in different ways, and tires of the same nominal width from different makers may vary by 3–5 mm. The ISO designation quotes the nominal width first, then the bead seat diameter, e.g., 28-630 for a 28 mm wide 27-inch tire (27 x 1⅛), 32-622 for a 32 mm wide 700C tire (700 x 32C) and 47-559 for a 47 mm wide mountain-bike tire (26 x 1.9). These traditional figures are also usually molded on the tire wall, in parentheses. Use the table on the next page for an overview.

Even if a shop hasn't got a particular size in stock, it will be able to order one for you—though delivery might take a few days, particularly over a weekend.

ISO	Common name	Ease of purchase
25-630 to 32-630 (3 width categories)	(27 x 1) to (27 x 1¼)	Common, but use is decreasing
18-622 to 35-622 (6 width categories)	(700 x 18C) to (700 x 35C)	Virtually universal, especially mid-range sizes, 23–28mm
32-597	(26 x 1¼) (unique to Britain)	Quite difficult
28-590 to 37-590 (3 width categories)	(26 x 1⅜) or (650 x 28A) to (650 x 37A) (European size)	Quite difficult: often heavy 37mm tires only
32-584 and 40-584	(26 x 1¼) or (650 x 32B) and (650 x 40B) (European size also used by some tandem builders)	Rare, except possibly in specialist tandem shops
18-571	"racing 26 in." or (650 x 18C) (front wheel of low-profile time-trial bike, also used by some makers of small-frame bikes)	Rare except in racing-oriented shops
32-559 to 54-559 (4 width categories)	"26 in. mountain bike" or (26 x 1.25) to (26 x 2.125)	Virtually universal
28-541 to 37-541 (3 width categories)	(600 x 28A) to (600 x 35A)(used on some quality bikes for children and by some makers of small-frame bikes)	Fairly rare
32-540	(24 x 1¼) (British version of previous, used for children's bikes)	Fairly common
37-507 and 47-507	"24 in. mountain bike" or (24 x 1.5) and (24 x 1.9) (used on small mountain bikes)	Common

Be sure that any tubes you buy have the correct valve. Most tubes of touring-bike width, whether in 27-in. (700 mm) or 26-in. (650 mm) size, are fitted with the narrow Presta valve; most mountain bike–sized tubes have the car-type Schrader valve.

If you are unfortunate enough to need a damaged rim replaced, check that the valve drilling is one you can use when you get home. Provided that you bought your bicycle in America, Australia or Britain, all other components should be of standard fitting. If, however, you bought a bike in France or Italy, threadings on the cranks for pedals, on the hub for screw-on freewheels and for the bottom-bracket bearing cups may be different. Specialist lightweight bike shops should be able to help if you need replacements.

Equipping a Bike for Britain

You can travel the whole length of Britain on paved roads, so you don't need any special equipment for British touring. However, rain fenders (UK = mudguards) are likely to be useful even if it's not raining. With Britain's rapidly changeable weather the sun may be out after a heavy shower or a wet night, with the roads still wet with puddles of water. We've known riders, too, who have been very grateful for the protection of fenders as they followed the tracks of obviously well-fed cattle being driven home from the fields to the farm for milking.

We've already mentioned—and you'll hear more of it—that there are some surprisingly steep grades on British hills. These are as common, even more common, in the "lowland" areas as in the mountains. These hills are often short, and presumably many of the lines they follow date from the days when travel between villages was on foot or horseback and paths took the shortest route that a horse or human walker could manage. In mountainous areas progress was more measured, probably over longer distances, so gentler but longer grades are more common. Anyway, low gears are useful; mountain bikes are equipped with suitably low gears, as are most modern touring bicycles. If yours isn't, we'd recommend a lowest gear of at least 26 or 27 in., or gear development of 2 meters—that is, with the largest cog on the rear cluster at least as large as the smallest front chainring (28 or 26 teeth on both is a common combination).

Security

In Britain as in many other places, cycle theft is a problem, particularly in London and other large cities. The best place to leave a bicycle is indoors, locked and under somebody's watchful eye. If you have to leave a bicycle on the street or in a public place such as a rail station, make sure it is locked to some immovable object, preferably in clear view of passers-by. Many public places now have a bike park with "Sheffield" cycle stands—a simple inverted square U-shape of 50 mm (2 in.) steel tubing cemented into the ground and to which bicycles can be locked. Make sure that the lock links a closed section of the bike frame to the loop of the stand so that it cannot be manipulated clear.

If you cannot find an "official" stand, find some railings or a similar fixed feature to lock the bicycle to. Don't forget that it is quite easy to lift bike plus lock bodily off plain metal poles. Choose a very public position but do not leave it where it obstructs the sidewalk: people with visual impairment may not easily be able to detect it, and wheelchairs must have room to pass. It may be possible to hang the bike on the inside (i.e., not the sidewalk side) of railings. Nowadays—in London particularly—highly suitable railings often carry notices stating that bicycles left there will be removed and impounded. They often mean what they say.

Use a good lock, such as a U-shaped shackle lock or one with a hardened thick steel cable, and make sure that easily removable quick-release wheels, etc. are also locked. Front wheels are easily removed for locking; some cyclists prefer to remove the back wheel and lock that too if the bike is to be left for any length of time. Components, fittings and baggage are also vulnerable; remove pumps, bottles, lights, cycle computers and bags if you are in any doubt.

It will undoubtedly be cheaper and easier for you to insure your bicycle against theft before leaving your home country. It may also be possible to get at least some coverage for a bicycle from your travel insurance. British cyclists can insure bikes through the CTC if they are members, or often, by paying an extra premium, as an extension to a household policy. Any insurance a non-British cyclist may effect in Britain for a bicycle alone is likely to be expensive and hedged about with a great many restrictions on where you can leave it.

1. Organizations and Addresses

Numbers quoted are phone numbers unless indicated "fax."
To call Britain from abroad, access the international network,
then dial 44 plus the number given without the initial zero.
Don't forget possible time differences when calling offices.

National tourist authorities

British Tourist Authority and English
Tourist Board
Thames Tower, Black's Road
Hammersmith, London W6 9EL
(0181) 846 9000

Wales Tourist Board
Brunel House, 2 Fitzalan Road
Cardiff CF2 1UY
(01222) 499 909

Scottish Tourist Board
22 Ravelston Terrace
Edinburgh EH4 3EU
(0131) 332 2433

British Tourist Authority offices outside Britain

Australia:
BTA
210 Clarence Street
Sydney, NSW 2000
(02) 261 603

Canada:
BTA
111 Avenue Road, Suite 450
Toronto, Ontario, MR5 3JH
(416) 961 8124

Ireland:
BTA
123 Baggot Street
Dublin 2
(01) 661 4273

Japan:
BTA
2-4-6 Tokyo Club Building
3-2-6 Kasumigaseki
Chiyoda-ku, Tokyo 100
(03) 581 3603

New Zealand:
BTA
Suite 305 3rd Floor
Dilworth Building
cnr Customs and Queen Streets
Auckland 1
(09) 3031 446

South Africa:
BTA
PO Box 41896
Craig Hall 2024
(211) 325 0343

U.S.A.:
Chicago:
BTA
625 North Michigan Avenue,
Suite 1510
Chicago, IL 60611-1977
(312) 787-0464

Los Angeles:
BTA
PO Box 711087
Los Angeles, CA 90071-9670

New York:
BTA
551 Fifth Avenue, Suite 701
New York, NY 10176-0799
(212) 986-2266

English regional tourist boards

Cumbria Tourist Board
Ashleigh, Holly Road, Windermere
Cumbria LA23 2AQ
(01539) 444 444

East Anglia Tourist Board
Topplesfield Hall, Hadleigh
Suffolk IP7 5DN
(01473) 822 922

East Midlands Tourist Board
Exchequergate
Lincoln LN2 1PZ
(01522) 531 521

Heart of England Tourist Board
Woodside, Larkhill Road
Worcester WR5 2EF
(01905) 763 436

London Tourist Board
26 Grosvenor Garden
London SW1W 0DU
(0171)-730 3450

Northumbria Tourist Board
Aykley Heads
Durham DH1 5UX
(0191) 384 6905

North West Tourist Board
Swan House
Swan Meadow Road
Wigan Pier, WN3 5BB
(01942) 821 222

South East England Tourist Board
Old Brew House
Warwick Park,
Tunbridge Wells, TN2 5TU
(01892) 540 766

Southern Tourist Board
40 Chamberlayne Road
Eastleigh, SO5 5JH
(01703) 620 006

West Country Tourist Board
60 St David's Hill
Exeter EX4 4SY
(01392) 76 351

Yorkshire and Humberside Tourist
Board
312 Tadcaster Road
York YO2 2HF
(01904) 707 961

Youth hostels organizations

Youth Hostels Association
(YHA–England and Wales)
St. Stephen's Hill
St . Albans, Herts AL1 2DY
(01727) 855 215

Scottish Youth Hostels Association
(SYHA)
7 Glebe Crescent
Stirling, FK8 2JA
(01786) 451 181

Fiona Maudeville
Fossil Bothy
13 Lower Breakish
Isle of Skye, IV42 8QA

Camping organization:

Camping Club of Great Britain and
Ireland
11 Lower Grosvenor Place
London SW1W 0EY
(0171) 828 1012

Cycling organization

Cyclists' Touring Club
69 Meadrow
Godalming, Surrey GU7 3HS
(01483) 417 217
fax (01483) 426 994

Organizations covering admission to historic buildings, etc.

National Trust
36 Queen Anne's Gate
London SW1H 9AS
0171-222 9251

National Trust for Scotland
5 Charlotte Square
Edinburgh, EH2 4DU
(0131) 226 5922

English Heritage
PO Box 1BB
London W1A 1BB
(0171) 973 3000

The Royal Oak Foundation
285 West Broadway
New York, NY 10013, USA
(212) 966-6565

Map producers and suppliers

Goldeneye Map-Guides
Mill Street
Prestbury, Cheltenham GL52 3BG
(01242) 244 889
fax (01242) 237 177

CTC Shop (mail order or callers)
69 Meadrow
Godalming , Surrey GU7 3HS
(01483) 417 217
fax (01483) 426 994

The Map Shop (mail order or callers)
4 Court Street
Upton-on-Severn , Worcs WR8 0JA
(016846) 3146

Stanfords (mail order or callers)
12-14 Long Acre
London WC2E 9LP
(0171) 836 1321

2. Glossary of UK and US Words

UK	US
Allen key	Allen wrench
Bank holiday	national holiday
(road) bends	curves
Campag (for Campagnolo)	"Campy"
candle wax	paraffin
(cycle) cape	(rain) poncho
carriageway	pavement
cattle grid	cattle guard
chainset	crankset
chemist(s) (shop)	pharmacy
(long-distance) coach	bus
crossroads	four-way road intersection
Drain cover	(drainage) grate
dual carriageway	divided highway
dynamo	generator
Elastoplast (trade name used as generic term)	"Band-Aid" (trade name used as generic term)
Fag	cigarette
fortnight	two weeks
Freephone	toll-free phone call number
(freewheel) block	freewheel) cluster (on screw-on hub)
(freewheel) cassette	(freewheel) cluster (on freehub)
freewheeling	coasting
Garage	gas station (usually with car repairs)
gear change	gear shift
"gents"	men's rest room
gradient	grade
gravel rash	road rash
groundsheet	groundcloth
guard's van	baggage compartment on train
gully grate	(drainage) grate
Junction	three-way road intersection
Knickers	panties
Ladies	women's rest room
large-flange (hub)	high-flange (hub)
level crossing	railroad crossing
lorry	truck

Metalled (road)	paved (road)
motorway	freeway (no bikes)
mudflap	mudguard
mudguards	rain fenders
Nipple spanner	Spoke wrench
notes (bank notes)	(money) bills
Pacing (while cycling)	drafting (with riders taking turns at the front)
Pannier carrier	(pannier) rack
paraffin	kerosene
paraffin wax	paraffin
pavement	sidewalk
petrol	gasoline
plaster	"Band-Aid" (trade name used as generic term)
public conveniences	public rest room
puncture	flat (tire)
purse	coin purse
Queue (pronounced "cue")	line, wait in line
Railway	railroad
rear light	tail light
roadway	pavement
roundabout	traffic circle
rubber solution	rubber cement
Saddle	(bicycle) seat
saddlebag	seat pack
saddle-pin bolt	seat binder bolt
seat-bolt	seat binder bolt
seat pillar	seat post
"sitting-in" (while cycling) drafting (probably without the consent of the leading rider)	
slope	grade
small-flange (hub)	low-flange (hub)
spanner	wrench (although adjustable wrenches are the same)
spoke key	spoke wrench
Tarmac	asphalt, blacktop
tent pitch	campsite
torch	flashlight
track mitts	cycling gloves
transfer charge (phone) call	collect call
tubular (tyre) or "tub"	sew-up (tire)
"tucking-in" (while cycling)	drafting
tyre patching canvas	(tire) boot
Unmetalled road	gravel road
Wired-on (tyre)	clincher (tire)
Youth hostel warden	youth hostel keeper

Index

Title	Author	US Price
All Terrain Biking	Jim Zarka	$7.95
The Backroads of Holland	Helen Colijn	$12.95
The Bicycle Commuting Book	Rob van der Plas	$7.95
The Bicycle Fitness Book	Rob van der Plas	$7.95
The Bicycle Repair Book	Rob van der Plas	$9.95
Bicycle Repair Step by Step (color)*	Rob van der Plas	$14.95
Bicycle Technology	Rob van der Plas	$16.95
Bicycle Touring International	Kameel Nasr	$18.95
The Bicycle Touring Manual	Rob van der Plas	$16.95
Bicycling Fuel	Richard Rafoth	$9.95
Cycling Canada	John Smith	$12.95
Cycling Europe	Nadine Slavinski	$12.95
Cycling France	Jerry Simpson	$12.95
Cycling Great Britain	Hughes & Cleary	$14.95
Cycling Kenya	Kathleen Bennett	$12.95
Cycling the Mediterranean	Kameel Nasr	$14.95
Cycling the San Francisco Bay Area	Carol O'Hare	$12.95
Cycling the U.S. Parks	Jim Clark	$12.95
A Guide to Cycling Injuries*	Domhnall MacAulley	$12.95
In High Gear (hardcover)	Samuel Abt	$21.95
The High Performance Heart	Maffetone & Mantell	$10.95
The Mountain Bike Book	Rob van der Plas	$10.95
Mountain Bike Maintenance (color)	Rob van der Plas	$10.95
Mountain Bikes: Maint. & Repair*	Stevenson & Richards	$22.50
Mountain Biking the National Parks	Jim Clark	$12.95
The New Bike Book	Jim Langley	$4.95
Roadside Bicycle Repair (color)	Rob van der Plas	$7.95
Tour of the Forest Bike Race (color)	H.E. Thomson	$9.95
Cycle History – 4th Intern. Conference Proceedings (hardcover)		$30.00
Cycle History – 5th Intern. Conference Proceedings (hardcover)		$45.00

Buy our books at your local book store or bike shop.

If you have difficulty obtaining our books elsewhere, we will be pleased to supply them by mail, but we must add $2.50 postage and handling, or $3.50 for priority mail (and California Sales Tax if mailed to a California address). Prepayment by check or credit card must be included.

Bicycle Books, Inc.
1282 - 7th Avenue
San Francisco, CA 94122, U.S.A.
Tel.   (415) 665-8214
FAX (415) 753-8572

In Britain: Bicycle Books
463 Ashley Road
Poole, Dorset BH14 0AX
Tel.   (01202) 71 53 49
FAX (01202) 73 61 91

* Books marked thus not available from Bicycle Books in the U.K.